Still Kicking

My Journey as the First Woman to Play Division I College Football

Katie Hnida

Scribner

New York   London   Toronto   Sydney

SCRIBNER
1230 Avenue of the Americas
New York, NY 10020

SCRIBNER and design are trademarks of
Macmillan Library Reference USA, Inc., used under
license by Simon & Schuster, the publisher of this work.

For information about special discounts for bulk purchases,
please contact Simon & Schuster Special Sales:
1-800-456-6798 or business@simonandschuster.com

Designed by Davina Mock
Text set in Garamond BE Regular

Manufactured in the United States of America

1   3   5   7   9   10   8   6   4   2

Library of Congress Cataloging-in-Publication Data

Hnida, Katie, 1981–
Still kicking : my dramatic journey as the first woman to play Division One college football /
by Katie Hnida.
p.   cm.
1. Hnida, Katie, 1981– 2. Football players—United States—Biography. 3. Women football
players—United States—Biography. 4. Rape victims—United States—Biography. 5. Sex discrimination in sports—United States. I. Title.

GV939.H54 2006
796.332092—dc22   2006051201
[B]

ISBN-13: 978-0-7432-8977-1
ISBN-10:   0-7432-8977-3

To Frank DeAngelis, a man who shines bright
in even the darkest of times.

And

The Hnida Crew: Mom, Dad, Joe, Jim, Kris, and KJ.
You are my essence. 3 up, 3 down, forever. CURRAHEE!

"It's supposed to be hard; if it wasn't hard, everyone would do it. The hard is what makes it great."

Tom Hanks

A League of Their Own

Contents

Prologue

Rainy Night in Albuquerque

I WAS FREEZING. Teeth chattering, bone-cold frozen. At halftime, I put on everything I could find in my locker to hold on to what little body heat I had left. But a driving, pelting rain through the second half of the game made warmth impossible. I looked at the clock. Fourth quarter, 7:20 left to go. Just 7 minutes and 20 seconds until I could go back to the locker room and let my drenched and frozen body thaw out. My team, the University of New Mexico Lobos, was up 58–8 on Southwest Texas in our season opener. I'd abandoned any hope of getting in the game, figuring that I would have gotten my shot a few touchdowns ago.

Suddenly I felt hard jabs to my side. "Katie! Katie! Katie!" Several teammates were poking me. "Coach wants you, NOW!" Before I could move a frozen bone, my kicking coach was standing right in front of me.

"Katie," he said, pulling off one side of his headset. "Next time we score, you're up. Got it?" He was matter-of-fact. But I knew my make-or-break moment had come. A moment that could make my dream of becoming the first woman ever to score in a Division I football game a reality. A moment that had taken many years.

WHAT? I stared at him with flying-saucer eyes but managed a weak nod.

"Atta girl, Katie!" "All right! All right!" My teammates started thumping me on my shoulder pads and helmet. "Yeah, Katie!" Their faith in me had never wavered. I felt my adrenaline surge, but it seemed to be the only thing moving in my body. My arms and legs were frozen stiff. My feet were soaked; they felt like they weighed 50 pounds each. I had piled on so many layers of clothing, I felt like the Abominable Snowman. How the heck was I going to kick a football?

My team was driving down the field. I had to get ready, and fast.

I started jogging down the sidelines, hoping to make blood flow through my legs. Back and forth, back and forth, with a few stretches in between. The fans in the stands saw me warming up and began to chant, "KATIE! KATIE! KATIE!"

I barely noticed. My focus had turned inward. "Keep me calm," I prayed to God. "Keep me calm." I trotted over to the kicking net for a few warm-ups with the ball.

Our offense was driving closer and closer to the end zone. My heart felt like it was going to pound straight out of my chest. I was tense, anxious with excitement and nerves. Just a few more warm-up kicks, just a few more kicks. My legs were beginning to come back to life.

But then I saw the ball fly high into the air, snatched and cradled in for a touchdown. The crowd roared and jumped to its feet. My time had come.

I ran onto the field, plowing through a mass of teammates.

Breathlessly, I counted out the 7½ yards I needed to line up behind the ball, which was placed on the three-yard line. I was ready. My offensive line was ready. The crowd was ready. My family was in the stands. But my holder was . . . missing! The moment had arrived; my shot at redemption, a place in history—but no one was there to hold the football for me!

I started waving to the sideline and screaming, "I don't have a holder! I don't have a holder!" I had only 25 seconds to get the kick on its way. The play clock seemed to move at warp speed. At any second, the ref could throw a penalty flag because we were taking too much time.

Then Michael Brunker burst through the cherry-colored jerseys on the sidelines, sprinting and sliding toward me. He skidded to a stop in the sloppy grass and calmly said, "Let's do it."

As he kneeled in position, I tapped his helmet, measured my steps, and entered "the zone," a mental state of calm, intense concentration. Everything fell silent; the world moved in slow motion. Now it was the football and me. Brunk's eyes locked into mine. With a slight nod, I said I was ready.

He put his right hand up, and the ball came spiraling back as I began my approach. One. Two. Plant. Pop. In a swift motion, my leg swung back, then forward as the instep of my foot connected with the surface of the ball. My hips continued to rotate as my leg followed through on the kick. I had done this thousands of times before, but it never mattered as much as it did now. I hit the ball cleanly. Instinctively, I knew it would be on the mark before I even looked up. The ball sailed through the uprights. The ref's arms shot up in the air. GOOD!

Still in slow-mo, I turned to Brunk. He was grinning. In a split second, the world burst back into life. I jumped into his open arms and screamed, "We did it!" The crowd went crazy. Wave after wave of cheers hit me. My huge linemen ran back, hugging and squeezing me so hard, I had trouble keeping my balance as we came off the field. I was mobbed again by my teammates on the sidelines, who were picking me up, slapping my shoulder pads, and tugging my ponytail. It was my moment, but also our moment.

I then turned to the thousands of fans who had sat in the rain cheering for the University of New Mexico. They were the same loyal fans who welcomed me with open arms the day I set foot in Albuquerque.

The crowd went wild. "Thank you, thank you, thank you!" I yelled. With my right hand I formed the words "I love you" in sign language. The cheering exploded. My eyes brimmed with tears as I waved and smiled.

I turned back to my teammates, the players who treated me like one of them. The players who believed that a girl who trained and worked as hard as they did deserved to get in the game. The players I was so close to, we were like family. I would find out later that it was my teammates who had relentlessly pressed my head coach to give me a shot.

A beefy lineman put his massive arm around me and said, "Well, Katie, you did it." I looked up at him and grinned. I *had* done it.

But hardly anyone knew how traumatic my journey to that moment had been. Hardly anyone knew the struggles and agonizing assaults I endured playing for my previous team at the University of Colorado.

I was physically, verbally, and sexually harassed. I was fondled, groped, and called sexually explicit names. One player even threw footballs at my head. At the end of my freshman year, I was raped by a fellow teammate, someone I had considered a friend. We hung out, watched ball games and movies together, and sometimes went out for a quick bite. I respected him as a player and trusted him as a person. As a fellow teammate, he knew the stress I faced week after week. When he invited me over to watch a basketball game, I thought nothing of it. I never imagined what he would do to me that night.

The rape hurled me into unimaginable despair. It had happened more than two years earlier, yet I still felt ashamed and afraid. Since that time, I endured an endless string of sleepless nights, depressions, and flashbacks that would strike without warning. It was a hell on earth I still couldn't tell anyone about. There wasn't a single day I could escape it.

Yet my dream never died. It actually helped save me. Kicking was something I could believe in. There were long days with even longer nights, yet quitting was never an option. I could never surrender a dream I felt destined to fulfill. On August 30, 2003, destiny and I came together on a rainy night in New Mexico.

Hours later, after the cheering stopped and the high fives, hugs, interviews, and congratulations ended, I knew there was still something left to do. I turned and walked back through the tunnel and into the empty stadium. The lights were dimmed. The fans were gone. Silence had slipped into the stadium, and the rain subsided.

I walked slowly to the goalpost and knelt beneath it. As I had done hundreds of times before, I thanked God for the opportunity to play the game that had become a part of my soul. The first time I walked onto a football field as a player in high school, I knew I had found a home. I had never felt a deeper sense of belonging or a purer connection to life as when I was on the field. The simple rhythm and cadence of kicking are like poetry for me. The smell of the grass, the crunching of helmets and shoulder pads, the intensity of the game, and the passion of its players and fans are magic.

It had taken only 1.28 seconds to kick my way into football history—an instant that was eight years in the making. It was a dream that had tested me at every imaginable level. It was a dream some felt I didn't deserve to have.

The last place I ever expected to see my dream triumph was in a rain-soaked stadium in Albuquerque. But nothing in my journey has gone as planned. At times I felt I had a one-way ticket into the bleakest, loneliest corner of the universe. But I now know even more strongly than I did on that August night that I wouldn't trade even the most miserable moment of my journey for anything in the world.

On November 26, 2001, during one of the hardest years of my life, I wrote a promise in my journal that you now hold in your hands:

"Someday, I will write. I will tell it all, truth harsh as winter air, pain as blinding & thick as fog, and love—so pure and true it may only have come from God.

"My name is Katie Hnida. And this is my story."

1

Are You Here for the Girls' Lacrosse Meeting?

M OST PEOPLE QUIT FOOTBALL because of an injury. In my case, I took up the game because of one. My gridiron career actually started with an awkward slide on a soccer field. I was 13 years old and playing in a preseason game with my competitive club team. It was a cold, wet February weekend so the field was a swampy mess. I was chasing after a player who had the ball when I hit a particularly slick area of the field. I knocked the ball out from under her feet, and it squirted out of bounds. Unfortunately, one of my legs went one way with the ball, while the other leg stayed on the field. A sharp, searing pain shot through my left thigh. It felt like it had been torn in half. Before I even stood up, I knew it wasn't good. It took just a moment, but a slip and a slide on a soaking wet field changed my life forever.

I didn't know how long I would be out of action, but the days quickly turned to weeks and then to months. I spent a lot of time resting the leg, icing it, and stretching it. But every time I tried to run, I couldn't go more than a few strides before the shooting pains hit. Then I'd start limping. When the leg didn't get better, I finally had an MRI. As it turned out, the tearing feeling I had felt on the field that day was exactly that. The scan showed a complete tear of my left quadriceps muscle.

The next thing I knew, instead of spending most of my time on the soccer field with my team, I was spending it at a rehab clinic with a therapist. The season rolled by as I tried to nurse my quad back to health. It did start to heal, but it seemed like every time I made some progress, I'd hit a growth spurt. I would grow, but the injured muscle wouldn't grow with me. Every time I ran, it went into spasms.

Spring turned to summer, and summer to fall. Even after months of rehab, I still couldn't get the full motion and agility I needed to make the cuts and slides on the soccer field. Eventually I got to a point where I could jog, but I still couldn't sprint at full speed. I knew soccer, at the level I played at, was out of the picture. One year and three doctors later, I was finished—at least for an unknown period of time.

The reality hit me hard. I had been playing at the highest competitive level in the state and was preparing for high school. I would be going to Chatfield High School, which boasted one of the top girls' soccer programs in the state. And the University of Colorado, where I wanted to go to college, had just added women's soccer to their athletic program. Even as a 13-year-old, my goal was to play Division I college soccer. The thought that I might not be able to play soccer in college, let alone high school, was hard to swallow.

Then it happened. On a typical spring evening more than a year after my injury. After dinner, Dad; my younger brother, Joe; and I went to the backyard to toss a ball around. We had a big yard that held soccer nets, batting tees, even a makeshift baseball diamond for our own pickup games. That night, the ball we tossed happened to be a football. We jogged around, doing pass plays and chucking the ball back and forth. On one particular play, I propped the ball up and kicked it back to my dad. Just on a whim. The ball flew about 20 yards over his head.

"Holy smokes, Kate!" My dad was amazed. "Could you do that again?"

"I don't know, probably . . ." I shrugged. It wasn't any big deal to me, I'd just kicked the ball.

"Hang on a second." He grabbed the ball, ran over, crouched down, and held the ball for me. "Give it a shot." Joe ran back to the edge of the yard to catch it. I lined up behind the ball, took a few steps, and gave it a pop. BAM! The ball sailed over Joe's head and landed in a neighbor's yard.

"Stay there!" Dad yelled to Joe. Dad retrieved the ball and began counting his steps as he made his way back to me. "That went close to 40 yards!" Dad exclaimed. Chuckling, he said, "Well, kiddo, if you can't play soccer, maybe you can make a career out of kicking footballs."

I laughed, too, but after a second started thinking, "Football—could I play football?"

Maybe. After all, I had always loved the game. I was a diehard Denver Broncos fan and lived in an area where "Bronco-mania" ruled the fall and winter of football season. I followed the pros on Sundays, the University of Colorado on Saturday afternoons, and watched Joe play Little League football on Saturday mornings. I followed the sport so closely that when I talked to my guy friends at school, they were surprised at how much I knew about the game.

In elementary school, I had even written a short story about a girl who played football. She was a quarterback who would hide her long hair up in her helmet so no one would know she was a girl. She went on to lead the team to the championship and at the end everyone is shocked to find out she is a female. The next season, she wears her hair in a ponytail outside her helmet.

But that night in the backyard, something definitely felt right. It was 1995, and while it wasn't unheard of for a girl to play football, it certainly wasn't common. And I had thought due to my gender and size, I would always be stuck dreaming about the game from the stands. Little did I know that that would change in the weeks to come.

I used to joke that I grew up on sports and classic rock. Whether it was shooting hoops in the driveway or playing home run derby in the backyard, it was to the sound of the Doors, Steely Dan, and the Stones rocking the background.

In the Hnida family, we picked our lotto numbers by the jersey numbers of baseball greats—the Babe, DiMaggio, Mickey Mantle, and Roger Maris, as well as Stan "the Man" Musial. Football legends had their own place of honor: posters of Dick Butkus, Walter "Sweetness" Payton, Vince Lombardi, and Knute Rockne adorned the basement walls. You name the team, we had their pennant hanging somewhere. I simply don't remember life without sports—it was ingrained in our family.

We lived in Littleton, a suburb just outside of Denver, and each of us kids went through the local public elementary, middle, and high schools. If a school offered a sport, we played it. If not, we played on the club or county level. Sometimes we played both.

My father, Dave, had played baseball in college, then worked his way around the minor leagues before going to medical school. Even after starting his medical practice, he played in an adult base-ball league when we were young. I have the best memories of sitting in the bleachers on a hot summer night eating peanuts from the shell and yelling, "Heyyyyy battabattaaaaa, swing!" They were great nights. The smell of the grass, the bugs fluttering around the light poles, and the crack of the bat hitting the ball. It was more than a game; it was a way of life. Win or lose, we'd all be happy driving home with the deep bass of the Doors' "Riders on the Storm" booming inside the car.

As we got older, Dad continued to play but also started coaching—my brothers in baseball, football, and basketball, my sister in soccer, and me with my kicking. He also took on the role of team physician for the high school and community Little Leagues. Dad is well known in Colorado, but not just for practicing medicine. When I was ten, he took a job as a medical reporter for a Denver TV station, where he reports on the day's health news.

My mother, on the other hand, is the day-to-day glue that holds our family together. She's a homemaker—in the best sense of the word. She created and sustained a genuine atmosphere of love at home. Mom can do anything—from reining in her four "kidlets" as she calls us to baking the best chocolate chip cookies in the world.

When Mom went to high school, the only opportunities that existed for her in sports were cheerleading and gymnastics. Instead, she decided to keep stats for the boys' basketball team—a job that started her down the road of being a fervent sports fan. That's probably why she never complained when she had to get each of the four kids to our separate games or practices. And why she would spend her weekends shuttling from one game to the next, trying to never miss a swing, kick, or tackle. She loved it all as much as we did.

I was born in 1981, and quickly showed my parents and the world that I had a mind of my own. A typical firstborn, I was independent, stubborn, and, basically, a pain in the neck. I also was colicky. Some nights Dad would put me in the car seat and literally drive around for hours until I quit crying and fell asleep.

One night when the driving didn't work, my parents just put me in my crib to cry myself to sleep. After what seemed like an eternity of screaming, there was finally silence. Success! Moments later there was a giant boom and then more screaming. I had decided that if no one was going to come get me, I was going to get myself out. I simply climbed up the side rails and crashed to the floor. To this day, my parents shake their heads over the high-bars incident in my crib, saying only, "That's Katie for you."

I paid my parents back a few months later by using a set of car keys to scratch designs into their first-ever brand-new car—a 1981 Subaru. I was pleased with my handiwork, but I swear that deep down inside, Dad still hasn't forgotten.

After that, I think my parents seriously discussed having only one child, but then they decided to try their luck on a second. Fortunately, number two was Joe. Joe was a mild-mannered and easygoing baby, traits that followed with him as he matured. He is 2½ years younger than I, but quickly became bigger than his "big" sis. Joe grew to be six foot two and 240 pounds by high school and had an athletic build. He played football as well as baseball through the years.

Born in 1986, Kristen was number three and like Joe, she had a calm disposition. While she played soccer, lacrosse, and ran cross country, she also found her niche in academics. Kris was always on top of the honor roll and had a knack for foreign languages.

Jimmy came last in 1988, and my parents joke that if he had been born second, there would have been only two Hnida kids. Jim was a mirror image of me in personality, especially as a baby—in other words, he was a handful. Jim, like the rest of us, played a bunch of sports as he grew up and went on to high school, but he was also involved in theater and student government.

I loved being the big sister. From the time I was a toddler, I always wanted to help out with my brothers and sister. I would call them "the kids," a phrase I still use when talking about them.

KJ, the dog, rounded out the Hnida clan. She was a golden lab mixed with a chow and had a feisty spirit. She was definitely a Hnida.

We were an exceptionally close family.

We supported and loved each other unconditionally. Better yet, we liked, and still like, each other as friends. We stuck together. When one of us was going through a tough time, the rest of us made sure we were there for anything that person needed.

We weren't competitive against one another. As children, we were each other's playmates, confidants, and role models. We had strong bonds that our parents reinforced continuously. Mom and Dad made it clear that the standards in our family were high and we did things one way—the right way. We developed a sense of pride in ourselves and in our family that gives us stability that lasts to this day.

When it came to sports, our parents instilled in us a sense that if we were going to do something, we should do it to the best of our ability and then try just a little harder. If we took a chance and things didn't work out, we were still successful—simply for trying. We never feared "failure," because if we gave it our all, it was never failure.

The high point of the day was sitting down together for dinner. We waited for each person to come home so we could eat a home-cooked meal together nearly every night. Dinner didn't end when the food was gone. We'd sit for an extra hour or so afterward telling stories, joking, and listening to how our days went.

When we were young, we'd often build forts to sleep in, and if we were lucky, we'd get Dad to come in and tell us a story before we fell asleep. We would snuggle together to listen to silly, made-up tales where the four of us and our friends were the main characters. Sometimes Dad would tell us stories about the things he and Mom did before we were born; how they coupon-clipped his way through medical school and didn't have any "real" furniture for years.

By far, our favorite was the tale of how they met. Dad was born and raised in New Jersey. Mom moved around a lot but lived in New Jersey for two years in junior high school. They didn't know each other then, but met years later, when my mom returned for a wedding. Dad was "dragged" to the wedding under protest by some of his friends. He was a broke medical student, so he figured at least he'd get a free meal out of it. Little did he know, not only would he get a chicken dinner, he would also get to meet his future wife. In a twist of fate, Dad caught the bride's garter. He had to put it on the leg of the woman who had caught the bouquet. And who caught the bouquet? My mom. They hit it off immediately and spent the rest of the night dancing and talking. The next day, though, Mom returned home to Colorado . . . and her boyfriend. Still, she left Dad with her address.

Dad started to write her letters and the letters turned to phone calls. Finally, Mom agreed to see him again; and Dad somehow scraped together enough money to go visit. The rest is history and they were married only seven months after the night they met.

We'd ask Dad why he kept writing Mom when he was so broke, just starting medical school, and two thousand miles away. Or we'd ask Mom why she even wrote him back. Their answers were the same: "Sometimes, in your heart, you just know what's right." More than a response, their answer became a lesson, one that would prove to be very important to me as I grew older: your heart will tell you what's right to do.

Along with a close family, faith was a strong part of my life since I can remember. We prayed as a family every night before dinner and every night before bed. We attended St. Frances Cabrini Church every Sunday, our six blond heads almost filling an entire row. The church itself was a place of comfort, with the familiar and secure feel of a second home.

For me, believing in God was never hard. I found Him to be everywhere: in the night sky, in my mother's eyes, even on the football field. I believed that He had a plan for each of us and that even when I was going through a rough time, it was for a reason and He would give me the strength to get through it.

When I got older I would often just go sit in the sanctuary of the church at night. It provided a place for solitude and quiet, away from my hectic life. In the years to come, it became a place to reflect when things got tough and hard to understand.

After a few more evenings of tossing and kicking the football around in the backyard with my family, things began to fall into place; events made it seem that I was meant to play football for real. In the eighth grade, I worked as a student assistant in the main office of Deer Creek Middle School. I'd answer phones, deliver notes around the school, and do random office work. I just happened to be organizing flyers for posting around the school when one caught my eye:

FOOTBALL MEETING
If you want to play football for Chatfield Senior High
in the fall, come to the music room, Thursday 2:15.

I held my breath. I wanted to go. Thursday? That's today. Holy cow. I could feel my adrenaline start to rush. Football. After that night when I had first kicked the ball, the idea kept creeping deeper and deeper into my head.

Football. Was I crazy? Maybe, I decided. But I also decided that I would go to the meeting. It was one o'clock already and I didn't have long to wait. I spent my last period anxious and excited. The hands of the clock moved impossibly slow.

"Breathe!" I kept telling myself. It's just a meeting. But deep down, I think I knew that it was going to be more than that to me.

Finally the bell rang, and I was on my way. I hurried downstairs, then stood outside the music room. Tons of guys were filing in, joking with each other and being loud.

A wave of anxiety washed over me. What was I thinking? I hung back for a moment. Half of the guys were the most popular guys in school. The other half were guys who'd played peewee football since they could walk. They were *GUYS*. What made me think that I should be in there, too? "GO!" a voice in my head said. I swallowed hard, screwed up all the courage I could find, and opened the door. Oh, man. There had to be about 100 guys in there. And not an open chair to be seen. I scanned the room. Aha! There was one. Of course, it was right smack in the middle.

"Excuse me," I muttered as I weaved my way toward the chair, trying to draw as little attention to myself as possible. But to my embarrassment, I did not go unnoticed.

"Hey there, little lady!" a voice bellowed. Dang it. I had just made it to the chair. I could feel myself begin to go red. The room became noticeably quieter. A big man with a slight southern accent was addressing me. "Are you here for the girls' lacrosse meeting? Because—"

"No, sir." I looked at him straight in the eye and, with a boldness I didn't know I had, said, "I'm here for football." I flushed as the room erupted into whispers and giggles. The man held his hands up to quiet the room but chuckled himself.

"Hey, now, well, it is the nineties . . ." he said. "Have a seat."

I sat down as another round of snickers and giggles filled the room. A hundred pairs of eyes were staring at me, and I could feel every one.

"Okay, now that's enough. Let's get started!" the man boomed. "I'm Bob Beaty, the varsity head coach at Chatfield."

I finally started to breathe again as he began to talk. I can barely remember anything he said, aside from the basics—football camp would begin a week before school started in August, and there were three teams—varsity, junior varsity, and freshman. Since we were going to be freshmen, that's where a majority of us would be playing.

When the meeting was over, I filed out behind the rest of the guys amid stares and whispers. I even heard one guy say, "Why did she even come?"

I went home that evening and told my parents what I had done.

"What?" Mom said, shocked. "I thought you wanted to play volleyball."

"I did. But I want to play football more. Mom, the other night when Dad and Joe were tossing the ball, I kicked the heck out of the ball. I think I could be a pretty good kicker."

Dad raised his eyebrows. "You did hit that ball pretty good." I could tell he was mulling it over in his head, and I also sensed a glimmer of excitement in his eyes.

"You hit the ball pretty good, but what if one of those guys hits you? You only weigh 115 pounds! There are boys on Joe's Little League team who are bigger than you!" Mom exclaimed.

"Mom, that's why I would be a kicker, not a linebacker. I'd have a whole line of guys protecting me. I think I can do this."

But before she could protest any more, Dad intervened.

"I'll tell you what. Tonight I'll take Katie out to a set of goal-posts and we'll see how she does. If she can do it, I'll talk to the coach." My face broke into a grin, and I looked expectantly at my mom.

"I've already signed you up for volleyball camp at the high school . . ." Mom ventured, but she knew that wasn't going to sway me and she relented. "Okay. . . ."

That night, after dinner, Dad, Joe, and I dug out four old foot-balls from the garage and headed to the field. Dad had also managed to find a kicking tee and block, a special tee used to kick extra points and field goals.

It had been one of those beautiful Colorado spring days, and the air stayed warm into evening. I'd brought my soccer cleats and stretched out as Joe and Dad tossed the ball around. I was eager to see exactly what I could do.

"Okay, I'm ready!" I shouted. Joe went back behind the goalposts to fetch balls, and Dad came back to me with the kicking block. We went to the 10-yard line, the spot where extra points are kicked after a touchdown. Dad handed me the block and said, "Pick your spot." I put the tee in the grass and took about three steps back. I will never forget the next moment. Dad placed the ball on the tee, and I took off. BAM. The ball shot into the sky, high and straight down the middle of the uprights. The ball flew over Joe's head and landed on the track.

"Holy shit!" Dad muttered. "Sorry," he said to me. "How about another?"

"You bet," I said, smiling. Something had happened when I kicked that ball. I felt a feeling that I'd not felt before. It was just right; something had clicked inside.

Dad set the ball up again and I kicked another one onto the track. Joe went scrambling after it.

"All right, we're moving back." We backed up another 10 yards. And then another. One by one, I nailed each kick through.

"Let's go back 10 more." We went back and I shot one through. It cleared with a few yards to spare. Dad turned to me. "You just kicked a 40-yard field goal," he said.

"Are you kidding?" I knew we had been moving back, but I hadn't payed attention to exactly where we were; I just kept kicking. I counted the yard lines. He was right. But 40 yards? Wow. Dad was shaking his head in disbelief but smiling because he knew exactly what he'd just seen. "You are good. Very good. I will talk to the coach for you."

I smiled and looked at the goalposts.

"Thank you. But Dad . . ."

"Yes?"

"Can we keep kicking?"

He laughed. "Of course."

Dusk began to settle in as I booted ball after ball. I kicked until it was dark. As the air cooled and my leg tired, I fell into a contented state, a permanent smile fixed on my face. We drove home, and Mom greeted us at the front door.

"She can do it. Absolutely, she can do it," Dad told her.

True to his word, Dad got in touch with the freshman football coach. His name was Keith Mead, and I went in to meet him a few days later.

He was calm and to the point. He told me they'd be happy to have me. He cut no one—everybody who came out made the team. Plus, he hoped we scored a lot of points that season so maybe I'd get some chances to get into a game. It sounded good to me. I could tell Dad was relieved as well.

I spent that summer preparing for the upcoming season. I learned more about kicking, including how far I was supposed to be from the ball before I made my approach, and how to tilt the ball so I could get optimum height. I also learned there were standard place kicking guidelines, but each kicker had his own minor variations in style. There was a lot of trial and error, but I found the standard three steps back and two steps to the left side of the ball was just right. I also preferred that the ball be tilted slightly back and to the right to make solid contact.

Practicing was easy. Time would fly, and some days I'd get so into it that I had to make sure I didn't kick too much and make my leg sore.

To appease my mother, "just in case football doesn't work out," I still went to volleyball camp. But after the first day, I didn't go back. My heart was set on football, and somewhere inside I knew it was going to work. I could just feel it.

Before I knew it, in mid-August, it was time for the first football practice. Mom kissed my forehead before I left. "Good luck, sweetie. We'll pray for you." I had a funny feeling she wasn't just going to pray that I did well, but also pray I didn't get killed out there. I grabbed my cleats and jumped into Dad's pickup truck.

I was silent in the truck. Though I was excited, I still had a stomach full of butterflies. I even wished for a brief second that I was heading over to volleyball, not football practice. Dad kept giving me sideways glances. "It's going to work out fine," he told me, but I could tell he was a little nervous, too. I could understand my parents' feelings. Here they were, sending their firstborn, a scrawny five-eight, 115-pound daughter, out to play a game where there was cheering when one player crushed another.

The ride over to school was short, and the next thing I knew, I was standing in a noisy, crowded hallway with about 60 guys. I recognized a few, but there were a lot of unfamiliar faces. It seemed that there was some sort of line forming, so I wedged my way in. I didn't know what we were waiting for, but the guy in front of me answered my question. "We're waiting for helmets. You ever worn one before?" he asked me. I shyly shook my head no.

"It's not so bad. You'll get used to it quick. But what are you going to do with all that hair?"

"Oh, uh, just leave it in a ponytail, I guess. . . ." I stammered, pushing long, blond strands off my face.

"I'm Matt, by the way. And you must be Katie." He smiled at me. "Yeah . . . how'd you know?" I asked.

"Word got around pretty quick that there was going to be a chick trying out. I didn't expect her to look like you, though." I didn't know quite how to respond.

"Well, I'm just going to be a kicker . . ." I trailed off.

"It's cool; we could use a good kicker. The guy who kicked on our team last year sucked."

"Yeah, I heard no one really had any kickers . . ."

"What the . . ." a deep voice exclaimed. We had reached the front of the line. One of the biggest and most muscular men I had ever seen in my life stared at me. "Who are you?" he asked. I felt myself blush again. Fortunately, Coach Mead emerged from the stacks of helmets just in time. "That's Katie. She's going to try kicking. Katie, this is Coach Ackerfelds."

"Ack, for short. Nice to meet you. Sorry about the surprise." He stuck out his beefy hand.

"No problem." I smiled and relaxed the slightest bit.

"Let's get you a helmet. Hmmmm, let's try . . . this one." Ack handed me a white helmet. Tentatively, I put it on my head. Whoa. It was way too big. My head felt like the great pumpkin.

Ack laughed and handed me another helmet. "This will be better," he said.

I took the other one off and put the new helmet on my head. It was better, but I still felt weird. "Shake your head," Ack instructed. I shook it back and forth. The helmet didn't seem like it was going anywhere. "That's good," he decided. "Here's your shorts and T-shirt for practice today. Smallest we have—sorry." A phrase I would hear over and over throughout my career. "Now, go right over there"—Ack pointed to another line—"and get a lock for your locker. Then go . . . wait. I don't think you go to the regular locker room. Coach Mead?"

"Oh, yeah. Katie, when you get your lock, one of the trainers will take you upstairs, to the women's locker room. Then come back down and we'll be meeting in the wrestling room."

I went and got my lock and one of the girls showed me to my locker room. It was directly above the guys' locker room, right next to the weight room. "Does it matter which locker I take?" I asked the girl. "Nope. No one else really uses this locker room very much, so it'll just be you. The lockers the girls use for gym are in a different place."

I thanked her, then decided on the first locker. I put my cleats and helmet in and changed into the shorts and T-shirt they had given me. I looked in the mirror. "CHARGER FOOTBALL '95," my shirt proclaimed. Not bad, I thought. A little big, but not too horrible. The locker room was quiet, a welcome break from the mass of confusion and noise downstairs. It would become a haven for the next four years, a place where I could come and be alone. I sat on the bench for a second, closing my eyes to say a quick prayer that I would do okay once we got onto the field. Then I went back downstairs for our meeting. There were still a few guys getting helmets and locks, but most were going into the wrestling room. I followed. I was still getting a lot of stares, but some of the guys smiled at me. Soon Coach Mead came in, then Ack and a few other men.

Coach Mead introduced all the coaches and explained what positions they worked with. I didn't hear anyone mentioned for kickers. Then he went through rules and what we were to do the upcoming week. "You will tuck in your shirts. You address us each by 'sir' or 'coach.' No shoes in the building." He was practically shouting. "You got it?" A mumbling of yeses trickled through the room. "What was that?" he yelled. "YES!" came a chorus. "Yes, what?" he demanded. "YES, SIR!" the guys responded. "Good. Let's get on the field!" He was out the door, and the rest of the room was suddenly in a hurry to follow.

I made it back upstairs to my locker room, grabbed my helmet and cleats, and went outside. "Here we go," I thought. As I sat on the sidewalk and put on my cleats, I could hear the yells and hits from the upper practice fields. That must be where the older guys are, I thought. I knew that the varsity team had started earlier than we did. "Let's go, let's go!" I could hear Coach Mead yelling.

I scrambled up and went to the fields. Because the varsity and jayvee had the upper field, we were stuck down on a grassy spot between the baseball and softball fields. No goalposts, I thought, but that thought was cut short by more yelling from Coach Mead. "Helmets on! Lap around the baseball field, then back here in lines to stretch! GO!" We took off. "Faster! WE DON'T HAVE ALL DAY!" the coach barked.

Good grief, I thought. Do they ever stop yelling? Apparently not that day. We were yelled at as we formed stretching lines, we were yelled at as we learned how to do C-H-A-R-G-E-R jumping jacks, and we were yelled at as we broke off into position groups. There were no other guys who were just kickers, so I ended up all by myself, kicking balls into the soccer nets. Soon enough, we all joined back together and I got my first shot kicking with the team.

Since there were no goalposts, we used the soccer goals as our uprights. "Okay, anyone who can kick, hold, snap, let's go." I stepped up, feeling like I was going to puke all over my brand-new cleats. I didn't know the guy who was snapping to me, but I'd had a few classes with the guy who was going to be my holder. I did my steps back. This was it. The snap was low, but the holder scooped it up and got it onto the tee.

WHAM.

"What the . . .?"

"Holy shit!"

"Are you kidding?"

I looked up. The ball was sailing high, straight, in a perfect end-over-end rotation, and landed in the parking lot. The coaches were staring at me. The guys were staring at me.

I saw Coach Mead say something to one of the assistant coaches. "Let's do it again."

One-two-three. I did my steps again, and BAM. The second one was actually farther than the first. I started to relax and fell into my groove. We kept going, doing about six or seven kicks. Only one looked a bit off center, but would have easily been inside the up-rights.

"Well, I think we've got our kicker . . ." Coach Mead said. I was psyched. The team broke back into position groups for more drills, and I went to go back to the soccer net.

"Katie." Coach Mead was standing in front of me with a man I had never seen before. Oh, no. For a second my heart stopped.

What had I done? My kicks had all been good, hadn't they? Decent, at least? As my mind raced with all sorts of crazy, irrational thoughts, Coach Mead introduced me to the man next to him. "Katie, this is Don Jones. He's one of the varsity coaches and oversees the kickers."

"Hello, sir," I said tentatively. The man had a kind face.

"Hi, Katie. Saw you kicking there. You've got quite a leg," Coach Jones said.

"Thank you," I said, my mind still racing in all directions.

"We'd like to take you up to the varsity fields and have you kick up there. See how you look with some of the guys." What? Varsity?

I looked at Coach Mead. He was smiling.

"Man, you guys are gonna come down here and steal away our kicker the very first day of practice? Geez," he joked. "Go on, Katie. Go ahead." I stood there, a bit shell-shocked.

"Okay," I said, unsure that this was happening. Coach Jones and I started to walk up to the upper fields, and my nerves began to twitch again.

"We've got four other kickers up there that I'd like to compare you to. I was very impressed by what I just saw. How long have you been kicking footballs?"

"Um, about three months now, I guess," I said.

"Ah. Are you a soccer player?" he asked.

"Yes. Well, no. I mean, I was. But not anymore."

We were at the field. These guys looked HUGE compared to the guys I had just been with. Suddenly it was as if I were in another country. Coach Jones took me onto the field and introduced me to the other kickers. They all seemed pretty nice. We were kicking 25-yard field goals from an angle on the right side of the field.

As we began to kick, I quickly found that I could keep up with these guys. We would rotate through, each holding, kicking, and fielding the balls. Coach Jones kept a close eye on us. My competitive gene kicked in, and I started to gain some confidence. Finally I asked, "Okay, are we going to move back yet?" After all, we were only kicking 30-yard field goals.

"Can you kick farther back?" one of the guys asked in amazement.

"Well, yeah," I said. "Can't you?"

"A bit, but man, I don't want to push back too much farther. Coach Jones said we didn't need to go back very far today," he said. I looked to one of the other kickers, a kid with blond hair who had a cannon for a leg.

"Let's go back a bit," he said with a shrug. So we backed up, me and the kid with the cannon leg. We were about 40 yards away. He popped a few through—all with plenty of distance, but one or two went a bit wide.

"You're good . . ." I told him.

"Thanks. You aren't so bad yourself," he said, and proceeded to hold four balls, each of which I knocked through cleanly.

All of a sudden, I heard a whistle blow and a loud yell from the opposite side of the field. The four other kickers took off toward the whistle. I didn't know what to do. Luckily, Coach Jones found me.

"You looked good today. Great, actually. I'd like to keep you up here to practice with us. I'll let Coach Mead know. Can you be here at nine tomorrow, instead of 10?"

Of course I could. I'd be there at 4 A.M. for him if he'd asked.

And with that, my first official day of football practice was over. And little did I know, the rest of my life was beginning.

Dad was waiting for me after practice.

"What happened? Where'd you go? Are you okay?" Dad asked anxiously. He had a panicked look on his face.

"What?" I was totally confused.

"I saw you kick, I thought you looked okay, then I saw the coach and some other guy come talk to you. Then they took you away," he said rapidly.

"Yeah, they took me to the upper fields to kick," I said.

"The upper fields?" he said. "You mean they didn't cut you?"

"No," I said, laughing. "Dad, they took me up to kick with the older guys. I'm going to get a shot at the varsity team!"

His eyes widened. "You're kidding!"

"No!"

"I thought they cut you!"

"No!" I was cracking up.

"Well, all of a sudden this guy comes down to the freshman field and takes you away. I thought for sure they were telling you this wasn't going to work!"

He paused. "Varsity?"

"Yes. I know, I can't believe it!" I said.

"Kate-O! I'm so proud of you! I can't believe this!" He pounded on the steering wheel, then gave me a hug.

The next week was a blur. I worked out with the varsity guys, then would come down and watch the rest of the freshmen practice. I received the rest of my gear, and my teammates taught me how to put my pads in all the right places. I was becoming more comfortable by the day and more confident.

When school opened a week later, I got a big surprise.

I was sitting in my last-period class when Coach Jones walked in. What is he doing here? I wondered. He spoke to my teacher, smiled at me, then walked to the door.

"Katie," my teacher said, smiling at me. "Mr. Jones needs you. Get your stuff." Get my stuff? What was going on? I gathered my books into my bag and went to the hallway, where Coach Jones was waiting, a jersey in his hand.

"What's go—" I started to ask, but he interrupted me.

"Hurry, we've got to go fast. I forgot that you still had class now." The school was so crowded that we were on a split schedule—freshmen started and finished later than everyone else.

"Where are we going?" I asked.

"Locker room, then the field. We've got pictures today—and you're our backup kicker. You made varsity."

He handed me the jersey, which I held on to like a piece of gold.

"Change quick. Put this on and come on out."

Though all of my teammates tried to look tough and mean for the picture, I just couldn't do it. That day, I couldn't resist a smile.

2

"I'll Kick All Day
if You Let Me"

I QUICKLY LEARNED that there was a big difference between kicking in the backyard with my family, and kicking in a real game with a team. Football turned out to be
hugely different from any sport I had ever played, especially since I
was the only girl on a team with 60 guys. I spent the season as the
backup kicker on varsity, but also started for the freshman team. It
was a little intimidating to be a 14-year-old girl around a lot of
older, huge, popular guys. Not only was I the only girl on varsity,
but I also was the only freshman. It wasn't new just for me; it was a
whole new thing for them, too. None of them had ever had a girl
teammate. It had to feel weird. But I remember how a lot of the
guys went out of their way to make sure I was doing okay and
telling me they thought it was really cool to have a girl who could

kick so well on the team. Freshmen or varsity, I was in a good place with a bunch of good guys.

The 1995 season started quickly and well. My first kick in a real game came just minutes into my first freshman contest, against the Lakewood High School Tigers.

Wait a sec! I thought. I hadn't even settled into the flow of my first football game and suddenly I found myself standing in the middle of the field. Our team had scored a touchdown quickly and now it was my turn to take the field and kick the extra point. It was all automatic, though—I found my place, took my steps, and waited for the snap and hold. Just like practice, I told myself. I drilled the ball through the middle of the uprights. My teammates, who had been watching me kick for a few weeks, expected it. No big deal. The other team, however, was trying to figure out why the Chatfield kicker had a long, blond ponytail.

Dad was there videotaping the game because Mom was at Kristen's soccer game. When we scored the touchdown, he called her and she listened on a cell phone as I went on to attempt my first kick. When she heard all the yelling, she knew it was good. Parents of my teammates were coming up to Dad and congratulating him. I ran off the field, but before we knew it, I was out there again. And again. And again. We destroyed our first opponent, 48–0, and didn't stop there. My freshman team went undefeated that year, nine wins and zero losses. Not only were we beating teams, we were annihilating them. I kicked more than 40 extra points that year for the freshman squad.

My first varsity game that year was completely different. Instead of just some parents and relatives on the sidelines, like at the freshman games, we were in a stadium with a few thousand people in the stands. Our games were usually played under the lights, at night. The stadium would literally rock as the school band played and the cheerleaders performed their routines. I thrived on the electricity and intensity. The level of play was also a lot different at these games—faster, with much harder hits. As my puny frame stood on the sidelines, I watched guys weighing upward of 250 pounds crunch each other into the turf.

The first time I got into a varsity game, we were playing at Broomfield High School. It was a warm September night, and we led the entire game. When we scored with a few minutes left in the final quarter, our starting kicker took a few steps onto the field to kick the extra point. Then he suddenly stopped. What's he doing? I wondered.

Suddenly Coach Jones was pushing me onto the field. "Go kick the extra point, Katie." What? We were three weeks into the season. Was I ready to go onto the field with the big boys yet? Apparently my coaches thought so. I ran out, where my holder, Mitch Moret, put his hands up for a high 10. I threw my hands up into his and he grasped them.

Sensing the apprehension in my eyes, he said, "Relax, kid, we've got this." He was right. The snap and the hold were perfect. So was the kick. My teammates mobbed me, smacking me so hard on my back that it lifted me off my feet. The public address announcer stumbled, "Extra point good for Chatfield by . . . uh . . . uh . . . Katie!" No last name. Just Katie. I think the announcer was more surprised than anyone.

I was usually on the quieter side when riding the bus home with the older guys, but not tonight. The guys kept doing imitations of the announcer saying " . . . uh . . .uh . . . uh . . . Katie!" and we laughed the whole way home. When we got back to school, I walked down the main hall with my teammates, then parted to go to my own locker room as they went to theirs.

That first year, the janitors would sometimes forget to leave the lights on for me whenever there was a night game. A few times they would even lock the door and I'd have to hunt a coach down for the key. On this night, the door was unlocked, but the locker room was dark when I walked in. I went to flip the switch, and stopped. I stood in the quiet, cool darkness and leaned my head against the wall. Closing my eyes, I smiled. Football was awesome. It was working out better than I ever dreamed it would.

Then when I flipped on the light, I saw my own reflection in the mirror shoot back at me. I paused. My ponytail that had been mussed up by the helmet I held in my left hand; I had my muddy pair of cleats in my right. I stared at myself in my uniform and pads and thought it looked right. There were no other words to explain it. I felt like a football player.

As the season went on, I was lucky to have the experience of playing on two teams. There was the complexity and intensity of the varsity level, which helped me to learn more about the intricacies and finer points of the game. Then there was the practical experience of kicking regularly in freshman games. It gave me a chance to work on the mechanics of kicking in a game situation. At practice, I would simply prop the ball up and kick on my own. But it's a whole different experience to work with a snapper and holder, and then have opposing linemen charging at you.

Typically, the experience is a smooth flow—the snapper hikes the ball back to the holder; the holder catches the snap and quickly spins the ball onto the tee at the proper angle for the kick. This whole process is supposed to take place in about 1.3 seconds. With all the different motions, there is little room for error. Sometimes something will go wrong. The ball is snapped too high or the holder drops the ball. In that case, the simple extra-point attempt turns into what's called a "fire play." The holder yells the word "fire!" and suddenly the field erupts into chaos. Everyone scrambles to get the ball into the end zone in any way possible. It's a rare occurrence on varsity, but not at the freshman level. We had fire plays about once every four attempts. Coach Mead had given me strict instructions when we had a fire play: GET THE HECK OUT OF THERE– RUN AWAY! However, my freshman year, there were times I felt like I had a target on my back. Opposing players would take a free shot at me when we'd have a fire play. At other times, I'd get nailed on a late hit–after the kick was good and the whistle had blown– just because someone felt like taking a pop. A lot of testosterone and frustration boil when your team is being slaughtered by another team. Especially a team with a girl on it.

I'll never forget the first time I got hit. I had just kicked the ball. My leg was still in the air on the follow-through, and SMACK. A huge lineman plowed into my chest. I bounced as I hit the ground. Wow, I thought. These shoulder pads work pretty good. My holder was screaming about the late hit, then turned to make sure I was all right.

As he pulled me up off the ground he said, "Geez, are you okay?" His face was puzzled–I was smiling.

"Yeah, I'm fine," I said. "That was kinda cool, actually."

He just shook his head and laughed. My teammates were naturally protective of me and sometimes would shove and punch the other team's players when I'd get hit. The shoving and punching decreased when they found that my skinny frame could handle a hit better than anyone thought, including me.

It's funny, one of the hardest hits I took that year wasn't from a guy coming after me because I was a girl. In fact, he didn't know I was a girl–at least not at first.

I had just kicked the ball and was plowed into as the other team tried to block the kick. This time, though, one guy landed right smack on top of me. We opened our eyes at the exact same moment, and for a split second we were looking straight at each other from less than an inch away. The next moment, though, a look that can only be described as a mix of terror and shock came into his eyes.

"Oh, my GOD! You're a GIRL!" he screamed.

No kidding; I've been one for years, I thought.

"I'm so sorry! I am *so* sorry!" He was scrambling to get off me, then pulling me up and dusting me off. "I am so, so sorry, I had no idea. . . ." I wasn't hurt and thought it was funny to see the look on his face. I did feel sorry for him, though; it was a pure accident.

"Take it easy, I'm fine." I said. The guy still looked horrified. "REALLY," I said, starting to laugh. He staggered off the field, looking like he was the one who had been run over.

It wasn't the only time I managed to shock a player on the other team. As we went through the handshake line after the games, I never knew what to expect. More often than not, guys would be surprised when they saw what my face looked like. Players' eyes would get big, some would shake their heads, and a lot would turn back around after I'd passed, as if to make sure they were seeing straight. Occasionally I'd get hit on. Guys would hang onto my hand for an extra second, smile, and say something cheesy like "Hey there, blue eyes." But by far the best line I ever got came after a game against Doherty High School. I was going through the line as usual and in the middle of the line one of the opposing players stopped me. He winked and said, "So . . . do you have a number besides two I could possibly have?" I laughed and shook my head. "Good line, though." It was definitely an original.

Being a female also meant some "original" places to change into my uniform.

One of our games was in Colorado Springs, which is about a two-hour drive from Littleton. Since the game was so far away, we didn't change at the school. Instead we packed our equipment on a separate bus and put our gear on when we reached the stadium. When we arrived, I shuffled into the locker room with my teammates. Scanning the room with my eyes, I looked for a place where I could change. No doors on the bathrooms, so that was out of the question. Next I went to find out if they had a women's restroom or locker room, even a classroom that I could use. Everything was already locked; no one had expected a girl needing a place to change for the game that night. Finally one of the managers from the other school found an open door. It was a broom closet. I peered in. It was small, crowded, and musty, but it would work. I thanked the man and lugged my gear in. Before I shut the door, I tried to find a light switch. No luck. Oh well, I thought, pulling the door closed. There was a faint glow coming through the door and it was somewhere to change. The closet was crowded and I kept smacking my arms on brooms or shelves as I struggled out of my dress and into my football gear.

"Whoa!" I tipped over as I tried to pull my football pants up. As I steadied myself, I noticed something in the mirror that was crookedly stuck on the floor. It looked like another person. I spun around.

"Augh!" It wasn't another person, it was a headless mannequin shoved in between the mops and brooms. I rolled my eyes, laughing at myself. No light, in a musty cramped little room with a headless figure. Nice. I felt as if I had been transported into a scene of some cheap horror flick where an ax was going to come flying at my head. I was out of there. I hurriedly got on the rest of my gear and ran onto the field as fast as I could.

When I kicked for the freshman team, we played our home games at the high school rather than Jefferson County Stadium. Since we were at Chatfield, we wouldn't go into the locker room at halftime. We simply stayed on the field to discuss strategy. One game was played on a rainy day and with a fierce wind whipping through the air. Strands of my wet ponytail were blowing and getting stuck in my face mask. It was already hard to see in the blinding rain and having my hair poke through wasn't helping matters. I needed to get it into a braid, but I couldn't reach my arms back because of my shoulder pads. I scanned the crowded sideline for one of our female managers.

"Hey." I nudged one of my teammates. "Where are the managers?"

"I don't know. Somewhere. I can't see. What's up?"

"I need to get my hair into a braid, it keeps blowing and sticking to my helmet," I explained to him.

"Oh. Yeah, sorry, can't help you there."

I turned to search down the sideline, when someone grabbed my elbow. It was another teammate.

"Hey—step back." He nodded his head to the side. I frowned at him.

"I heard you," he said. Huh? He pulled me back and said under his breath. "I can braid."

"Really? You know how to bra—" I exclaimed.

"Shhhhhh," he hissed. "Step back and block me so no one sees." In about ten seconds, he had pulled out my ponytail and whipped my hair out of my face and into a tight braid.

"Wow," I said, reaching back to touch my hair. "Thanks. That's *really* good." I stared at him in amazement.

"I have five sisters," he explained. "Don't tell anyone I did that. The guys will give me hell." I promised and went on to kick three extra points in the second half, all without my hair smacking me in the face.

My best and most important kick of my freshman year didn't come on a high school field. It happened at Folsom Stadium in Boulder, Colorado, home of the University of Colorado Buffaloes. It was early April of 1996, and CU was having their annual spring game and fan participation day. Joe, Dad, and I went up and watched the game. Afterward we went down onto the field, where players were signing autographs. A number of activities were set up, and it was crowded with a few thousand people milling around the field or sitting up in the stands. While we wandered, we came across a miniature set of goalposts with little foam footballs.

How cute, I thought, as I watched a toddler run at the ball and take a swipe. My gaze followed him, and as I looked upward, I noticed the real goalposts in the distance behind the little fake ones. Hmmm . . . I thought. Dad could see the wheels in my head turning.

"Kate???" he asked.

"Come on," I said, grabbing Joe and pulling them toward the line. "I'm going to kick."

"Uh, Kate, those goalposts are a little small, don't you think?" Joe said.

"Look behind them," I said. They both took a look, not quite comprehending what I was thinking.

The real goalposts were somewhere between 35 and 40 yards away. There was also a pile of real footballs next to the little foam ones. I got into line and started doing a quick stretch to loosen up a bit. I soon got to the front of the line.

"Can I use a real ball?" I asked the player who was holding.

"Uh, yeah, I guess. Why?"

"I want to kick a real ball." He paused, sizing me up, and then shrugged.

"Whatever." He placed the ball on the tee, and I gave it a kick. WHAM! Dang it. I hit the ball well, but hooked it a little to the left. It didn't seem to matter. A murmur rose around us. The player was looking at me like I was from another planet.

"I kick at my high school," I explained to him.

"Oh . . . yeah." He kept staring at me.

"Well, look, I missed that one. Can I take another? Is that okay?" I asked the guy behind me. The man shook his head rapidly up and down.

"Please," he said, gesturing toward the tee.

The player set up another ball, still looking at me strangely as I lined up and took another shot. BAM. Ah. The kick was good.

"Damn." The player muttered, still staring.

"Do it again!" someone yelled. I turned back, and a small crowd of people had stopped to watch. I raised my eyebrows to the player.

"Yeah, sure . . ." He grabbed another ball. I banged it through. "Oooohhhhhh." I could hear the reaction of the people around us. I turned and grinned at Dad and Joe. The small crowd was growing. "Where do you go to school?" "How old are you?" "What's your name?" "Kick again!"

Sure, I thought, I'd love to. I'll kick all day if you let me. I kept popping them through, and I was starting to fall into my rhythm when I heard loud voices in the crowd behind me. I turned and was face-to-face with a man I had seen countless times, though never this close and in person. It was Rick Neuheisel, the head coach of the Buffaloes. I knew he was somewhere out there because I could hear him talking on a microphone every few minutes over the noise on the packed field.

"Hi there," he said.

"Hi . . ." Now it was my eyes that were wide.

"What's your name?"

"Uh, Katie. I'm Katie Hnida."

"Nice to meet you, Katie. I'm Coach Neuheisel. I hear you're kicking field goals over here?"

I nodded.

"Great," he said. It was only then that I noticed the microphone in his hand. He was flipping it on.

"Okay, people! Okay, let's quiet down!" he boomed. I looked at Dad and Joe in panic. What was he doing? It became so quiet I could hear my own breathing.

"I've got Katie Hnida here, from . . ." Coach Neuheisel covered the mike. "Where do you go to school?"

"Chatfield," I said.

"Katie Hnida, from Chatfield High, and she's going to kick us a field goal." A cheer rose from the thousands in the stadium. I looked at Coach Neuheisel, then turned, nodded my head, and lined up. Everything was quiet. I saw only the ball, the turf, and nothing more. I had tuned out the outside world, but I was still nervous inside.

"Okay, God. I know I promised I would never specifically ask You to make a field goal good, but if you could help me just do my best this once?" I asked silently as counted out my steps.

I took off. As soon as I hit the ball, I knew it was good. I nailed the sweet spot, and the ball rocketed right through the middle of the uprights. The crowd roared. Coach Neuheisel looked a bit stunned but recovered quickly. "I've got scholarship papers up in my office!" he joked into the microphone.

"Thanks, Katie." He flipped off the mike and shook my hand. "That was really, really good. Let's keep in touch."

I could only nod. With that, he headed across the field, followed by a throng of fans. I stood there. Keep in touch?! From the head of CU football?

I could've died and gone to heaven. Then I heard a small voice behind me.

"Can I have your autograph?" A little boy was at my side, holding a little football and a marker. I couldn't believe it. He wanted *my* autograph? Why?

"Sure," I said, kneeling down and taking the ball. I scribbled my name and handed it back to him.

"Here ya go." He gave me a toothy grin and skipped away.

"Will you sign mine, too?" It was a woman holding out her program.

I ended up signing a handful of things for people. "Will you write down where you go to high school?" one man asked.

"We'll be watching you."

Finally I got back over to Dad and Joe. We all looked at each other for a second, then broke into grins and started breathlessly talking at once.

"Kate, that was awesome," Joe said.

"I can't believe that just happened!" I said.

"Do you realize who you just kicked for?" Dad said.

"We've got to call Mom!" we all said.

As we walked out the stadium gate, I stopped and looked at the field. Neuheisel's comments had planted a seed in my head. Could I do this in college? A new goal began to develop in my mind.

"Kate?" Dad called.

"Coming," I said, shaking myself out of the daydream that I could be a college kicker. On this field.

There were a number of pay phones on the plaza outside the stadium. We stopped at one outside Gate 4 and called home.

"Mom!" As I told her about the day, I couldn't believe it had actually happened. Mom was speechless.

The drive home from Boulder had never been so sweet; the Flatiron Mountains at the base of the Rockies had never looked so beautiful, and it didn't seem like the air had ever been this fresh. With a Steely Dan melody floating in the background, I leaned my head back and fell into a contented state, dreaming of kicking field goals in a black-and-gold uniform.

A few changes to the program took place my sophomore year. Coach Beaty retired and my freshman coach, Keith Mead, was promoted to the head varsity spot. I moved up the chain of kickers. I now started for the junior varsity squad and continued to play on varsity. The novelty of having a girl around was long gone. Now it was time to do more. I still didn't do kickoffs because the coaches didn't want me getting run over when the ball was returned. But that year I started kicking field goals as well as extra points. Field goals meant longer distances and different angles on the field. I also got more playing time at the varsity level to prepare for my junior year, when I would take over as the number one kicker. I continued to kick the entire practice. I would kick so much that my teammates would tease me. "Don't you get bored?" they'd ask me. "No," I'd answer truthfully. I enjoyed just the feel of being on a football field. I kicked for hours on end. If the team was using the entire field for drills and I couldn't get a set of goalposts, I would drag the kicking net out of the storage shed or practice my steps on the sidelines. I found my natural flexibility was a big asset in my kicking, so I stretched as much as I could. I focused on every detail to make each of my kicks flawless. Even if a kick went through the uprights, I wasn't satisfied unless I had kicked it perfectly. Nice and high, right down the middle with lots of room to spare as the ball cleared the crossbar. It was my goal to be automatic from any angle, at any distance, and in any situation.

My sophomore year was busy. Like the year before, I'd suit up on Friday night for a varsity game, get home late, then get up early the next morning for a junior varsity game. But I couldn't complain. Life was good on the field. Off the field was good, too. I worked hard, got good grades, and made the honor roll. Though football was always first in my heart, it was hardly my only activity. In the spring, I ran sprints and pole-vaulted for the track team. I wrote for the school newspaper and eventually became an editor. I loved drama, but couldn't balance the spring or fall plays with my sports season. Instead, I became a member of the speech and debate team and took part in statewide competitions. I even found time to be a mentor to incoming freshmen. I also was a volunteer in the pediatric ward at Littleton Hospital. High school suited me.

Junior year, I became the starting kicker for the varsity. I was ready to roll. Unfortunately, that season my team didn't roll very well. We literally defined the term "rebuilding" that year. We only had eight seniors returning to our 60-man roster. Nearly all of our starters graduated, and we had a lot of young guys learning how to play at this level. Chatfield is a large school, and our football team plays in the largest division in Colorado. We also played in Jefferson County, the strongest conference in the state at the time. All these factors added up to a 1–9 record for the season. We didn't even score a touchdown until our third game of the season, which meant I didn't see the field very much that year. The season wasn't a complete loss, though, and a lot of that was due to Coach Mead. He knew I could kick and had been with me from the start, so we shared a special bond. He was a tremendous man who cared more about his players than what the scoreboard said at the end of a game. Even though he spent countless hours on the football field, I think he spent even more time off the field making sure his players were doing the right things in school and out. We had a lot of close games and tough losses. Even though it had to be frustrating for him, Coach Mead made it a point to instill a sense of pride and hard work. We were not to hang our heads, nor give up when the games didn't go our way. Instead, we were to fight until the last whistle. These lessons stayed with me and influenced other areas of my life as well.

One episode that year I will never forget. The season was winding down and we had just lost a close, physical, and emotional game. It was an away game, and after we shook our opponents' hands, we gathered and knelt in the end zone. The whole team was beat to the bone, weary, and sick of losing. I'd missed a 45-yard field goal, and though it didn't cost us the game, I hit the ball like it was a brick and it seemed to miss the goalposts by about a mile. All I wanted was to get home and crawl into bed. Coach Mead stood in front of us. He pulled his cap off and wiped his brow, then took a deep breath. "I know this was a tough one. You guys fought hard, and none of you quit. I'm proud to be the coach of this team." He paused. "Things didn't go our way tonight. But as dark as this night is, the sun will still rise tomorrow. No matter how dark the night gets, the sun always rises. And so will we. Tomorrow we will rise and start again." Ironically, as he was talking, the bright lights of the stadium began to turn off, gradually leaving us in darkness. As we got up and made our way to the buses waiting to take us home, the line repeated in my head: "No matter how dark the night gets, the sun always rises." The words brought a little solace to my tired body. But Coach is right, I thought. We'll get up tomorrow and go after it again. Little did I know just how important those words were going to be in my life.

Though that fall was a bit of a downer, new life came with the New Year; 1998 would turn out to be one of the best years of my life. Even though I knew I was rusty, I thought I would give soccer a try in the spring. I played on the junior varsity squad and had a blast. It was a little weird to be on an all-female team again, but I loved the girls.

The game was fun to play again, the pressure low at the jayvee level, and the sport conditioned my legs well for football the next fall. Football, though, was ingrained in me more than I realized. In a game against a league rival, I had to chase down a girl who was headed for the goal. The best way to stop her was to give her a solid shove and then knock the ball away. It is against the rules to push with your hands and arms, so I gave her a hard bump with my hips. The hit was clean, no foul was called, and play continued. Apparently, though, she wasn't used to that kind of rough play. As I dribbled up the field with the ball, she screamed, "Hey, what the hell do you think you are—a football player?" My Chatfield teammate closest to her ran by, laughing. "Actually, she is."

Then one day I got a surprise that made the spring even sweeter.

"Hi, Mom!" I called out as I came through the door from soccer practice. Mom emerged from the kitchen.

"Hi, sweetie," she said, giving me a hug and a kiss on the forehead. "How was your day?"

"Oh, good, the usual," I said, and plopped down on a stool to chitchat. She was beginning dinner. "Oh, shoot. I forgot to pick up the mail on the way home today. Let me call your dad and have him stop on the way home," she said. We didn't have the traditional mailbox in front of the house; ours was a group box at the end of the street.

"Oh, no, Mom, I'll run and get it," I said. "It's so nice out today. I'll take KJ with me.

KJ loved to go for walks, but you didn't walk her. Rather, she walked you.

KJ heard the word "walk"—and came galloping into the kitchen.

"Yes, I was talking about you," I said, rubbing her head. "We're going to go get the mail, KJ." I grabbed the mail key and the leash, and with that, my dog was dragging me down the street. We got to the mailbox, and it took me a minute to get her to sit still while I turned the key.

"KJ!" She had yanked me over toward a weed she wanted to sniff, and I almost dropped the stack of mail. As I was gathering it all back together, I noticed a flash of gold in the corner of an envelope. What was that? Was it a football helmet? Hastily, I rifled through the letters and magazines. There it was. An envelope with a golden football helmet embossed in the corner. CU Football Department. Addressed to a "Miss Katie Hnida." I stood there in surprise for a moment as KJ prowled around me.

"Hey! Sit!" I cried at her. "KJ!" I put the rest of the mail on top of the mailbox and I opened the letter. "Dear Katie," it began. "We would be honored to have you attend our annual junior day on April 17, 1998." It went on to describe junior day as a day for in-state football players to come up and check out the University of Colorado and its athletic facilities. Holy cow. Coach Neuheisel hadn't forgotten about me. All right! I was actually being invited to attend an official recruiting event.

I grabbed the pile of mail and gave KJ a tug. Now I was yanking her up the street. We ran up the cul-de-sac together and stormed into the house, both panting.

"What on . . . Kate, are you okay?" Mom came into the entryway. Grinning, I handed her the letter. She read it. "Oh, my gosh . . . congratulations!" She gave me a giant hug while KJ, sensing something exciting was going on, jumped all over us.

Two weeks later, Dad, Joe, and I went up to CU. Even though I had been on the field, being inside the athletic center was a whole different story. When I walked in, it literally took my breath away. It was a stunning building off the northern corner of the end zone. Immediately inside the door was an area for check-in. When we got to the front of the line, the girl automatically looked at Joe.

"Name?" she said to him.

"Oh, actually, it's me," I said.

"Oh! You're Katie! The kicker! I'm so glad you came!"

I was flattered. "I'm so glad to be here," I said.

"Let's see . . . here you are." The girl pulled my name off a list of sticky tags. It, too, had the embossed gold helmet. "Katie Hnida, Chatfield Senior High," it said.

"Follow the signs and go downstairs. They have a video for you, Coach Neuheisel will talk to you guys, then you get a tour." She lowered her head. "I really hope you decide to come here!"

I smiled at her. "Thanks." I turned back to Joe and Dad. Was this for real? Every time I came to this place, it just got better and better. We followed the signs and went down to the team meeting room, which was done like a small auditorium. This was where CU football players actually met before games. I had just walked by their locker room! Suddenly the lights dimmed and a video began on the huge wall screen. It was a highlight reel of the team, set to music. The song was Chumbawamba, "I get knocked down, but I get up again." I felt a chill go down my spine as I watched Buff players lay crushing blows on opposing teams. Oh, my God, I thought. I love football so much.

After the video, Coach Neuheisel got up, thanked us for coming, and said a few words about the program. He finished by saying, "I hope you all enjoy your day and decide to come out and play for the Buffs." I gave a look at Dad and Joe. I didn't need any more convincing. We spent the rest of the afternoon touring the facilities, looking at the locker room, the field, the gigantic weight room that overlooked the stadium. I looked out onto the field and once again imagined myself clad in the black and gold, kicking field goals. Oh, this was too good to be true.

When we left that day, I was sold. Or rather, I was in love. Everything about this place seemed perfect. It was the start of summer and I was ready to train for my senior season. I would train harder than ever before. A new fire was burning.

So far, all of the formal kicking instruction from my coaches had been pretty basic: kick the ball through the uprights. That's often the case at the high school level. Most coaches just don't have the time or the expertise when it comes to the details of place kicking. Often I was left to work on my own, so that summer, I decided to get some expert instruction. I attended a football camp run by the kicking gurus Ray and Rob Pelfrey. They travel the country, putting on kicking camps for high school and college kickers and punters. They had seen the best players America had to offer. When I signed up, Dad checked to make sure it was okay that I was a girl. Sure, they said. We get girls from time to time. I was excited to finally work with people who had a deep, specialized knowledge of kicking. Kicking was an art form to me, and I hoped the camp would help me with the finer points.

The camp was at CU, and many of the guys were from out of town and staying in dorms on campus. But since I lived relatively close, I drove up for each of the three days.

We met for check-in on day one. When I got to the front of the line, there were two men behind the desk. One I recognized as Ray Pelfrey. Ray was about 70 years old; he'd kicked for the Green Bay Packers in the 1950s. The other guy looked a little older than I. He sat with a cocky little smile on his face. Arms crossed, he looked me over.

"You're a kicker?" he asked me incredulously.

"Yes." I said somewhat defiantly. And not a bad one, either, I thought.

He snickered.

"C. W., can it. Let's get her checked in. You must be Katie," Ray said. He scanned up and down his list. "I'm Ray and this is C. W. He's one of our camp counselors." I looked back at the guy. He still had that cocky little smile on his face.

"Okay, you're set. Just hang around here. After we get everyone checked in, we'll have a quick meeting, then head down to the field," Ray said.

Dad and I stood against a wall and surveyed the scene. The room was hot and packed with people. There were kickers, along with parents and other family members milling about. Finally Ray came out and quieted everyone down. He went over dorm rules and the schedule of what we would be doing the next few days, and then he led us across campus to the stadium. I was pumped to be back inside Folsom. That field just carried a magic for me.

When we got on the field, they divided us into kickers and punters, and then told us to warm up by kicking across the field to each other. I went down to the farthest end of the field, feeling out of place; I didn't have anyone to kick with. I was placing my ball and tee down when I heard a voice.

"Hey," It was one of the guys next to me. "Come kick with me," he said in a southern drawl.

"Thanks," I said, a feeling of relief washing over me. He went back to the other side of the field, and we booted the ball back and forth. I was impressed: this guy had one of the strongest legs I had ever seen. After about five minutes, Ray called us in. My kicking partner met me in the middle of the field, and we walked over together.

"You're pretty good," he said. "I bet you're going to outkick a lot of the guys here."

"Oh, I don't know about that . . . but thanks," I said.

"Trust me. I've been here before. What's your name?"

"I'm Katie."

"They call me Tex."

Tex? I wondered. "Where in Texas are you from?"

"Wyoming, actually." As in the state. Seeing my confusion, he answered, "It's because of my accent." That made sense. I would later find that lots of the guys had nicknames, relating to almost any subject under the sun. For example, we had "Mozart" at camp that year. He was an accomplished concert pianist who also happened to be a kicker. The first night he played in the dorm everyone thought someone was playing a classical music CD.

Each kicker took a turn kicking while C. W. taped us from various angles. When it was my turn, I walked up, and the usual wave of whispers went through the group. I looked up at the goalposts—these were the same pair I had kicked the football through for Coach Neuheisel. Time to do it again. I took my first shot and crushed it. The ball went high and straight and far. C. W. almost dropped the camera. I gave him a wink and a little smile.

Not bad for a girl, huh?

Then I heard the usual mutterings of shock: "Oh my God." "Holy shit." "Damn."

I grinned and then drilled three more perfect balls through the uprights. Ray was astonished.

"Why, we've had girls before, but I've never seen . . ." he muttered. "Okay, okay, everyone quiet down. Next guy, step up." I walked back and stood next to Tex.

"Way to go D-I," he said. I looked at him quizzically. "D-I," he repeated. "You're going to kick D-I." Apparently, I had gotten my own nickname. D-I. It meant Division I, the highest level of collegiate football.

Not only had I gained a nickname, I also was accepted into the fraternity of kickers. Kickers are often considered a little "different" from the rest of the team. Most of us don't look like "typical" football players. We're at the bottom of the football food chain—a combination of hero or goat, depending on if we make the kick.

Ray took me under his wing all through camp. C. W. and I ended up getting along great, especially after I found out he was the kicker for Colorado State. Since I wanted to go to Colorado, we spent a lot of time razzing each other about which school was better. We spent the day kicking, analyzing film, and then kicking some more.

I left kicking camp that day sunburned, tired, and happy. I had spent the day doing what I loved most, on the field of my favorite stadium in America, and had learned more about my kicking style in one day than I had in four years. I also had a group of kickers—many of who would be playing at Division I schools—think I was good enough to kick at that level, too.

The next day was more of the same. In the last 15 minutes, while we kicked longer field goals, Ray came over and took my arm.

"I want you to kick a 50-yard field goal. I ain't never seen a girl kick so far, and the next time I'm talking about my kickers, I want to say I got a girl who can kick 50-yard field goals." All right, I thought. I'd hit decently well from 45 earlier in the day, but I knew my leg was pretty tired from two full days of straight kicking.

I set up the ball for a 50-yarder and give it a pop. I could feel the fatigue in my leg when I made contact with the ball. Surprisingly, it still flew far—close to the goalposts, but not close enough.

"You're tired, aren't you? Well, that still came close. Try it again," Ray said.

"Come on, Katie! You got this, girl!" one of the other nearby kickers said to me.

I took another swing. Ohhh. I knew that one wasn't good.

Ray looked at me. "What happened?" He knew what had happened.

"I tried to kill it," I admitted.

"Yes, you did. Move it up a bit. And kick it just like you would an extra point."

I nodded and scooted up a few feet. It took all the juice I had left in my bones, but I got a good hit off. I keep my head down during my follow-through, but pulled it up in time to watch the ball going through the air. I'd kicked it straight; it just needed a few more yards. "Come on, baby," I muttered. The kickers down by the goalposts threw their arms in the air. It had cleared the crossbar. Ray looked at the yard line.

"Forty-eight yards. Good girl." With that, Ray called the guys over. Not a bad way to end, I thought. That was the farthest field goal I had ever kicked.

3

The Queen Wears a Helmet

AFTER THE PELFREY CAMP, I developed a new confidence. I had kicked with some of the nation's best high school kickers and could keep up with them. I was kicking better than ever and was ready to get onto the game field. I knew a good season was crucial to continuing my football career after high school. I had come to love playing the game so much, I couldn't imagine life without it. I also knew that the University of Colorado was definitely the place I wanted to pursue my career.

Going into the fall of 1998, there had been only three women who had been part of college football programs. One was Liz Heaston, who in 1997 kicked extra points in two games for Willamette College, a small program in Oregon. Another woman, Kathy Klope, had suited up for a game at the University of

Louisville in 1995, and Heather Sue Mercer had made the spring roster at Duke University that same year. But no woman had yet to play and score in a Division I college game. I wanted to be that woman.

So my days and nights were spent working out. Like most high schools, Chatfield held a summer training program for its football players. Four days a week, there would be open weight room hours. Joe was going to be playing for the freshman team the next fall, so he and I would go in and lift together. For a lot of guys, it probably wouldn't have been seen as "cool" to be working out with your sister. It never was an issue for Joe, though. I was a built-in part of the Charger football program, and he and I were like any other two siblings on the team. Of course, I just happened to be his sister and not his brother. We were great training partners, knowing exactly how to push each other to our limits. On days when we weren't lifting, we'd run together and he'd fetch footballs as I kicked. We spent long hours preparing for his first high school season and my last.

Some evenings, the whole family got into the act. Mom would snap the ball, Joe would hold, I would kick, and Dad videotaped the motion for us to analyze later. Jim and Kristen would shag the balls and punt them back.

The closer the season got, the harder I worked. Our team wasn't expected to be world-beaters, but we sure would be better than the previous year's 1–9 disaster. I knew that the best approach was simply to do my best and let things happen the way they were supposed to happen.

Our first game my senior season was against Overland High School, a traditionally strong team. I went through my usual game-day rituals: I wore my jersey to school, carried my kicking tee in my backpack with me to classes, then headed over to church quickly at lunch to pray and bless my cleats with holy water.

The bus ride to the stadium was its usual quiet journey, some whispered conversations, a few headsets with music, and lots of minds lost in thought about the battle to come.

As the stadium filled, I went through the warm-up I followed for years. Start 20 yards out from the goalposts, then 25, 30, and ending at 40 or so. Then I'd change angles, going from the right side of the field, then the left. I'd paid close attention to the breeze during warm-ups. The slightest bit of wind can have a major effect on a kick, making the ball sway from its course in whatever direction the wind is blowing. If there was any wind, I would make adjustments to get the ball through the uprights. For example, if the wind was blowing toward the left side of the field, I knew the ball would drift to the left, too. To compensate, I would aim the ball a bit farther to the right so it would be blown straight. After my warm-up, I would go over to tell Coach Mead how I felt.

In the game's first half, it looked like the powerhouse from Overland was just going to roll over us. But we fought back in the second half to win, 38–20. I had a 35-yard field goal plus was five for five on extra points.

We lost the second game of the season the following week to Highlands Ranch High School. I put us on the scoreboard first with a 28-yard field goal, but we just didn't have it that day. I was three for three in extra points plus the field goal. We lost, 35–24.

Game three that year was against another team that was predicted to beat us handily: Eaglecrest High. My leg got a lot of work that day and we won, 51–27. We were in a smaller stadium and I could really tell how much stronger my leg had gotten during this game. I kicked several balls onto the roof of the locker rooms and a few more over the fence and into the parking lot.

The following week the team came back to earth as we lost to a league rival, Arvada West, 34–14. I went two for two in extra-point kicks that night but had no more chances as our offense sputtered. Ironically, the week following the loss would be one of the most significant and best of my football career.

Every year, the Colorado State High School Newspaper Awards ceremony was held at CU in Boulder. There were workshops in the morning and then an awards ceremony in the afternoon. I was an editor for our paper, the *Chatfield Charter*, and each year the whole staff would take the school day off and go to Boulder. Debi Kuhn, our newspaper adviser, would take us to lunch and then give us some time off to wander around the campus before the awards ceremony started. As a group of us started to walk back from lunch, I had a thought.

"Hey, Nate," I said. "You wanna go check out the stadium?"

Nate Johnson was a sophomore who wrote for the sports section and also played football. I was especially close with a lot of my sophomore teammates. They were backups on the varsity squad and usually spent most of the game on the sidelines. If our team wasn't on offense, I'd usually hang out with them and watch the game.

"Oh, heck, yeah!" he said.

We separated from the group and made our way across campus to the stadium. As we got near Folsom Field, I got a rush.

"I love this place," I told him. "Have you been inside the athletic building before?" He shook his head no. "Okay, we're going in, then. It's incredible inside." I led him back around to the other side of the stadium where the complex was.

"Are you sure we can go in?" he asked me.

"Yeah, let's just watch the time. I don't think Ms. Kuhn would be too happy if we were late to the awards ceremony." I pushed through the double doors.

"Whoa . . ." Nate muttered as we entered the lobby. "This place is awesome."

I nodded. "I love it."

We wandered toward the weight room, looking at the trophy cases. As we were standing there, another thought crept into my mind. I turned to Nate. "Hey . . . I'm going to go upstairs and see if

I can get in see Coach Neuheisel. He's probably not here, or busy, but what the heck," I said. "Will you be okay just hanging out for a few minutes?"

He nodded.

"I'll probably be back in the next 30 seconds, but if for some reason I'm not and it gets late, go back without me," I said.

I turned and went up the marble staircase. I can't believe I'm doing this, I thought. Coach Neuheisel is a head coach who's right in the middle of a busy season with a game just a few days away. I'm sure he's got plenty of extra time to sit and around and chitchat with a high school kicker. I crossed through the office doors and turned to the right into Coach Neuheisel's office. I approached the secretary's desk, stuffing down the apprehension that was starting to make its way through my body.

"Can I help you?" the woman at the desk asked politely.

"Yes. I was wondering if Coach Neuheisel was in," I said with a boldness that surprised me.

"Do you have a meeting scheduled with him?" she asked me.

"No," I said. "I just happened to be in the area and wanted to say hi."

"What's your name?"

"Katie Hnida."

The secretary studied me for a moment, and I caught a brief look of recognition flash across her face.

"Okay," she said. "He's on the phone, but should be off any minute. Have a seat."

I sat, trying as hard as I could not to fidget. I didn't really expect that he'd be available.

In reality, I probably waited only a minute or two, but it felt like an eternity. Finally the secretary called for me.

"Katie? Coach Neuheisel will see you now."

"Thank you," I said, smiling at the woman.

As I stood up, the door behind the secretary's desk opened. It was Coach Neuheisel. My heart stopped for a second, and so did I.

"Hey, Katie. Come on in," he said. I regained my composure and walked into his office.

"Oh, wow," I said under my breath. The view was stunning. The pristine Folsom field was out the window, framed by the Flatiron Mountains at the base of the Rockies and a bright blue sky.

"Pretty nice, huh," he commented.

"Unbelievable," I said, almost unable to take my eyes off the field.

"Have a seat," Coach Neuheisel offered.

"Thanks," I said. "And thank you for seeing me."

"Sure." He smiled and sat behind his massive oak desk. "How are things going?"

"Good," I said. "We had a high school newspaper thing up here today, so I thought I'd drop by and say hi."

"I'm glad you did. Saw you in the paper last week. Looks like you're doing really well this season."

I smiled. Coach Neuheisel had an easygoing manner about him that put me at ease.

"Yes, it's been going well so far. I wish our record was a little better, but hopefully we can pull stuff around." I paused. "Coach, I'd really like to be a Buff next year."

A smile played across Coach Neuheisel's face.

"I know I came up for junior day and you saw me kick a few years ago . . . but how would you really feel about having a woman play on your team?"

Neuheisel rocked back in his chair. "I don't see any issue with it. If you can kick, you can kick." He paused. "And you can kick." The smile returned. "I think you'd make a great Buff."

I couldn't move for a moment. Though I had been invited to junior day and knew that Coach Neuheisel thought I was a good kicker, hearing the words come out of his mouth had just helped to solidify my dream.

"So . . ." Coach Neuheisel said. "You write for your high school newspaper. What else do you do?"

"Well, I run track . . ." I told him. We chatted for a few minutes about other things I was involved in, stuff at school, and even a bit about my family. He was easy to talk to and I couldn't believe he would take time out of his day just to shoot the breeze with me. Finally, I got up to go.

"Thank you so much for seeing me," I said.

"Of course. Good luck the rest of the season," he said. "Katie, we'll be in touch."

I grinned. "Sounds good. Thanks again."

I bounded down the stairs and out of the athletic facility. Outside, I could barely contain myself. I'd make a great Buff? We'd be in touch? This was really going to happen. Suddenly I realized I'd been in there longer than I thought. Nate was long gone. I looked up at a tower clock. Crap. I was really late for the ceremony. I started running back across campus, my excitement and adrenaline pushing me all the way.

I finally made it back to the auditorium. The awards ceremony had already started, so I tried to slide in as quietly as possible. I looked for Ms. Kuhn. Still panting, I fell into the seat next to her. "I am so, so sorry," I breathlessly began. " I—"

"Shhh, it's okay. Nate told us. How did it go?"

I broke into a smile. "I'm going to be a Buff next year!" I whispered.

"Oh, Katie!" Ms. Kuhn gave me a squeeze. I couldn't stop smiling.

My entire newspaper staff was staring down the row at me. Nate raised his eyebrows. I nodded my head at him and grinned.

I was finally beginning to catch my breath when I heard my name. "Finalists for the best feature article in the state for 1998 . . ." With everything that had happened that day, I had completely forgotten I had been nominated for anything.

"Winner . . . Katie Hnida, Chatfield Senior High!" Applause started, but I just sat there.

"Um, Katie," one of my classmates said, poking me, "you won it. You have to go up there."

"Oh! Right." I jumped up and went to the stage to accept the award.

Once again, I had another great day up in Boulder. I was beginning to think this place was heaven.

Our next game was traditionally the biggest game of the season. It was against our hometown rival, Columbine High School. The players all knew each other from Little League, church, and other community activities. The stadium was always jam-packed, and the game always was a good one. Even when we were 1–9 the year before, we took the game to the wire and lost a close one at the very end.

It meant the hitting was extra-fierce and the adrenaline pumping a bit harder. Right before halftime, I gave us the lead with a field goal from 33 yards. Watching it on film, the ball cleared the crossbar with at least 10 yards to spare. It was easily my best kick of the season. I wish I could say the game turned out as well as that kick. After halftime, a bigger Columbine team simply wore us down. We lost, 33–23.

On Tuesday after the loss to Columbine, I got a tap on the shoulder in Economics as I was chomping down an apple.

It was a girl from the student council.

"Katie, you're up for homecoming royalty this year," she said.

"Oh, yeah? What do I have to do?"

"Nothing yet. The school will be voting the next two days. But good luck."

"Thanks," I said, and went back to my apple.

Two days later I was called into the main office. Coach Mead also was an administrator, so I figured he'd called me down for something to do with football. But it was another girl from the student council who'd called me to the office.

"Well, we just finished tallying the votes, and you won."

I looked at her blankly.

"You're homecoming queen," she said.

"Oh! Really?" I was surprised.

"Yes. Congratulations!"

"Thanks . . ."

She went on to explain where I needed to be for the school assembly on game day and then at half-time of the homecoming game. The homecoming game. It was an extremely important game.

With a 2–3 record, we needed a win to pull us up back up to .500 and turn the season around. If we lost, any hopes of getting into the postseason playoffs would be gone. Well, maybe the homecoming thing would be fun for my family to see, but that was it. How little I knew.

On game night, I had finished my warm-up and was heading over to the sidelines to do some stretching when Coach Mead stopped me.

"Katie, there's a woman from the *Rocky Mountain News* who wants to talk to you." He nodded to a woman standing near our bench.

"What for?" I asked.

"I'm not sure. Homecoming, I think," Coach said.

Okay, I thought. I didn't even make it to the bench before the woman rushed toward me.

"Hi, Katie, I'm from the *Rocky;* I just wanted to ask you a few questions." She thrust a mini tape recorder toward my face. "First, how does it feel to be homecoming queen?"

I was taken aback. How did she know I was going to be homecoming queen? They didn't announce it until halftime.

"Uh . . ." I stammered. "I haven't really thought about it that much," I said. Truth be told, the only thing I was really thinking about at that moment was that I needed to stretch out my right quad muscle.

Suddenly another person appeared. "Hi, Katie, I'm with the *Post;* congratulations on being named homecoming queen. Must be an exciting night for you." A flashbulb went off. What the heck? I was caught completely off guard. Where did these people come from? The woman reporter started to open her mouth again, but I cut her off.

"I'm really sorry, but I can't answer any questions right now. I have a game to play and I need to finish warming up," I said, turning to jog down the sideline.

"Katie!" Another reporter had joined the group and was calling after me.

"I'm sorry—I will talk to you after the game!" I yelled back.

"Just a few questions!" a man yelled. The group swarmed after me. Luckily, Coach Dave Bolger was a few feet down the sideline and saw the commotion. "I'll take care of them," he said. "You go do what you need to do."

"Thank you," I said. I ran toward the end zone. A pack of my teammates were doing drills there. I hid behind them and started to stretch.

"Hey, Katie. Going to be running a few plays tonight?" Chris Jones, a sophomore running back, asked me.

"No, just hiding from the reporters. Don't ask," I said, rolling my eyes. I went on with my stretching, trying to refocus myself.

Soon enough, it was game time and we were back in the locker room. Coach Mead gave us a last pep talk and we were back onto the field. The night was warm. The stands were overflowing, and the lights lit the field. I felt a thrill go through my body. It was time for some football!

FLASH! SNAP! FLASH! And also time, apparently, for some photo ops. The reporters had been sent to a roped-off area behind our bench, but it didn't stop the cameramen from snapping away. I quickly wedged myself between some teammates and weaved down the sideline until I found my special group of sophomore guys.

"Hey, guys . . . I might need a favor tonight," I said. "There are a bunch of cameramen and reporters here for homecoming stuff and they are driving me nuts!"

"Here you go, Katie." Chris Jones, the player I'd spoken to in the end zone, was tucking my ponytail into my jersey. He patted my back. "Now you look just like one of us."

I gave him a look.

"I'm kidding, I'm kidding," he said, laughing. "You know we got your back. We'll block you from the cameras." The other guys nodded in agreement.

My little sophomore army surrounded me, helping me keep my focus during the game. It was a good thing, because I had to be ready to go. My team scored quickly, and I jogged out to put the first extra point through the uprights. I gave no thought to the reporters or the cameramen on the sidelines. I nodded to my holder, Chad Antonio, and popped the first one through with ease. The scoreboard changed from 6 to 7.

The team was thriving off the energy from the homecoming crowd and also the extra attention from the media. I put through two more extra points in the first half, each time trotting back into my group of sophomores to hide out. The gun sounded for halftime, and I began my jog toward the locker room.

"Katie, I think you're supposed to stay." It was Chris, grinning, next to me. "Sorry we can't stay out and guard you now."

Whoops. That's right; I had to stay out for homecoming festivities. I jogged back to the other side of the field. Since I had played on the varsity squad since my freshman year, I had never seen what happened at halftime during a homecoming game. I had no idea how this worked.

"Katie! Oh, good, we thought you had headed into the locker room!" It was one of the girls from the student council. "Come with me."

She gathered all of the royalty together. The other girls were dressed in skirts and heels. I had on a sweaty uniform and cleats. We were then paired off by class. Luckily for me, the homecoming king was Eric Schmidt. Eric was a forward on the basketball team and one of the nicest, most easygoing guys I knew. "This might be a bit crazy," I said to him before we walked through flags. "I'm sorry, I have no idea where all these reporters came from."

"Hey, don't worry. It's all going to be good," Eric reassured me. I smiled at him gratefully and then took his arm to walk through a row of upraised flags. When we got to the end, the camera snapping started. Dear God, I thought. I just wanted to escape back to the locker room. They announced the royalty from each class, crowning the freshmen as Duke and Duchess, the sophomores as Lord and Lady, and so forth. Finally they got down to me and Eric.

"And finally, your 1998 Homecoming King and Queen . . . Eric Schmidt and Katie Hnida!" The crowd erupted into cheers, and I was blinded once again by camera flashes. I tried to smile as Eric and I were crowned, but I couldn't see anything. They crowned Eric easily, but my bulky shoulder pads made it more difficult to get the sash on. The photographers ate it up, snapping away as we struggled to yank the "Queen" sash on over my pads. Flowers in one hand and helmet in the other, I smiled for the cameras once more and then waved to the crowd. "I gotta go now. Is that okay?" I asked the student council girl. I handed her my flowers and tried to strip the sash off. The damn thing kept getting twisted and stuck under my shoulder pad. I knew there were other football players who'd been royalty before; they seemed to be able to get their sashes on and off relatively easily. What was the problem with mine? The student council girl answered my question.

"Oh, yours is smaller . . . since it's made for a girl." Right. I should have figured. Finally I won the sash battle and sprinted to the locker room. I got stopped by a TV reporter who wanted to know how it felt to be the kicker and the homecoming queen. All I can remember coming out of my mouth were snippets of sentences—

"I'm sweaty. Hair's a mess. I don't look much like a homecoming queen, but who cares? We're winning. Got to keep it up."

Safely in the locker room, I stretched out on one of the tables, then refocused my mind back to football. We were back on the field in minutes. My team hadn't lost any of the fire from the first half, and we kept scoring. Point after point, I kept nailing them through. We won the game, 42–15. I was a perfect six for six on extra points. When the clock ran down, I went through the handshake line. Waiting for me on the other side were the reporters.

I woke up the next morning with the contented feeling I always had after we won a game. We had a short practice in an hour, just some light running and film. Later that night was the dance. I was glad we had the homecoming game on Friday night. For the first time ever, I'd actually have time to get ready. In years past, homecoming games had been on Saturday afternoon and would leave me little time to get ready for the dance. Most girls would spend a few hours getting ready, often having hair appointments and getting their nails done. I was lucky to get a shower in before my date would pick me up.

I walked down the stairs and into the kitchen. The whole family was up.

"Hey, guys," I said as I pulled out a box of Cheerios. In mid-pour, I noticed they were all looking at me.

"What?" I asked.

Mom smiled. "You might want to come look at the newspapers," she said.

"Yeah?" I said, carrying my cereal to the table.

"You made the cover of both the *Denver Post* and the *Rocky Mountain News*," Dad said.

"The front page? On both?" I asked incredulously. I pulled a paper over. Wow. There I was, smiling in my burgundy uniform. I scanned the articles as I ate. Not bad. A line in one of them caught my eye. "With her six extra points last night, Hnida now leads the state in kicking."

"Dad, would you pass me the sports section?" I asked. I quickly flipped to the high school football stat leaders and found the kicking section. There it was, at the top of the list. "Hnida, Chatfield." All right! Now, this was something to get excited about. I had been in the top group of kickers since the season had started, but I hadn't gotten as many shots as some of the other guys who played for teams with high-scoring offenses. Fortunately, though, I had made all my attempts, and it put me at the top.

I finished my cereal, slid into my sweats, and drove over to practice. A group of my teammates were sitting on the ground, stretching. Everyone was in a good mood from the win the night before.

"Hey, superstar!" one of the guys said to me as I sat down to stretch. "Front page!" "Homecoming queen! Leading the state in kicking!" They teased me good-naturedly, grabbing my ponytail and giving me a noogie.

"Hey!" I protested. But I was smiling. "Knock it off," I said with a laugh. Practice was quick that day. I was glad to get back home and I wanted to snooze a bit before the homecoming dance that night. When I walked back into the house, the phone was ringing. I walked into the kitchen. "Oh! You're home early! The phone has been ringing off the hook since you left," Mom said. "*Sports Illustrated* just called."

"WHAT?!" I said. My eyeballs almost popped out of my head. "Are you kidding?"

"No. Rick Reilly, the back-page columnist, you know, he lives in Denver?" Mom asked.

"Oh, yeah . . ." I recalled.

"Well, he saw you in the paper this morning and wants to interview you. I told him you had practice and were over at the school. He said he would go to Chatfield and track you down."

"What?! He's going there now? I gotta get back there!" I grabbed my keys and raced back out the door. *Sports Illustrated?* The magazine I read cover to cover each week? Wanted to interview me? I flew back to school. I had rolled out of bed for practice that morning, thrown on my sweats, and pulled my hair into a ponytail. I don't think I even brushed it. Too late now, I thought. I ripped up the main driveway to school and saw a dark-haired man leaning against one of the walls. It was Rick Reilly; I recognized him from his picture. He was dialing his cell phone when I jumped out of the car.

"Rick?" I called out. "I mean, Mr. Reilly?" The man looked up.

"Katie! Call me Rick!" He said jovially and started walking toward me. "I didn't see anyone here, so I was going to try your mom again."

"Yeah, we had a pretty short practice this morning. Sorry if I made you wait," I apologized.

"No, actually, I just got here myself. Man, what a great night you just had! Read it in the paper in this morning and thought, now, this is a cool story!" Rick said. He had a dynamic and animated personality. I liked him right away.

"Is there somewhere we can sit and talk?" he asked.

I checked the doors to the school, but everything was locked. We settled on the bleachers next to the soccer field.

"So let's start at the top. How the heck did you ever end up on the football field? Soccer?" Rick asked.

"Well, sort of. It kind of happened by accident." I told him the story of kicking in the backyard and deciding to play for the team. "It just snowballed. Now I can't imagine my life without it."

"Wow," he said, scribbling on his notepad. "You still play soccer in the spring, though?"

I shook my head.

"Actually, I did last season, but it was the first in a long time.

This spring, I'll go back to track," I continued. "That way I can focus more on my football training. Football is my main sport."

"No kidding. . . . Okay, let's talk homecoming. What was it like out there getting crowned in your uniform?"

"It was a little crazy. I didn't have much time and I was so focused on the game. It'll be fun tonight, but to tell you the truth, it's really not that big of a deal to me."

"Seriously? I would think most girls dream being homecoming queen."

"Aaah, I'd rather be kicking field goals," I said, shrugging. Rick looked a little surprised.

"But you're still so . . ."

"Girly? No way. I am not 'girly,'" I explained. "But I am feminine. I wear skirts. I curl my hair. I'm looking forward to getting dressed up tonight. But put me on the playing field and I'll kick the crap out of you. And I'd much rather watch *Field of Dreams* than some weepy chick flick."

Rick was chuckling. "Okay, I got it." He then went on the pepper me with questions about everything under the sun. We talked about my teammates, "great guys, don't mind when they burp and fart around me," to my family, "they are everything to me," to getting hit and hit on by opposing teams, "big difference between those two." Rick asked about the school newspaper, drama, and my favorite classes. We'd been talking for close to two hours when I realized what time it was.

"Rick, I don't want to cut this short, but I actually have to start getting ready for tonight. Want to come back to the house?" I asked.

"Actually, that'd be great. I'd love to talk to your parents," he said.

"I think my dad is at my brother's game, but I know Mom is home. We're not far away. Just follow me." I went to my car and waited until Rick was behind me before taking off.

I called home from my cell. "Hey, Mom, it's me."

"Hi, honey. How did the interview go?"

"Actually, it's still going. Rick and I are coming back to the house."

"What?! How about a little warning? This place is a mess!"

"Oh, Mom, it is not, and even if it was, Rick wouldn't care anyway. He's totally down to earth. You're going to love him. We'll see you in about five minutes. Love you!"

When we got to the house, I introduced Mom to Rick, hung around for a few minutes, and then went up to take a shower. When I came down, they were just finishing up.

"It was great to meet you," Rick told us.

"Likewise," I said. "It was fun talking with you," I said. "Better than most interviews."

"Good luck with the rest of the year—and hey, call me if you ever need anything—and keep in touch." He gave me his number scribbled on a piece of paper.

"Take care!" Mom and I waved good-bye.

"Whew," I said when the door shut. "This has been some 24 hours."

"Well, it's not over yet," Mom said. "We've gotten over a dozen interview requests for you this morning. Both *Sports Illustrated* and the *Post* are sending photographers over to the dance, and one of the local stations is going to come film."

Was she serious? I was going to go blind if I saw another camera flash.

I finished getting dressed in record time. When I was pulling on my shoes, I happen to notice how high the heels were. Oh, boy. Eric and I had to walk down a huge set of stairs after we were crowned. What if I took a dive? Not only would the entire school see, but also cameras would be there to record me falling on my face.

Luckily, the evening went perfectly. Dinner was good. The sash slid over me with ease. I made it down the stairs smoothly. And I actually ended up having fun as the homecoming queen.

I thought the media would start to die down after the dance. Instead, the opposite happened. It completely exploded. I was in newspapers around the country and made Paul Harvey's news broadcast. I did radio shows as far away as Boston. The *Sports Illustrated* article came out the next week and produced another flurry of media. CNN and *Dateline* producers called. I received my first offer for a television movie based on my story. I even made the tabloids. Letters asking for autographs poured in. I also started to receive mail from colleges other than CU. Notre Dame and Stanford sent letters and applications to me. A number of other schools, including Missouri, Harvard, and Arizona, contacted me to express interest in having me walk onto their football teams. While it was hard not to look at a school such as Notre Dame, I knew CU was where I wanted to go. My heart felt like it belonged there. The season continued on, and the media settled into a more steady flow. I got used to cameras constantly snapping at games.

In late October, a few incredible things happened. One came when I opened my door to give out candy on Halloween. In front of me were two girls in football jerseys and tiaras. They were little Katie Hnida costumes! I was flattered and humbled; I made sure to give them extra candy. Then, *Teen People* magazine named me their number one "Teen to Change the World" for 1999. I was going to be featured in their February issue and go to New York for an awards luncheon. The second event was an honor as well: I got to kick with Jason Elam, the Denver Broncos' placekicker. One Sunday afternoon, I was lying on the couch watching the Broncos play Jacksonville. The Broncos missed a first down and it looked like they were going to have to punt. All of a sudden, I noticed Elam running onto the field. I sat up. What were they doing? They were barely at midfield. Were they going to run a fake? The broadcasters announced it would be a 63-yard field goal attempt. Incredible: 63 yards would tie the NFL record for the longest field goal ever kicked.

"Dad! Mom! Get in here!" I yelled. "Elam's going to attempt a 63-yarder!" They raced in. Elam approached the kick. He hit the ball cleanly and it was traveling straight. Would it have the distance? I held my breath. It did! "Yeah!" I jammed my fist into the air.

The ball cleared the crossbar with room to spare. "That was amazing!" I cried. More amazing was the next day. The phone rang at about ten. Dad's television station was doing a piece on Elam, and they wanted to know if I would kick with him. Were they kidding? Of course I would. Jason Elam was one of the best kickers in the NFL. Mom and I drove over to the Broncos' training facility that afternoon. The cameramen introduced me to Jason and started filming as we talked about kicking. He gave me some advice about kicking off the ground, since I wouldn't use a tee in college. Then he got down and held the ball so I could take a few kicks. "Wow," he said after my first kick. "That's really good, Katie." After a few more, Jason looked directly into the camera and exclaimed, "The girl can kick now, the girl can kick! I wouldn't change a thing!" I thanked him. To this day, it's still one of my favorite memories.

4

Where Did He Go?

BY NOVEMBER, high school football was coming to a close. Our offense wasn't producing quite as much as we had at the beginning of the year, so I wasn't on the field as much during our last four games. Still, I continued to do my job, tacking points onto the scoreboard whenever I kicked. My last high school game came on a gray November day. After dropping two games, our record was 5–4; even with a win, it didn't look like playoffs were in our future. I don't know if it was the weather or the fact that it was our last game, but our performance wasn't very good. We scored once in the first half and I booted the extra point. I kept hoping to get one last shot at another field goal. The clock was winding down. I didn't get a field goal, but I did get a final extra point attempt. I went through the motions, automatic as breathing. Bang! The ball went off my foot. Well, that was it. The final kick of my high school career. It wasn't until I was pulling my mouthpiece out that I realized the refs were signaling "No good."

"WHAT?" My holder and I both started screaming. The ball had gone a bit to the right, but it still was inside the goalposts. The problem was, I'd kicked the ball so high, it had soared way above the tips of the goalposts. Coach Mead was yelling at the ref on the sideline. I stood there for a brief moment, then jogged off the field. I hadn't missed the entire season, and on my last attempt, my kick gets called no good.

With the 5–5 finish and the season over, it was time to look to my college career. Most people knew I was headed to CU, but I tried to downplay it in the press, and according to NCAA rules, CU couldn't talk about me either—or, for that matter, any of the players they were recruiting. Coach Neuheisel was interviewed on TV and asked about the possibility of a girl ever playing college football. All he could say was that with the right player, it was possible. She needed to be able to kick the ball off the ground without a tee, since tees weren't allowed in college ball. And a girl could make it as long as she could kick the ball high and kick it quickly, since the college game was a lot bigger and faster than high school ball.

Though my name was never used, it was clear I was the "girl" being talked about. I was ready to go.

Then the bomb dropped.

I was out shopping with a friend on a Saturday night in January. I was in the middle of trying on some new clothes in the dressing room when my cell started ringing.

"Kate, it's Dad. I'm not sure what's going on, but I just got a call from my TV station. There's a rumor that Neuheisel is leaving to take a new job."

"What? Where?" I asked, stunned.

"I don't know. I don't think it's true, but I'll keep you in the loop."

"Okay . . ."

No way, I thought. Here we were in early January, at the height of recruiting season. A coach doesn't just up and leave in the weeks before a school is about to announce which new players would be joining the team. It's literally called "signing day," and it's probably the most important day of the year for any football program. No way would Neuheisel be leaving CU now.

The ring of the cell phone jolted me back to an uneasy reality.

"Kate, it's Dad again." He paused. "I'm so sorry. It's true. Neuheisel is leaving for Washington. There's a press conference in about an hour."

I told my friend I had to leave and went straight home. Driving, I tried to sort through my feelings. What did this mean? This was something that had never crossed my mind. For a minute I cursed myself for not taking the time to seriously look at some of the other schools who had expressed interest in me. Then I shook my head. No, I loved CU. I had always wanted to play in my home state, for the Buffs. I had already applied and was accepted by the university. But who would the new coach be? And, more important, would he be open to having a woman on his team? If he wasn't, would I think of going to Washington, or even somewhere else?

I got home in time for the news. The bright lights at the hastily called press conference that night emphasized the confusion on a lot of people's faces. CU's athletic director had a short, terse statement, saying, "Coach Rick Neuheisel informed me earlier today he has accepted a position as the new head coach at the University of Washington. A search committee will begin to work immediately on filling the vacancy here at the University of Colorado." That was it. Nothing more.

* * *

It was January 9, 1999, and my solid, bright future was hanging in limbo. Since it was right near the tail end of the recruiting season, it was agreed by both universities that no players or recruits would be allowed to follow Coach Neuheisel to Washington. That meant going there was out of the question. Other schools were going to be a tough possibility, too—most application deadlines had passed or were passing as the days went by.

The decisions I would have to make depended on who would be the new coach at CU. A lot of names were thrown around, including Gary Kubiak, a popular assistant coach with the Denver Broncos. It looked as though he was going to accept the offer. At the last minute, Kubiak changed his mind and turned the job down. Finally, on January 20, it was announced that CU had their man. The new coach would be Gary Barnett, from Northwestern University, just outside Chicago. It seemed like a good choice, especially since Barnett had led Northwestern to the Rose Bowl just a few years earlier. He also had started his coaching career out in Colorado, and had been part of the CU staff that won the National Championship in 1990.

Since signing day was just weeks away, I thought the best thing to do was to let Barnett settle in and get the program running his way, with his staff. So I waited until mid-February to write a letter, explaining who I was and what my situation was. A week or two later I got a call from David Hansburg, the new director of football operations. He had worked under Barnett at Northwestern for a few years in the same position. Hansburg invited me up for a visit and a talk. We finally met in mid-March.

There was definitely a different feel in the air when I went to Boulder for the meeting. It seemed a little stiffer and a little more formal. Hansburg and I talked privately for about 45 minutes. He seemed like a nice guy. I was able to express to him my seriousness about playing college ball; I was a football player, not a novelty or a publicity stunt. He asked me if I would ever sue the school if anything went wrong. Went wrong? No, of course not. What could go wrong enough that I would want to sue? The question did have a new relevance—the woman who had made the Duke roster in the spring of 1995, Heather Sue Mercer, had been cut before the fall season. She claimed she was cut because she was a woman and sued the school on grounds of gender discrimination. Just a few months earlier, a jury ruled in her favor and she was awarded two million dollars (although the Supreme Court would later overturn the damage award). I told Hansburg that I didn't know very much about the case, which was true. I just wanted to come and give kicking a shot. I left him an audition tape, and he told me they would be in touch soon.

I spent the next few weeks on edge. CU was up in the air, and I started to wonder again if it would be a good idea to get in touch and send audition tapes to a few other colleges. A few weeks later I finally got the word: I would be invited to "walk on" as a kicker at CU. "Walk on" meant no scholarship—I'd pay my own way—but that was fine with me. That's all I expected anywhere. The majority of kickers in college start their careers as walk-ons. Content and satisfied that I would be getting a shot, I realized things had worked out pretty well. It had just taken a little longer than expected, and the coaching change was simply a bump in the road.

I felt even better when I read a couple of articles in the paper that talked about me coming to CU. Gary Barnett told the *Rocky Mountain News,* "It's not so much about honoring [Neuheisel's] commitment. We went in knowing we had no obligation. But our kickers and Jon Embree [tight-ends coach who will work with the kickers] saw her on tape and liked her more than any other candidate we saw."

It was a statement that he would later backpedal from when I joined the team the following fall.

5

Columbine

MY NOSE WAS PLASTERED against the window as I tried to see the island of Manhattan come into view. It was April 20, 1999, and I was on my way to New York City. I'd just been there for the first time about a month earlier, on a trip with my family during spring break. I had loved the hustle and excitement of the city. This time around was going to be even better—I was coming to accept the honor of being named *Teen People*'s #1 Teen to Change the World in 1999. Dad was with me. He was working for *CBS News* at the time and would routinely travel to NYC. What a great few days this was going to be for us.

We landed and taxied down the runway. I could barely contain my excitement. But all that changed in seconds.

Dad's cell phone began ringing the moment he turned it on. He answered immediately. I watched his face as a brief look of confusion crossed it. "My daughter? No, Katie goes to Chatfield." This sparked my attention. "Columbine? Yes, of course. It's right down the street. No, I don't know anything; I've been flying the past four hours. Mmhmmm. Yes. I'll get back to you."

Columbine was our rival, neighboring high school. My school, Chatfield High, had been built years earlier to accommodate the overflow of students. My father snapped his phone shut. I stared at him expectantly. "There's been a shooting at Columbine." My stomach lurched. "That was CBS. I don't know what's going on. I'm going to call your mom." We filed off the plane as I tried to figure out what could have happened. Shooting at Columbine? Nah. Surely it was a mistake. Something small. Maybe a kid brought a BB gun to the school and shot out a window or two. At worst, maybe someone was shot in the arm or something minor like that. After all, this was Littleton. We were just a regular middle-class suburb, like thousands of others across America. As soon as I stepped off the plane, though, I knew I was wrong. This wasn't some kid shooting a BB gun. TV screens throughout the terminal were flashing pictures of SWAT teams and students running out of the school.

Oh, my God, I thought. SWAT teams? Why do they have SWAT teams there? What was going on? My brain immediately shifted to my friends at Columbine—Nick, the guy I had been dating on and off, dozens of friends from church, sports, and work. I even knew the principal of Columbine, Frank DeAngelis, who attended my church. I'd just seen him at Saturday night Mass. As I stared at the television screens, I was overcome with anxiety. Tears filled my eyes. I began to pray as fast as I could. Please protect my friends. Please let everyone be okay. This couldn't be happening. Not in Littleton. I didn't grow up in a place where shootings occurred, let alone school shootings.

Dad was telling me to stay calm as he dialed Mom over and

over. He wasn't getting through. All circuits were busy. We sat for a second as he continued to try to reach her. He finally did. "What's going on?" he asked. All I could hear was "Okay . . . okay . . . okay. The rest of the kids are all right? I'll check back in with you soon. I love you." It would be our last contact with Littleton for hours.

Dad turned to me. "No one knows completely what is going on. It looks like some kids brought guns to school and opened fire. There have been injuries, but no one knows how bad they are." I stared at him, questioning eyes blurred with tears. I couldn't open my mouth, but he seemed to know what I was asking. "We don't know yet if anyone has died." He squeezed his arm around me, then wordlessly handed me his cell phone.

I called Nick's home. All circuits busy. I dialed a few friends whose phone numbers I knew off the top of my head. All circuits busy. Damn! I stared at the TV screens, which were zooming in on SWAT teams combing through a park right next to the school. The reporter was explaining that three men wearing black trench coats had been spotted in the park and they somehow might be related to the shooting. A bomb had gone off a few miles away from the school. Dad was right—no one seemed to know what exactly was going on, except that it was bad. All other schools in the area were in lockdown, including the elementary, middle, and high schools my brothers and sister attended.

I didn't want to leave the TV screens, but finally Dad pulled me away. Nothing new was coming on. "Let's get our bags, and we'll go straight to CBS. Hopefully there will be more information by then." Reluctantly, I wiped my eyes and we retrieved our luggage. As soon as we stepped out of the taxi at the CBS studios in Manhattan, the producers put Dad on the air to describe Littleton and Columbine. While Dad was able to maintain his composure and professionalism, I could barely hold myself together. The tears hadn't stopped since they began at the airport. "Wait until you know more," I tried to tell myself. But from the feeling in my gut and the images on the screens, I knew this was a very serious situation.

Dad came off the set and held me as I cried.

We spent the next few hours upstairs. Someone gave me an office with a phone to use, and I began to call as many of my friends who attended Columbine as I could. The circuits continued to be jammed, and it was impossible to get through to anyone. Frustrated and scared, I sat at the desk, crying quietly and staring out the windows. The city outside continued on, hurried and unbothered. Taxis weaved down the streets, people scurried across streets, racing back and forth in the rush hour traffic.

"Stop!" I wanted to scream. How could anyone be functioning when this was happening? Don't they know what's going on in our country right now? How could the world keep going when my little corner of it was shattering before my eyes? More news began to trickle in: there were definite fatalities but still no names. There was fresh footage of bloody students lying on the grass outside the campus. Interviews with shaking, terrified students recounted how two boys were shooting fellow students right in front of them. An injured student escaped into the arms of waiting rescuers by heaving himself through a broken window. Someone held up a white Magic Erase board to the window with "One bleeding to death" scrawled across it. I kept my eyes glued to each of the screens, not daring to miss a face that passed on the screen. Every once in a while I thankfully saw someone I knew make his or her way to safety. "This isn't right, this can't be," I thought. This has to be a bad dream. It was Tuesday. Just the Friday before, track had gotten out early and I'd gone over to Columbine to see Nick. I knew the school well, both inside and out. I had spent so much time at Columbine for sporting events, debate and speech tournaments, and just visiting friends. That Friday, as I made my way down Columbine's hallway, I had run into some fellow female athlete friends and stopped to chat.

Everything was so normal then, just four days before. And now—this?

For hours, the networks and cable channels just played the same footage over and over, burning it into my mind forever: bloody students, students running out of the school with their hands above their heads, students crying, and desperate parents waiting and hoping to reunite with their children outside the school.

By 4:30 P.M. local time, 6:30 in New York, the Jefferson County sheriff's office finally issued a statement saying that the situation was under control and that the two presumed suspects had taken their own lives after the rampage. Police and detectives were now combing the school for homemade bombs and any other students who were still hiding and afraid to come out. There were dozens of injuries. Fatalities? It was believed there could be as many as twenty-five.

I had finally gotten hold of Nick, and we were able to talk for a few minutes. He had been able to get out quickly. But Rachel Scott, a close friend he'd just taken to the prom, was missing. I'd met Rachel on a few occasions but didn't know her well. "I'm sure she's okay . . ." I said, knowing neither of us believed my words but saying them anyway. I hung up and tried to let everything sink in. But it was still too overwhelming, too incomprehensible. I sat for a minute, staring off into space, and then returned to the room with Dad and his producer. We all just sat there, with the televisions droning on in the background. Dad continued to try to reach Mom. Last we'd heard, they'd reopened all the surrounding schools and Joe, Kristin, and Jim were home safely. Mom was now apparently headed to our church, which was on the same street as Columbine High. People were gathering there to pray and wait for information. When my dad finally reached Mom again, she was able to give us much more information than what was coming through on the newswire.

At one point, Dad took his mouth away from the receiver, then looked at me. "Isaiah Shoels?" I shook my head. No, I didn't know him. By my father's demeanor, I knew Isaiah must be one of the presumed dead. Then Dad hastily grabbed a pen and began to scribble names. My eyes followed his hand as he wrote, anxiously scanning each name. Val Sch— He paused when I gasped in recognition. Val was a friend from church. "She's fine, she's going to be fine," he reassured me, even though he didn't really know the full extent of her injuries. Dad's producer came and held my hand as my eyes refilled with tears. My father kept his eyes on me as the names kept coming. More were familiar, but none were my closest friends. I closed my eyes and remembered that I had seen Val a mere two weeks before. I had been at Columbine for their spring play. When we saw each other we hugged, talked about how long it had been since we had seen each other, and agreed that we should get together soon. The usual. It occurred to me that I had seen Rachel then, too. She had a lead role in the play, and I had congratulated her on a great performance. About an hour later, it was reported that most of the students who were still missing were most likely dead. Parents of the missing kids who were still gathered at a local elementary school were told to get everything from clothing descriptions to dental records to help identify the dead. As numb as I had become, that news put me over the edge. Dental records? Feeling that I might vomit, I stumbled toward the nearest trash can. Closing my eyes, I willed myself to breathe. As I clung to the side of the can, I started to pray—for Val, for Rachel, for Isaiah, for Nick, for Mr. DeAngelis, for everyone. This was undoubtedly the worst day of my life in my 17 years. The wave of nausea passed, and the producer brought me water. News was coming over the wire, printing on the machine in the middle of the room. Two presumed dead: Isaiah Shoels, 18. Rachel Scott, 17.

Eyewitness accounts reported that Isaiah, an African American, was shot in the library after being singled out because of his race. Others reported seeing Rachel's body outside, where she had been eating lunch. Hospital bulletins began to come as well, listing the number of students who'd been admitted and the severity of their injuries. Dad and I sat and waited in disbelief. When it looked like that would be the last of any new information coming for a while, Dad's producer suggested we try to get some rest. It was already after 11 o'clock when we stepped onto West 57th Street.

The cold Manhattan air was welcome after so many stress-filled hours. My contacts were completely fogged over from all the crying I'd done all day. My head ached horribly. Dad took my arm and we silently walked the few blocks back to our hotel. My father, the strongest and most honorable man I've ever known, had no words. There were none. Nothing could be said that would ease the pain or make anything more understandable. He simply held on to me and we grieved together in silence.

CBS had sent our bags over to the hotel and ordered food for us from room service. Neither of us had much of an appetite, but Dad urged me to eat. I sat, picking at shrimp cocktail, while Dad phoned home again. He spoke to Mom, then each of the kids, and finally handed me the receiver.

"Hi, Mom," I said, my eyes spontaneously refilling with tears. "How are you guys doing out there?"

"We're hanging in there. How are you, sweetie?" Her voice was hoarse; I could tell the day had taken its toll on her. She went on to list the people she had seen at church, naming more people whom we now knew were safe. She told me that Val was shot multiple times in the library, but knew no further concrete details. I closed my eyes, letting tears squeeze out, and wishing to God that I was home. I should be there, I thought. This is my home. This happened in my home. I needed to be there, to be with the people I loved and who loved me. I needed to be there to help.

"Mom, how are the kids?" I asked.

"I think they are holding up," she said.

"Can I talk to them?" My voice was breaking. It was like I had to hear their voices to know that they were okay. I talked to Joe first, then Kristen, and finally Jimmy. Joe sounded like he was doing all right. I asked him what Chatfield, our high school, was like that day.

"Pretty rough," he said. Most people had friends, some even had siblings and parents who worked at Columbine. By the time they locked down our school, classes had been canceled and people spent the day gathered together around the TVs or in groups, praying and comforting each other.

"Take care of everyone until Dad and I get back," I told Joe. "I love you." Though I routinely told my brothers and sister that I loved them, that night the words had a special significance. I talked to Kristen next and then to Jimmy.

Jimmy was the hardest. He was only ten years old and couldn't understand why this had happened.

"Why would somebody do that, Kate?" I don't know if it was the innocence of his question or the fact that I didn't have an answer for him that broke my heart.

"I don't know, Jim . . . I don't know." I wiped my eyes. I finally handed the receiver back to Dad.

I was exhausted, emotionally and physically, but sleep wasn't easy. I drifted in and out of half consciousness for a few hours. Images I had seen on TV blurred and mixed with my own memories. Twenty-five possibly dead. I couldn't get that number out of my head. At some point I finally fell into an uneasy sleep.

I woke up the next morning in a state of confusion. I didn't know where I was, and my eyes were stinging. Columbine. No, I thought, pressing my face into the pillow. The events of the previous day came back to me. It felt all too real. I felt lifeless, drained from the intensity of emotions that had been flooding through my body. We had tickets to go home, but the first available flights weren't until late afternoon.

Dad had to go back to CBS. We still thought it was the best place to get the latest information. After that, we decided to stop at the Time Warner building, where my awards banquet was being held. With everything that had transpired in the past 24 hours, I'd forgotten why we had come to New York in the first place.

I didn't care anymore. All I wanted to do was get back to Littleton, back to my friends and family. When we got to the studio, the morning show's producers ushered my dad off to talk about putting him on the air again that morning. I was left in a room that had four or five TV monitors. I sat motionlessly and stared up at the screens.

On one TV there was footage of the studio where Dad was; on another screen, footage of running Columbine students; on another, a shot of Littleton. Again, I felt a stabbing pull to get home. I had called *Teen People* to let them know I wouldn't be making it to the banquet. On our way out of the city, we stopped at their offices to apologize and thank them for being so gracious.

By the time our plane landed in Denver on Wednesday night, it had been more than 24 hours since the shootings. It felt like it had been a hundred years. It was my first experience with how time is warped by trauma. As soon as I stepped off the jetway, I could feel that something was different in the air. It felt as though it was the complete opposite of the bustling city we had just left. Now we were in a place where everything seemed to be in slow motion. Littleton had stopped, and Colorado had stopped with it.

The Denver Nuggets canceled their basketball game scheduled for that evening. Parents took days off from work and kept their children close to them. Schools were closed, churches were open, prayers services and vigils were held. We were a community in shock and in mourning. Nothing mattered outside our own little world.

As Dad drove home, I stared out the window at the lights of Denver. I thought, My God, how could You allow this to happen?

At least at this point, more facts were known. Thirteen had been killed, 12 students and a teacher. The two student gunmen had committed suicide. Dozens were wounded. At this point it appeared that all of the wounded students would survive. Val, though she'd been shot more than nine times, was in stable condition.

When we walked into our house, it was quiet. Usually I'd hear the clinking of KJ's tags and collar as she raced over to greet us, but tonight she waited for us to enter the family room. Even she could sense the somber tone in the air. My parents embraced, and I turned toward Joe, Kris, and Jim. We shared a group hug and I thanked God for keeping my brothers and sister safe. KJ weaved herself into our legs, and we broke apart to let Mom and Dad come into our circle. We embraced for a minute, all six of us and our dog. I was never so glad to be home. Though it was getting late, I knew I wanted to go over to the church. Joe came with me. Dad went to visit families of the wounded and slain students. He'd had a private medical practice for years in Littleton, and many Columbine students and their families had been his patients for a long time, including a number of the dead and wounded. Joe and I drove over to the church, not saying very much. We were both numb and still in a partial state of disbelief. The church was dark, lit only by candles. There were a few clusters of people, softly weeping. I went to our usual pew, knelt, and began to pray and cry at the same time. Joe sat next to me, his hand on my back.

Chatfield had suspended classes for two days, but I had to go in anyway—I had newspaper work to finish because I'd been away. Security was tight at the entrance to the school. I had to show my ID and carry a pass with me at all times. But before I went down to the newspaper room, I knew there was someone I had to see first: Coach Mead.

His daughter had graduated from Columbine the year before, and his family lived literally a minute away from the school. As soon as he saw me, he opened his arms to me. Though I thought I was all cried out, tears flowed from both of us as we embraced. "You doing okay?" he asked me. I nodded. "Sort of," I answered softly. "Thanks, Coach. Are you?"

"Yes. You know we'll make it through this," he said.

As I walked through the halls of my high school, I was haunted by the idea of a shooting happening here. Among school and all of my sports and activities, I spent countless hours in Chatfield. The building was practically my second home. With our long, packed hallways, where would I hide if the shootings had happened here? STOP! Don't think that, I told myself. At the same time, I knew it was true. If it had happened at Columbine, it could happen anywhere, including my school.

The rest of the week was surreal. Chatfield briefly discussed canceling our prom for the upcoming weekend. I spent a lot of time at candlelight vigils and churches. The funerals were beginning to be held; we had four at our church alone. The funerals were packed with thousands of mourners. On top of that, the media were everywhere. Satellite trucks lined block after block. If reporters couldn't get inside the funeral service itself, they'd be poised outside waiting to capture images of mourners coming or going. It was a scary time as well not only was the community shaken by what had happened, but threats of further violence were circulating across the Internet and to local schools.

Our church received a bomb threat the day of Matt Ketcher's funeral. There was no bomb, and thankfully the authorities were able to defuse the situation quickly so the service could continue.

The prom went on as scheduled, and everyone tried to make it as normal as possible. But it felt strange because everything around us was so different. It was impossible for me to find "normal." I had spent the morning at Rachel Scott's funeral and was not in the mood to even try to be a carefree teenager that same night. I had bought a beautiful golden strapless gown I had been so excited to wear. Now the gown didn't fit. In the days between the shootings and my prom, I had eaten so little I'd dropped weight. Mom had to safety-pin the dress to get it to stay put. All of the "normal" events that were supposed to be a big deal leading up to graduation seemed so trivial now.

The day after the prom, the largest memorial service was held. More than 70,000 people gathered in adjoining parking lots to pray and listen to then vice president Al Gore and other community leaders speak. We attended as a family and huddled close to one another. As the ceremony began, a silent trail of steady tears began to slide down my cheeks. Joe, my "little" brother, had passed me by in height years ago. Wordlessly, he put his arm around me and I cradled myself on his shoulder. I don't remember much of the ceremony itself, but I vividly recall my brother holding me up throughout it. This would not be the last time my "little" brother comforted his big sister.

My last month of school was even more abnormal for another reason: the Columbine students were going to finish their year at Chatfield. Columbine was so physically damaged by the shootings that it was compared to a battlefield. There was no way students could return, so it was decided that we would share our high school. We finished the school year on a split schedule, with Chatfield students using the school in the morning and Columbine students taking classes in the afternoon.

Security became even more intense. Only the front entrance of the school was accessible; all other doors were locked and guarded by police officers and parent volunteers. In the week leading up to the Columbine students' arrival, I spent hours in preparation. We made banners and ribbons to welcome Columbine to our school.

Finally graduations came. I attended Columbine's graduation with Nick's family. The ceremony was by ticket only, in efforts to keep the media out. The ceremony was emotional but filled with hope. Though I had been watching Mr. DeAngelis bring hopeful messages throughout everything during the past month, I was particularly struck by his words on graduation day: "We will not be defeated." He urged his students never to forget what happened, but to keep moving forward into our bright futures. Some of the most powerful moments came when students who had been injured came forward to collect their diplomas.

When I watched Val walk onto the stage on her own, barely a month after being riddled by bullets, I was overcome with emotion. As the crowd cheered, tears slipped out of the corners of my eyes. In the mass craziness of the past month, I had spoken to her only briefly and knew she was still mostly bedridden. It was remarkable to watch her walk, gracefully as she always did, across that stage.

The next day, the *Rocky Mountain News* ran a full front-page shot of Val after she had picked up her diploma. I cut it out and saved it. Several years later, I would dig it out of an old box to take to New Mexico. That picture hung in my football locker for the three seasons I played at the university.

A few weeks later, I would visit her after her first surgery, to remove one of the four bullets left inside her body. She had many surgeries to come.

My own graduation was a relief. I was ready to move on from high school life and was excited at the prospects ahead—especially playing for CU. There was little mention of Columbine at our graduation, except to thank us as students for responding so well in sharing our school. We'd all been overwhelmed by Columbine, yet our administrators wanted to try to keep graduation what it was meant to be: a celebration of the end of our high school education, our entrance into the "real world."

But even on the bright, sunny morning, we couldn't help but feel the tragic pull of Columbine. The shootings were still too fresh, too disturbing.

While waiting for my name to be called, I quietly thanked God for the opportunity to be standing there. I had never taken the blessings in my life for granted, but Columbine made everything more precious.

To say that my life changed because of Columbine would be an understatement. As clichéd as it sounds, I started to give thanks every day just to be alive and felt a driving force to make my life as meaningful as possible. Though I saw the worst of humanity in the shootings itself, I saw the best of humanity in the way our community responded. I saw how powerful the human spirit infused with hope could be. I saw bravery, love, and strength in their purest forms. My belief in God did not waver; rather, it made my relationship with Him stronger, and my faith unbreakable. Though the question of why Columbine happened may never be fully answered, I knew one thing for sure: the world we lived in was the kind of world where an event like this could happen. I was determined to live a life that would help to change that. I never wanted anyone ever to have to experience the terror and grief that our community went through as a result of those shootings. I internalized each of these lessons and they became a part of who I am. I would use them as I made my way through the world and dealt with unseen ordeals to come.

A few weeks after graduation, I went to Clement Park, adjacent to Columbine, just before dusk. I walked toward Rebel Hill, then crossed over to the fence that bordered the Columbine campus. It was as close as I could get to the school. I stood silently and stared at the school, where I could still see bullet holes and shattered glass. Many of the library windows were boarded up. Yellow police tape still wrapped around the grounds fluttered with the evening breeze. I shivered, partially from the breeze and partially from the scene before me. The scene of a massacre, I thought. The pain I felt was intense, but there were no tears. Instead, on that night, I stood there as a typical kid from an average American town, trying to find answers to questions that had none. So I just stood there. Finally, when I turned to go, I gazed at the sun, which was melting into the foothills that frame Littleton. A single beam of light glittered across our town. Littleton. A town that had earned a grim place in American history. A town that would eventually regain a sense of normalcy. But on that night, as I stood there on the cold, hard ground staring out at Columbine, I knew my life would never be the same.

6

"Go Home, Prom Queen"

Though I had four years of high school football under my belt, I knew that the jump to college football—especially Division I college football—was going to be huge.

I also knew I was ready to make the move, but I was naturally nervous about the unknown world waiting for me in Boulder. When I had met with Coach Hansberg months before, I found out that the team had a voluntary summer conditioning program that would start in the first few weeks of June. I decided that it would be a good idea to check it out; I wanted to introduce myself to the strength and conditioning coach as well.

E. J. "Doc" Kreis had been around a long time and was a legend not only in Boulder, but also in football circles throughout America. He had been at CU for years and was best known for his unforgiving workouts and unconventional personality. He took high school football players and turned them into elite athletes. I had heard all the rumors about him: Doc was tougher than rawhide, uncompromising, and intense. I also knew that he was set in his ways. I wasn't quite sure how the rough and tough Doc was going to react to having a woman on "his" football team. I shouldn't have worried. Our meeting went great. Doc seemed intrigued and ready to take on the challenge of turning a skinny female into a Division I college football player.

He showed me around the weight room and introduced me to several players. The few guys I met were friendly and seemed cool with the idea of me joining the team. Then Doc explained to me the summer conditioning program: players ran at one of the four scheduled running sessions a day and then came in to do the weight lifting. He was on his way to run a session now, so I decided to tag along and check it out. Before we left, Doc loaded my arms up—a summer conditioning workout plan, medicine ball, and training guides. He also invited me to come up and work out whenever I wanted.

The running sessions were held about half a mile from the stadium, at Potts Field, where the track and cross-country teams trained. I took a seat in the stands and watched. There were about a dozen guys and—to my surprise—two girls as well. Occasionally some of the women's volleyball team members would join in the workouts. I watched as Doc took everyone through their paces. The workout looked tough but doable. I can do this, I thought. I wanted to make sure my body was ready first, though, so when I got home that night, I studied the workout manual. It was thorough, listing each drill, number of repetitions, and the rest time in between. I recognized one description as the workout I'd watched that day. The next night I grabbed some orange cones and headed over to the high school field. I set up the cones for the drills described, did a quick warm-up, and started the workout. The first exercise was long sprints. I jogged

10 yards, sprinted 100, and jogged 10 more. I repeated this distance eight more times, with a 28-second rest between each run. Then I moved to 80-yard sprints, eight times, then finally 60-yard sprints, 12 reps. By the end of that portion I was already breathing hard. Next I moved to agility drills, short sprints around cones set up in "L" or "T" shapes. These were shorter distances, with concentration being on doing a quick turn around the cone. Last was a drill I knew well: "suicides," aptly nicknamed because it felt like you were working your body to death. Suicides were a type of shuttle drill, where cones are set up in five- or 10-yard spaces. Today the cones were placed on the 50-yard line, the 40-yard line, the 30-yard line, the 20-yard line, and finally the 10. I started at the goal line, where I sprinted out to the farthest cone on the 50, turned, and sprinted back. I touched the goal line, turned again, and raced out to the cone at the 40. Back and forth I went, sprinting out to the next farthest cone and back to the goal line, until I had reached each cone. I was panting, and my legs were burning. There were only three reps of suicides on that day's schedule and by the time I finished, the burning in my legs had changed to deadweight. It had been a grueling workout, but I had made it. The next day, I returned with my conditioning guide and a pair of sore legs. Luckily, the schedule for that day was slightly less intense, with shorter suicides and 20 minutes of 50-yard "on/off" drills around the field. On meant you sprinted 50 yards; off meant you walked 50 yards. I did the workouts for the rest of the week and then decided I was ready to give it a go up in Boulder.

The following Monday, I made the 45-minute drive from home to CU and did my first official workout. Day one of conditioning wasn't too bad—the summer heat beat down, but I was able to keep up pretty well. During the workout Doc turned into a screaming lunatic from hell. "Katie! GO! GO! GO!" he roared. "Pick up your legs!" "Quicker cuts!" I was running as fast as I could. I was used to a lot of yelling on the football field, but I had never been singled out like this.

Between two of our last sets, I bent down, sweat dripping off my face, and gasping for air. "KATIE! GET YOUR HEAD UP!" Doc bellowed. I did as I was told. This man is trying to kill me, I thought. One of my new teammates stepped toward me. "Put your hands on your head. And don't worry about Doc. It means he likes you." Seeing the look of confusion cross my face, he lowered his voice and explained. "The yelling means he cares about you and wants to make you better. Watch who Doc yells at; you'll see."

It was true. Doc yelled the most at some of the guys who were the best players on the team. His method worked, though. Doc pushed me beyond limits I didn't know I had, and it released a new hunger inside me to train like an animal.

At the end of the session we gathered in a circle. Doc introduced me, and a number of the guys came up and said hello. I was sweaty and exhausted, but now it was time to hit the weight room. I had lifted weights through high school, but never like this. The workouts were intricately designed to complement our running and the specific needs required for each position. I had lifted free weights but never had done Olympic-style lifts before. Doc introduced me to the assistant weight-lifting coaches and turned me over to them.

First things first. Every day we came in, we went straight to the scale to monitor our weight. It was important for many of the guys to be at a certain weight for optimum performance at their position. I stepped onto the scale: 127.2 registered.

"What is she at?" Doc had taken notice and yelled across the room.

"One twenty-seven, sir," the assistant answered. I cringed. I wasn't terribly body-conscious, but had always been aware that I was "on the slender side." Okay, really, I was a skinny puke, especially for a football player. I had managed to get up to 135 before my last football season, but it had quickly fallen off as the season began.

Doc came over.

"One twenty-seven?"

"Point two," I added, as if that might make it better.

"How tall are you? Five-eight? Five-nine?"

I nodded. "Five-nine."

"You could stand another 30 pounds on your frame. Don't you worry; we'll get you there in no time. See me before you leave." Doc walked away.

Thirty pounds? I actually wanted to put on some weight, but I had a naturally small frame and an athlete's speed-train metabolism. Well, if anyone could put the weight on me, I had a feeling it would be Doc.

The assistant then took me through the workout, which was written on a dry erase board in the middle of the room. Each day we had a warm-up, a core workout that would focus on our upper body or lower body, an abdominal routine, and finally some auxiliary exercises that were oriented for each position.

The workout took just under an hour, and by the end I was dead. It actually hurt to pick up my keys out of the little cubby I had left them in. I popped my head in to see Doc.

First he handed me a big tub of protein powder—"Mix it with whole milk, ice cream—drink it EVERY NIGHT." Then he led me to the area of the weight room where the coolers of water, Gatorade, and energy bars were kept. Between the coolers and the sink, there was a shake dispenser. Doc grabbed a cup and pulled the lever. "And every day, after workouts, you drink one of these." He handed me the cup. It had the density of a milkshake but sure didn't smell like one. Tentatively, I took a small sip and gagged. It tasted like ground-up cow manure with chocolate flavoring mixed in. Doc chuckled at my face. "You'll get used to them," he said, turning to go. Pausing, he looked back at me. "Good first day. I'll see you tomorrow."

That being said, I began making the 45-minute trip up to Boulder four days a week to train under Doc. I was happy; it was a good way to get familiar with the program, get in shape, and meet my new teammates. They weren't all there for the summer, but I was beginning to learn some names and faces. It looked like things were going to go smoothly. But I hit my first potential snag.

It was only my second day of running when I met my first teammate who didn't seem to like the idea of a woman on the football field. He was an extremely large guy. I figured he had to be an offensive lineman. I was lacing up my cleats when I noticed him looking at me. Or glaring. Maybe it was the sun? Whatever. I got up to stretch. I didn't notice him again until we were running our 50 ins, 50 outs. I turned at a cone and slowed to a walk.

I wiped the sweat from my brow as I walked past him. "Are you *the kicker*?" he asked sourly.

"Yeah, that would be me," I answered. He crunched his large face up.

"Why? Weren't you the prom queen or something like that?" he asked with a snarl.

"Something like that."

"Well, go home. You're not a football player. You're a girl."

"What?" I wasn't quite sure I heard him right.

"I said, go home, prom queen." We were approaching a cone and I broke into a sprint a few steps early. Out of a hundred guys, I knew there were sure to be a few who weren't going to like me. I had found one of them, but I didn't care very much. As long as he didn't give me too much trouble, I'd just ignore him. In the weight room later, I asked one of the guys who'd run with us who the enormous guy was.

"Oh, the really big one? That's Spanky."

"Spanky?"

"Well, Chris Morgan, but we all call him Spanky. Out of *The Little Rascals*."

I smiled to myself; he did look like a bigger version of Spanky. I figured I could handle this guy.

The rest of summer flew by, a flurry of weights, sore muscles, running, and protein shakes. I met the equipment managers, and toward the end, more guys came back to Boulder, and I met all of the kickers. I had corresponded with Jeremy Aldrich, the starting kicker, a few times via e-mail. I'd followed his career since he started at CU. Jeremy was one of the best kickers I'd ever seen. He also turned out to be an incredibly nice guy. I then met Mark Mariscal, the second-string kicker and punter, and later the two other kickers: Derek Moore and Matt "Rat" Altman. I also met Coach Jon Embree, the tight-ends coach who also oversaw the kickers. He had a quiet warmth about him, and I liked him immediately. On one of the last days of summer, I met the man that I had wanted to meet most.

I was under the bar doing squats when Doc came over to me.

"When you're finished in here, go on upstairs."

"Why?" I asked.

"Coach Barnett would like to meet you." Doc had a gleam in his eye. "He was surprised to hear that you had been doing the workouts up here." He continued. "I told him that you had been here a long time and have been working your tail off." I smiled. That was high praise coming from Doc.

"Thank you."

As soon as I was done working out, I went straight upstairs. Finally, I was going meet Gary Barnett, the man. I had been reading about him in the papers but was finally going to see what he was like in person.

There was a new secretary behind the desk, and I introduced myself. Her name was Jane, and she was very sweet. We chatted for a few minutes before she buzzed Coach Barnett. He appeared in the doorway.

"Katie . . . come on in," he said, smiling. I walked into the familiar office, once again struck by the breathtaking view.

"Sit down." Barnett motioned to a chair. He sat behind his desk. I had an odd feeling of déjà vu. The office was the same as the last time I had been in it. The only difference was the man behind the desk. "I was surprised to hear that you had been coming up for summer conditioning. How's it going?" I was a little perplexed. Why was he so surprised that I had been doing the summer workouts? Wasn't that what players were supposed to do?

"It's going well," I said. "I like Doc, I like the training." Though he was smiling, I had a gut instinct that he was studying me.

"Good, good. When I heard you were up here, I asked Doc to send you by. It's great that you're working out."

"Well, I want to be in the best shape possible for the season. It's been good to get to know the program a bit."

Coach Barnett nodded, still smiling. I smiled back, but felt vaguely uncomfortable. We talked for a few more minutes, about Boulder, what I was going to study, and so forth.

"I'll let you get back to work. It was nice to finally meet you. I'm looking forward to the season starting," I said, getting up. "Thank you for introducing yourself."

"Of course. Keep up the good work." Barnett stood as well and shook my hand.

"Definitely."

I left his office, said good-bye to Jane, and went home. That went well, I thought. He seemed friendly. It was a relief to see him as an actual person. The season would be under way in only a few short weeks.

7

Welcome to the Big Time

I DON'T EVEN REMEMBER what my first day of college classes were like; I was too busy thinking about football practice that afternoon. Even though I had done the summer workouts and met a number of the guys, this was the first time I would be around the entire team and the coaches. I had made a decision with the media director, Dave Plati, that I'd be off-limits to the media for the first few weeks. I was adamant about not creating a distraction for the team or a media circus. I wanted to be taken seriously. Regardless, I knew media would be there and I'd be under the microscope whether I was doing interviews or not.

As soon as my classes were over, I raced across campus to the athletic facility. Since I'd been around during the summer, I'd already been fitted with my shoulder pads and helmet. When I got to my locker room, they were sitting in my locker, along with a number two practice jersey and the rest of my gear. I went across the hall and looked at the board in the hallway where the guys' locker room was. "Team Meeting: 1:30," it said. It was only about 12:45, so I went back to my locker room.

"Oh!" There was another girl in there. It was Megan Rogers, the only female equipment manager in the football program. We'd met briefly in the summer.

"I'm sorry, you scared me. I forgot you used this locker room, too," I said. Out of the 20 or so lockers in the room, only three or four were in use, including hers and mine. All the other female teams used locker rooms at their respective practice areas.

She turned and smiled briefly at me. "Ready for your first day of practice?" she asked.

"Yeah. I'm pretty nervous, though," I admitted. "The team meeting room, it's the auditorium next door, right?"

"Yep." She finished tying a bow in her half ponytail. "See you out there."

"Okay. Thanks," I said, smiling at her as she left the locker room.

She wasn't rude, but certainly wasn't very friendly. Megan was only a year older than I, and one of the few other females around. I had hoped we'd be friends, but I had a distinct feeling that she didn't care much for me. I shook my head; maybe she was just having a bad day. I had much more important things on my mind. I was glad that the locker room wasn't used much. I had liked having my own place in high school and was glad to have the same advantage in college. They were like my own little refuge, a quiet place after long practices. I looked at my watch and saw that it was only 12:50. I changed into my practice pants and pulled my jersey over my shoulder pads. For a moment I looked at the golden helmet. I was really doing this. In spite of my nerves, I felt a thrill flicker through my body. I was getting ready for practice with the University of Colorado Buffaloes, the team I had glorified while growing up. Heck—I *was* a Buff. I rechecked my watch. It was 1:00 P.M. Okay. I sat quietly, trying to keep my nerves in check and stay mentally focused. The ability to concentrate intensely was one of the strongest parts of my game. On the field, I was able to block out everything except kicking the ball. I knew with all the pressure and attention today, it would be especially important to get into my zone. Man, I was nervous. I must've checked my watch every 30 seconds. I closed my eyes, praying and making sure to control my breathing.

Finally, at 1:15, I made my way out of my locker room toward the meeting room. As I opened up the door onto the area outside the meeting room, I froze. I thought it would be empty. Instead, there were about 25 of my new teammates standing there. And they were all staring at me. I gave a small smile and slid in, placing myself against the wall and trying to blend into it. There were murmurs, but then conversations resumed. I exhaled, not realizing I had been holding my breath. As soon as I dared, I looked up and scanned the room for a familiar face. *Any* familiar face. Finally I saw one. It was Jeremy Aldrich, our starting kicker. He gave me a small smile from across the room. I smiled back, grateful to see someone I recognized. Within minutes a manager came and unlocked the doors. The guys all filed in and I joined in line. When I got through the doors, I saw Jeremy already sitting in a row closer to the top. I sat next to him.

"Hey," I said.

"Hi there. Welcome to 'kickers' row.' This is where we usually sit," Jeremy said.

"Okay. Can you fill me in on how this usually goes?" I asked. Aldrich was such a great kicker; I was a little in awe of him. But he was so easygoing, I felt really comfortable around him.

"Sure." He explained to me that we would meet for a few minutes as a team, then the other players would go to their position meetings, and we kickers would go out and get warmed up. We would kick during the first part of practice and then be on our own.

As he spoke, Mark Mariscal wandered in and sat next to us, followed by Derek Moore.

The room filled up quickly. I saw guys from the summer, including Chris Morgan, the lineman who'd told me to "go home" while we were running. When he saw me, he made a face at me. I drew back in amazement. Seriously? I thought I had just started college, not kindergarten. I didn't get the chance to think about it for long. Coach Barnett entered at the front of the room, and everyone quieted down immediately. I looked at the man standing in front of me. I hadn't gotten a good feel for him yet. Barnett had seemed friendly, but there was something about him I just couldn't put my finger on. He spoke briefly about practice that day and then went on to the Colorado State game. It was less than two weeks away and already getting a lot of attention in the press and among the public. It was the first time in 13 years that we would be playing each other, and the renewal of the rivalry was a big deal. If you were a football fan in Colorado, you were either a big booster of CU or of CSU. There was little love between the schools and their fans. We were ranked 14th in the country in the preseason, and were expected to bulldoze the CSU Rams by a few touchdowns at least.

It was a quick meeting and we split up, the guys into their meeting rooms, and me back to my locker room. I grabbed my helmet, cleats, and shoulder pads. Saying a quick prayer, I headed out to the field. As I sat outside, lacing up my cleats, Doc passed by, giving me a quick wink. "Go get 'em," he said. I grinned at him, feeling the rush of excitement again. "You got it." I walked down to the hill to our practice fields. There were four fields encased by a high fence. The fence was covered with black tarp. Weird, I thought. I didn't remember that ever being there. Then I remembered something I'd heard a few weeks before, something about Barnett bringing a very different atmosphere to Boulder than Coach Neuheisel had created. Not only was there privacy fences, he would also have closed practices, something few coaches did at the time. That meant if you were a fan, you couldn't come in just to watch. And if you were a member of the press, you better have the proper credentials. Hey, if that meant there'd be less people staring at me, I wasn't going to complain.

My cleats crunched as I crossed the dirt parking lot in front of the fields. As I got near the entrance, there was a large group in front of it: the media. They parted as I walked through the gate. I held my head high, nodding and smiling briefly in acknowledgment as cameras flashed. I crossed to the other side of the field, where Jeremy and Nick Pietsch, our starting punter, were beginning to warm up. I said hi and then began my own warm-up. I took my time, wanting to make sure I got my muscles warmed and stretched out properly. Warming up was a ritual for me; I would get my body loose, but my mind relaxed as well. I grabbed a ball and started doing my steps. I started with no-step kicks, then one-step kicks, and finally my full kicking motion. I set the ball on the tripod and gave it a pop. Ugh. That wasn't a usual kick for me. It wasn't horrible, but it certainly wasn't me. Unfortunately, it was the only full practice kick I got. Our snappers and holders had come onto the field. Coach Embree set me up with John Donahoe, another freshman, who would be one of the two holders I would work with throughout the fall. Practice hadn't officially started yet, but most of the players and their position coaches had trickled onto the field. John took a few practice snaps from the snapper and then was ready for me. I took a deep breath. I had snapped my helmet on but could feel eyes from everywhere watching me. Now was time to get into the zone. I lined up and nodded to John that I was ready. The ball was snapped back, and I went for it. Oh, no. The second my foot made contact with the ball, I knew that it was a bad kick. Grimacing, I looked up. The ball flew with a weird spin and missed the left goalpost. Stay calm, hit your next one. Focus. One good hit and I'd fall into my rhythm.

"Let's go again," I said. I lined up. The ball came back. Again, as soon as my foot hit the ball, I knew it wasn't a good one. This time the ball was low and rotating sideways. I cursed under my breath.

"Relax." Coach Embree was next to me, and I knew he could sense my tension. "Just kick like normal."

I nodded, shook my body out, and got in place for my third kick.

Another bomb. What was going on? Usually I kicked my best under pressure. Instead, balls were going all over the place. I had never kicked a string of balls that bad in my life. Luckily, a horn blew and the team came together to warm up and stretch. After we stretched, the next few minutes were "live" kicking drills, which meant kicking in a gamelike situation. There would be snap, hold, and kick as an opposing group of linemen tried to break through and block the ball.

There were two groups set up, one with Mark and one with Jeremy. They alternated, moving back after each kick. "You won't get to do this for a bit," Matt Altman, the third-string kicker, said to me. "You gotta pay your dues first—it took me three years before I kicked in live drills." I nodded, a bit relieved. I didn't want to be kicking with the team—not after that horrific warm-up I'd had.

Soon enough, a horn blew again. I quickly learned how college practices were structured. They were sectioned into five-minute blocks; each block was called a period. Practices would usually range between 12 and 24 periods, depending on how close to the game we were.

After the first period was over, the kickers and punters were on our own. There were seven of us total: me, Jeremy, Nick, Mark, Derek, Matt, and Mike Twisselman. We didn't have a coach who was with us, so we'd do our own drills and move around the fields to wherever there was space.

"How'd it go?" Jeremy asked me. I just shook my head.

"That bad?" he asked. "You were probably just nervous." I nodded, but I'd never had nerves affect me like that. Granted, this was a new experience with high pressure, but still . . . it was kicking. The thing that came as naturally to me as breathing. I didn't know what had happened, but I was going to find out right now. I grabbed some balls and went to kick into a net hanging on the goalpost. I wanted to kick into the net so I could study my form, and not be concerned with how the balls looked. I went back to one step, making sure my foot was hitting the ball correctly. When I was satisfied that my foot was in the right place, I did my full motion. Just like in the backyard with Dad and Joe, I said to myself. It took a hit or two, but I fell into my rhythm. I was hitting the ball cleanly. Before I knew it, the team was running a scrimmage and we went to join the rest of the guys on the sidelines. I had wanted to keep kicking, but figured I'd better go with the other guys for now.

As I stood there, a few of my teammates came up and introduced themselves. One asked me how I liked my first college practice.

"Not bad," I answered, smiling. It hadn't been, minus the hideous warm-up.

The last horn blew, and Coach Barnett called us in. We circled around him and he wrapped up practice with a few words of praise and criticism. When he was done, we all stood and formed a huddle. As I got squeezed into the mass of bodies, I felt a hand move onto and rub my buttock. What the hell?

We broke, yelling "BUFFS!" I quickly turned around, but there were about 30 players behind me, going in all directions to see their position coaches. Strange. Maybe we were just crunched in so tight that someone's hand got accidentally pushed into my butt. After all, 100 guys trying to huddle together means everyone is smashed up against one another. I shook it off and saw Ben, one of our head equipment guys.

"Hey. Is it okay if I stay out and kick a bit?" I asked.

"Sure. Just bring in the kicking bag when you're done and lock the gate behind you," he said. "How'd it go today?"

"Not bad, except at the beginning. Bad kicks. I think I got it straightened out, but I'd like to hit a few more balls—make sure it's out of my system," I said. "I won't be too long."

I went to find the kicking bag. On my way, I passed by my face-making friend, Chris Morgan. He looked at me with disgust.

"I thought I told you not to come out here," he said.

"You did," I answered.

"So why are you here?"

"To kick footballs." I went on my way. He muttered something and I spun back around.

Morgan was making another face at me. Honestly, what was with this guy? He was a senior and was supposed to be a leader. Instead, he made faces like a five-year-old.

Shaking my head, I reached the ball bag, took off my shoulder pads, and restretched my muscles. I was alone on the fields now and was ready to work on nailing down my suddenly lost form. I started with extra points. Pop! Pop! I banged them through, one after another. They were high and rotating end over end like they were supposed to. I worked my way back from the goalpost, going from the left and then from the right, finally ending somewhere around 35 yards. The balls were clearing the crossbar without a problem. I was fine. The sun was melting into the sky as I gathered the balls and walked back up to the complex. What had happened earlier? It was so uncharacteristic of me, but I figured I shouldn't overanalyze. What mattered was that I was back on track and tomorrow would be a new day. I went in through the front around the guys' locker room to the equipment room.

"Thanks, Ben!" I called out as I placed the ball bag on top of the others.

"No problem. You were out there a while—get everything worked out?" He appeared out of the back shelves.

"Yeah, I think so. Don't know what the deal was earlier." I shrugged. "I feel good now, though."

"Good," Ben said. "Anytime you want to use the balls, just let me know."

I smiled and thanked him, then walked into the hallway. I had dropped my shoulder pads and helmet when I entered the hallway so I didn't have to lug them with the giant ball bag. I walked back to grab them. The hallway was basically empty, as most of the guys had already showered and changed.

I bent down to pick up my pads when a group of five guys walked out of the locker room. They were loud and hooting at each other when they noticed me. I gave a quick smile, stood up, and went to take a step toward the door. One of the players blocked my way. I didn't know who he was, except that he was huge. He looked me up and down, undressing me with his eyes. I was still in my football pants.

"Not bad . . ." he remarked.

I was immediately uncomfortable and stumbled backward. The four other guys joined him, grouping around me. It was like a pack of hungry wolves surrounding their prey.

"So . . ." the first guy said. "How do you like black dick?"

I was startled. "What?" The other guys chuckled.

He looked at me expectantly. "Have you ever had it before?"

I was silent. I didn't know how to respond. I realized that in stepping back, I was now backed against the wall. Shit. They were all staring at me, two of them laughing. I now was terrified, knowing I was stuck.

"Well?" the first player pressed me.

"Uh," I stumbled. I didn't now what to say or do. He started to move closer and closer to me. At that moment, the locker room door banged open and another guy came out. Two of the guys in the group turned and started razzing with him. Thank God. I slid to the side and to safety.

"Later," the original guy said creepily, raising his eyebrows at me. He stepped away and I blasted back down the other direction.

I pushed through another set of doors and stepped into the dark corridor where my locker room was. Why weren't the lights on over here? Fumbling, I punched in the code and got inside. I was literally shaking inside and out. It was the first time in my life I'd felt cornered and helpless.

I finally went back to the dorms. I was exhausted. It had been a heck of a long day—literally and emotionally. Even though I hadn't known exactly what the day was going to bring, the events that occurred weren't what I had expected. I talked to my parents and told them how practice had gone. But I didn't tell them what happened after practice.

The next few days didn't go much smoother. I was still shaken up about the incident that had occurred after the first day of practice and couldn't completely focus on my kicking. At the end of the week, I had my first dinner with the team, up on the third level in a room called "training table." I went through the food line and walked into the large eating area. I felt like I was a junior high kid in a high school cafeteria, nervous that I wasn't going to have anyone to sit with and be the outcast eating alone. Where were the other kickers? Luckily, as I stood there, one of the linebackers, Ty Gregorak, called out to me.

"Hey, Katie, come sit with us." Relieved, I carried my tray over and sat down next to him. When I first met Ty, I was incredibly intimidated by him. Not only was he a titanic man, he also was tough and wasn't shy about speaking his mind.

A few of the guys at the table looked up to say hi, and I felt myself start to loosen up. Between my kicking being off and the harassment, I had been constantly stressed and edgy since I started at CU. My relaxation, however, was ended by the sound of knives clinking on glasses. As it got louder, I stopped in midchew. One of the other kickers had warned me about this. The clinking of the glasses was a signal that one of the freshmen was going to have to stand on his chair and sing. Being that this was my first dinner with the team, I had a feeling the clanking was for me. Sure enough, it was.

"Katie, it's time for you to sing!" someone yelled, and the players roared their approval.

Okay, stay cool, I told myself. Ever since I had found about this little initiation, I had been thinking about what I would sing. I thought maybe I could have some fun with it. Shania Twain's "That Don't Impress Me Much" had come to mind, a song about guys who thought they were studs, but were actually superstars only in their own imaginations. I figured I could switch around some of the lyrics to make them pertain to guys on the team and the football field. But after a week of mixed reactions from teammates, I thought it better to play it safe. I stood up, not knowing one to sing.

"Any ideas?" I asked my table.

"Have you seen *My Best Friend's Wedding*?" Dave Andrews, a fullback, asked.

I nodded, and a smile came to my face. I knew he was referring to a scene in the movie where the cast sings Dionne Warwick's "I Say a Little Prayer for You." That would be it, I decided. I stood up on my chair and said a little prayer that I wouldn't fall off it.

The guys all yelled as I stood up. Here goes nothing, I thought.

"In the morning, when I wake up," I began, "before I put on my makeup . . . I say a little prayer for YOU." I had emphasized the "you" and pointed at Sean Jarne, a friendly player I had run with often in the summer. The rest of the team went wild, hooting and hollering.

"Yeah, Jarnes!"

"Whoo-hoo!"

I continued on, each time pointing to a different player whenever I got to the line "I say a little prayer for you." And each time the guys would go nuts and I'd have to wait a few moments before I could start singing again. The last time, though, as the noise was beginning to die down and I was getting ready to start again, a voice yelled through the crowd.

"God, her singing is WORSE than HER KICKING. That's IM-POSSIBLE!" The room fell silent as I looked to where the voice had come from. There he was, sitting at a table in the middle of the room: Chris "Spanky" Morgan. I should have known. Everyone was staring at me to see what I was going to do. Instead of sitting down in embarrassment, I stayed atop the chair. I was pissed; this guy had given me nothing but trouble since I'd met him. I threw out my arms as if to say "What?," then nodded my head in the direction of the door. Come talk to me outside. He glared at me, arms crossed and shaking his head. I glared right back at him. Morgan mouthed what looked like the word "bitch" to me. Right. I raised my eyebrows at him. He just kept glaring and shaking his head at me. Finally, I shook my own head in disgust and climbed off the chair. What a jerk. The noise slowly resumed in the room and I picked my fork back up.

"Don't worry about it. Spanky's just like that," Ty said. I just nodded. Frankly, I didn't care what he was like. How could someone who didn't even know me hate me so much?

I finished my meal and went to go next door to study hall. On my way out the door, I ran into "Spanky" himself.

"It wasn't me," he grumbled.

"Whatever," I replied. "Just leave me alone." I started to walk away.

"I didn't say it." I just kept walking. Was I really *that* offensive because I happened to be a female on the football field? A few steps later, Coach Embree came up and stopped me.

"Are you okay?" he asked.

"Yeah, I'm fine," I reassured him. "It's fine."

"No, it isn't," he said. "I'll make sure it gets taken care of."

"Really, I'm fine," I protested. I didn't want Coach Embree to have to deal with anything extra because of me. The last thing I wanted was to cause a stir. I could handle whatever Spanky would dish at me.

Sighing, I went in to study hall. I knew it was somewhat impossible, but I just wanted to blend in. I tried to open my sociology textbook, but my mind kept wandering. This week had not gone very well. My kicking wasn't on the mark, I was getting harassed by a rude lineman, and had had a few creepy sexual encounters. My body kept getting grabbed in the huddle at the end of practice. It was no accident. At one point, I had even felt a hand sliding up between my thighs. Alarmed, I kicked one of my legs back into whoever was behind me. The hand dropped, but again when I jerked around, it was just a mass of bodies. A day later, I was in the stairwell headed up to the weight room when a voice called up to me. I had paused and looked to the bottom of the stairwell.

"Check this out!" One of my teammates had yanked off his shorts and was exposing his penis and part of his testicles to me. I was disgusted, didn't say a word, and sped up the rest of the stairs.

Then there had been the incident of the guys surrounding me after my first practice. Though nothing had ended up happening, it had scared the hell out of me. Next week will be better, I thought. This is the first week, I'm still settling in. Our first game was next week, and the season would be under way.

The next day, though, I had a bit of a surprise. I was in the weight room, just about to start lifting, when Zac Colvin, one of the backup quarterbacks, came up to me.

"Hey, Katie . . . I just wanted to apologize for what I said yesterday. I was just kidding around," he said. I looked at him. What was he talking about? Then it hit me. At dinner the night before, Zac was sitting next to Chris Morgan. He was the one who'd made the comment about me, not Morgan. Chris had been telling the truth when he told me he hadn't said it.

"Oh . . . it's okay. Don't worry about," I said. He smiled at me and went on his way. I was a bit perplexed. I had run with Zac a few times during the summer conditioning and he'd never said anything rude or inappropriate to me. Actually, I even thought he seemed like a pretty nice guy. What had prompted last night's comment? Maybe he was just kidding, but it really hadn't been that funny. Oh well, it really wasn't a big deal. Probably just hazing. I went along with my workout.

It wasn't until a week or two later that I learned Zac certainly didn't care much for me, when I was walking by him during warm-ups.

"Cunt," he muttered as I passed. I stopped, shocked. I had rarely ever heard that word come out of anyone's mouth, let alone have someone call me one. I looked at him. Zac stared back at me for a moment and then turned away. It wouldn't be the last time he called me a name, or harassed me, for that matter. I would continue to have problems with him the rest of my time on the team.

My first college game wasn't quite what I expected it to be. Since I had joined the team late with the rest of the walk-ons, I wasn't allowed to suit up for the game. So a large group of us stood on the sidelines in our warm-ups with our jerseys on top. We played on a warm Saturday night in Denver's Mile High Stadium against Colorado State University. Since the crowd was expected to be large, officials knew the stadiums at CU or CSU wouldn't be big enough. They were right. More than 74,000 attended the revival of the in-state rivalry, and I'd never been in a noisier stadium in my life. It was certainly different from what I was used to at Jeffco Stadium. It was incredible.

The mood of the team on the bus ride down was a little looser than what I had experienced in high school, and we were confident. A little too confident. Before anyone blinked, the score was 21–0 CSU. Our players and coaches were in shock. Colorado State was known as a "midmajor" school—meaning they supposedly didn't play as tough a schedule as we did in the Big 12. It also meant we were supposed to annihilate them, not the other way around. As the

scoreboard rang like a slot machine, we fell farther and farther behind. I didn't know what to do or where to go when the halftime
whistle mercifully blew. By that point it was 28–0 and when I went
to the men's locker room with the rest of the team, I found I
couldn't get in. I was left standing uncomfortably outside the door.
Literally an outsider. When we came back out, CSU didn't let up.
My old counselor from the Pelfrey kicking camp, C. W. Hurst, was
Colorado State's kicker, and he kept banging field goals with ease. It
was 41–0 before CSU put in their second- and third-team players.
We scored a couple of late, meaningless touchdowns that made the
final score 41–14.

As the teams shook hands, words were exchanged. Then fights
broke out in the stands, and suddenly my eyes felt like they were on
fire. Police in full riot gear had launched tear gas and Mace. As I ran
off the field toward the locker room tunnel, a couple of bigger
teammates shielded my head from beer bottles being launched from
the stands. Since I didn't suit up, I didn't have a helmet to protect
me from flying objects. It was chaos.

Since the game was in Denver, we didn't have to travel back to
Boulder on the team bus. So when things seemed to have calmed
down, I was able to track down Dad and Kristen, who had come to
the game. We arranged to meet away from the stadium. I thanked
God for cell phones as we made our way through the masses to
meet up. The three of us drove back to the campus. We were told to
meet the buses in Boulder, so we waited in the dark outside the Dal
Ward Center for the rest of team to arrive. The players looked like
zombies as they shuffled off the bus. No one had anything to say.
The only noise came from coughing and runny noses. Everyone
seemed to wander away in silence. I stayed for a couple of minutes,
and then just went back to my dorm, still stunned that we had lost
the game. My whole experience had not been anything I'd ever expected college football to be like.

I did my best to settle into a routine. I would wake up at about

7:00 A.M., get breakfast, and then head over to study hall. All freshman players had mandatory study hall every Monday through
Thursday from 8:00 to 9:00 A.M. and then we had to log an additional five hours on our own time. After study hall, I'd either head
straight to class, or I'd go downstairs and get in our required weight-
lifting workout for the day. The order of these would vary, depending on my class schedule for the day. All football players had their
classes over and done with by 1:00 P.M., and at 1:30, meetings
would start. Then it was onto the practice field. After practice, I'd
usually stay out for an extra 45 minutes to an hour to continue kicking and then go in, grab a quick dinner, and put in more hours at
study hall. Depending on my study hall hours, I'd usually get back
to the dorms between 7:30 and 8:30 P.M. They were long days, to
say the least.

Dorm life wasn't that great. My roommate, Deb, was very
sweet. But the floor we lived on wasn't very sociable. Most people I
knew hung out a lot with the people they lived by in the dorms,
but I didn't even know a lot of the girls' names. I'd also occasionally get weird visitors and phone calls. We had gone to great lengths
to make sure that my personal information was protected at CU,
for both my privacy and safety. There was a slip-up, though; my
name and room number was printed in a directory book that was
given out at the dorms. Fortunately, most people would use the Internet directory when looking up people, but some people still
came across my name. I'd have people knock on the door "just
to see what I looked like." I'll never forget the knock I got one
evening.

Deb had gone home for the night and I was reading my sociology textbook before bed.

I heard a knock and looked at the clock. It was getting close to
midnight. Who was out there now? I answered the door in my paja-
mas and glasses.

"Dude . . .are *you* Katie Hnida?" Some guy I had never seen before was standing outside the door. He smelled like alcohol and seemed to be drunk.

"Yeah, why?"

"Oh mannnnn, I thought you were supposed to be hot!" He fell against the door frame, laughing to himself.

"Get lost," I said, and shut the door. Apparently, my glasses and pjs hadn't done much for him. What a moron, I thought, and went back to my textbook.

On the field, I was adjusting to kicking off the ground instead of the two-inch tee I used in high school. I'd asked Jeremy for some tips, and not only did he teach me about the mechanics of kicking off the ground, he was also kind enough to stay outside and work with me after practice. He'd usually stay with me for about 20 minutes, watching my form and talking to me about technique. Then he'd head in and I'd stay outside for a while longer, working on the details and getting more reps. I was working hard but having more and more trouble dealing with the select few teammates who decided to make my college experience hell.

Late one evening, after dropping off the balls, I checked the bulletin board. Nothing new, just articles on this weekend's opponent. Today has been such a long day, I thought as I headed to shower. As I pushed open the door, I almost knocked into one of my teammates, a guy I knew fairly well. He was a smart-ass, but he'd never given me any problems.

"Oh!" I said in surprise. "I'm sorry; usually no one is around here."

"I forgot my keys in the locker room." He looked at me. "Why are you still in your pads?"

"I stayed out a bit longer to kick a little more," I explained. "I'm actually on my way to change now. I just came this way to check the boards." He was still looking at me, studying me.

"You know, I've seen a girl football player before, but never one who looked like you. Most are pretty butch. You're small, even for a kicker." I was suddenly very conscious of the fact that I *was* small, especially in comparison to him.

"Yeah . . . well . . ." I shrugged. I was uncomfortable, but I was always uncomfortable these days. Still, something in my gut was telling me to get out of there. I started to the other door. "See you tom—" I didn't get to finish my sentence. The player grabbed my jersey. My eyes flashed back up to him. "What are—" I protested.

"Just wait a second. I want to see how these shoulder pads fit a little girl," he said. He still had his hold on my jersey and was grabbing at the strap on the side that hooked the pads in place.

"Oh, is this a little tight?" he said mockingly at me, still pulling at the strap. "I can't seem to get a hold."

"They're fine," I said, twisting away from him.

"No, I don't think so." He shook his head, pushing the side of my pad up into my neck. "We don't want your tits to get squished down there, now, do we?" His hand grazed the side of my breast.

"Stop it." His hand was working its way farther across my chest. "Get OFF me," I hissed. I threw my other shoulder down, trying to bring my pads with it. I turned my body, and he released his hand.

"Oh, now don't go crying about this to anyone," he said, seeing the contorted look on my face. "Barnett hates kickers to begin with, but he's REALLY got a special place for you."

He went toward the opposite door.

Safely in my locker room, I felt my eyes well with tears. Damn it. Could I not walk around these halls safely? Was there anyone I could talk to about this? And what's the deal about Barnett? I didn't know what to do.

I knew I should tell someone, but I didn't want to. Even though I knew it wasn't my fault, I was humiliated and ashamed of what was happening. I was scared of causing a problem; all I wanted was to try to blend in. I was also scared of the players who were doing this to me. That last incident, the player had specifically told me not to say anything. What would he do to me if I did? The thought terrified me. I was 18 years old, on my own for the first time.

If I told my parents, they'd surely make me tell someone in the program. And if I wouldn't, they would. I didn't feel comfortable with Coach Barnett and he wasn't very approachable. Coach Embree? He always seemed like he genuinely cared about me. But he was so busy with the tight ends that I rarely saw him. Any of my other teammates? They weren't all bad guys by any means. It was only a core group of the same 10 or so guys who gave me problems. A lot of the guys on the team were friendly. Just the other day I had been doing squats in the weight room when Kane Cullum, a senior offensive lineman, had come by and said, "Katie, I don't care what anybody says or tells you. You keep going because what you're doing is cool as hell!" Kane didn't know it, but with a simple comment he had turned my day around. Yet I felt stuck. I just didn't know what to do. Could I talk to a guy like Kane about what was going on? I just didn't know him that well.

I made it through the week, though, and we hit our second game of the season, San Jose State at Folsom Field. Once again I didn't dress for the game. Neither did the rest of the walk-ons. This game was a complete turnaround from the CSU contest and we romped 63–35. After all these years, I was elated to be on the sidelines at Folsom for a ball game. Yet I still was stressed out by what was going on the rest of the time. I knew it wasn't supposed to be like this.

The third game of the season was against Kansas. We would be playing at home, and I would finally get a chance to suit up. It was a bright, sunny Saturday when I was in full uniform for the first time. Game time was 1:30 P.M., and the kickers went out as a group to warm up two hours before kickoff. The game was on national TV, and my family came up to Boulder early to watch. As the stands slowly filled, I stretched first and then went through the same warm-up routine I had followed for years: one-step kicks, two-step kicks, then my regular approach and kicking motion. A crew from ABC Sports followed my warm-ups, and I could see my family standing at a railing in the stands watching me in my gold pants and black jersey with my name and number 2 on the back. It was a day I had been waiting for for a long time. My pregame kicks weren't perfect, but they were better than I had done in weeks. The game turned out to be a rout. We beat the Jayhawks, 51–17. My family had taped the game on the VCR at home, and it lifted my spirits to hear the ABC announcers saying good things about me during the game. "We watched her warm up and she can kick. It's not a fluke. He didn't have to invite her out here. He wanted her out here. She's a quality kicker." I was having my doubts about "he"—meaning Barnett—wanting me, yet I had to be happy with TV announcers saying I was good enough to play. I knew they saw kickers across the country every week.

Our fourth game of the season was a big one. The reason: We were playing the University of Washington, coached by none other than Rick Neuheisel. The game was played in Seattle, so I decided to drive home to Littleton to watch the game on TV. The game itself was important; so was the subplot of Barnett versus Neuheisel: the coach who took off for greener pastures versus the new savior of the CU football program. The papers covered that angle more than the game itself. We lost a close one, 31–24, but what happened after the game got as much attention as the score. Although Barnett didn't care much for Neuheisel, the same couldn't be said for a lot of the CU players. They had been recruited by Neuheisel, and many had played for him in years before. As the teams went through the handshake line at the end of the game, it was amazing to see the number of guys who hugged Neuheisel. One of our star players, Ben Kelly, even invited Neuheisel to his graduation as they shook hands and hugged at midfield. It was clear that many on the team loved their old coach, and that made for a bit of an uncomfortable situation back in Boulder.

Once again, those of us who didn't make the trip were told to be at Dal Ward that evening to meet the team after they got back from Seattle. Either celebrate a victory or console after a defeat. It was the concept of "team" that had been drilled into us by Coach Mead at Chatfield. But this was strange. As the buses pulled up and dropped off the players, I realized I was the only player there to meet them. So much for "team." The players got off the bus and wandered away. I never went to meet another bus again.

The week following the Washington game was an important one. I would finally talk to the press. Plati told me he wasn't sure how much longer we were going to be able to keep the media at bay. "They were chomping at the bit," and as much as I wanted to blend in, Plati reminded me that I was in a unique situation. And, of course, he was right. We were the only college team with a woman on it, we were well into our season, and I had suited up for my first game, making me only the second woman in history to suit up for a Division I contest. Might as well get it over with, I thought. I told Plati I was ready, for him to talk to Barnett and then decide whatever they thought was the best way to handle it. It was decided that the best way to meet the press was a one-shot deal, a press conference on Wednesday—everyone invited. When I walked into the room, I was stunned. I thought I had seen the media before, but this room was jammed full. People seemed to be on top of each other among the cameras, microphones, notepads, and video cameras. So much for avoiding a media circus, I thought. Barnett was on his way out as I came in. As we came face-to-face, the news members seemed to zero in to watch our interaction. I smiled tentatively at him, trying to convey to him that I didn't like having to do this much either. Barnett smiled back at me and I felt relief pass through me. "Thank you," I said softly, quiet enough to be out of the media's earshot. Barnett smiled again and left the room. Whew. Thank God, his interview must have gone okay. I still had trouble reading him, never sure exactly how he felt about me. But he had smiled. It was okay.

Taking a deep breath, I was joined by Dave Plati, who guided me to the head table along with Jeremy Aldrich.

As soon as I sat down, a mass of people pushed toward the table, all placing minirecorders around me. I was a little nervous but loosened up quickly. It was like any other interview I had done; it just happened that instead of one person asking questions and jotting down answers, there were more than twenty. The questions were standard and what I expected: How do you like it up here? Where do you change? How do the guys treat you?

I blinked at the last question. "They've been very cool," I said. Well, most of them, I thought. Really, only a handful of them had been giving me trouble. Still . . . I quickly pushed the thought out of my mind. Smiling, I looked up, ready for the next question.

After a few more questions, the reporters turned to Jeremy. I watched him as he answered questions about how I was coming along. He was kind as he told how I reminded him of himself when he first came to CU. He struggled when he was a freshman, but with more practice he got better, just as I would as I adjusted to kicking off the ground.

Plati spoke up from the back of the room. "Okay, let's get one more question; then these two need to get to practice."

It was directed to Aldrich, who was asked what strengths I had at this point. His answer was interesting. Along with saying I had a lot of experience and skill, he noted I knew what it was like to be part of a team and be "one of the guys." But that was high school, and I didn't exactly feel like "one of the guys" here.

It wasn't until the next day when I opened up the papers that I found out exactly how "well," or rather how poorly, the press conference had gone.

It had been a bomb. Barnett had completely changed his tune. Now, after the incident with my teammate, I had little doubt in my mind: Barnett didn't like me, and not only that, he didn't want me. Barnett had started the press conference by saying this was the first time he'd ever had a press conference about a walk-on place kicker.

He then went on to talk about how I needed to improve. Stronger leg. More height on my kicks. More distance. Then he admitted he'd seen me kick only six balls since the first day of practice.

What bothered me the most, though, was that he said I'd "been given a special situation." He claimed he was honoring a commitment made by the previous coach—Rick Neuheisel—and insinuated that was the only reason I was on the team. He then went on to say there were probably 15 other guys who couldn't walk on as place-kickers because I had taken their spot. Later in the press conference he said he had to turn away 100 guys who wanted to walk on as kickers. I kept on thinking back to his earlier comments widely reported in the press that out of all the kickers they had seen, I was the best. I had kept the articles. The reality struck hard that my head coach didn't want me around and was made worse by the way he changed his story.

Even though it didn't seem possible, the days after the press conference just got worse and worse. I was still working out after practice. Jeremy would still usually stay an extra 20 minutes or so to keep checking on my form. I appreciated his help, but could feel myself beginning to close off. I was starting to feel discouraged on top of the frustration. I was spending hours upon hours each week, on the field or watching film, trying to straighten out whatever this problem was with my kicking. I was sick of being called vulgar names and having my body groped. I was sick of watching "Spanky" stand in a group of linemen, cracking jokes at my expense. I had quit going to training table, skipping dinner, and would just head straight into study hall after extra kicking. There I could at least hide in a cubicle or bury myself in a textbook. My body was becoming constantly achy and tired. My running and lifting had slowly begun to deteriorate week by week. I tried to reason with myself that it was natural, I just needed to get more rest, that I went nonstop from seven in the morning until at least nine at night. Then I'd usually go back to the dorm, study more, and try to avoid any uninvited strangers who'd drop by to see what I looked like.

After getting in my street clothes, I went out to wait for the elevator to go up to study hall. I was thankful that no else was waiting; I didn't feel like dealing with any crap today. My body was worn out, and I couldn't seem to kick a cold that had been lingering for more than a week. God, I was so tired. I closed my eyes and leaned my head up against the wall. I just wanted to go back to the dorm and sleep for an eternity.

"Daydreaming about me?" A voice shook me back to the present. Great. It was one of my least favorite guys on the team, one who was always dropping sexual innuendos. He had made comments about my breasts, my buttocks, my legs. "Looks like you're growing a bit there, Katie," he said, thumping on his own chest and nodding his approval. "Very good." I'd walk by him at practice or in the weight room and he'd say, "How about a blow job, Katie? You up for it? I am." Then he'd laugh at his own joke. For the most part, I would just let his comments roll off my back.

I shook my head, not even bothering to answer him.

"Aw, come on." He reached over and put an arm around me, pressing his body up against my side. I felt something hard pressed against my hip. Oh, dear God. He had an erection.

"See, I got the goods. You're missing out," he said. I brought my hand to my mouth, disgusted. I physically shrugged him off, as two more of my teammates walked into the foyer. Thank God. I just stared at the floor as the ding signaled the elevator arriving. I didn't know whether I wanted to cry or hit him as hard as I could.

On October 9 we played our fifth game of the season. At this point we had a 2–2 record and needed a win against Missouri to get above the .500 mark. The game was at Folsom, which meant I got a chance to suit up. When I woke up to head over to the stadium, I had to drag myself out of bed. This cold was no longer a cold; I was coming down with something. I was achy and my throat was starting to hurt. I made it through pregame warm-ups, then settled onto the sidelines for the game.

We jumped on Missouri quickly and had a comfortable lead as the clock ran down late in the fourth quarter. It was one of those games where you are beating the other team so badly, thousands of fans start filing out early to beat the traffic. Suddenly Missouri recovered fumbles, picked off passes, and scored several times to tie the game as the clock ran out. We eventually pulled the game out in overtime, winning 46–39. It was a victory, but a costly one.

The next day, Sunday, was our usual film and running day. Though we had won the game, we'd blown a big lead and almost gave the game away. We were going to pay for it during our gassers. Gassers consisted of sprinting across the field from one sideline to the other, then turning around, touching the sideline you started from and doing it again. Ever since I'd begun football as a 14-year-old, gassers were my least favorite form of conditioning. I was especially dreading them today, since my body felt so bad. I waited for the whistle to blow and took off running. I fell behind my teammates, but finished the first few sets. I was determined to get through these, even if I had to crawl. On the last one, though, I crashed. My vision was blurred with big, blotchy spots and I tumbled to my knees. Our trainer, Steve Willard, rushed to my side. I didn't know if I was going to pass out or throw up. I could feel my head start to fall forward.

"Whoa there," Steve said, grasping my arm to keep me up. He guided my head back up and tried to slow my breathing. "What's going on?"

"I don't know . . . spots . . . I can't . . . my throat . . ." I was burning up and couldn't even manage to get words out. The team had finished the last set. My breathing was slowly returning to normal.

"I'm okay," I told Steve as my teammates straggled off the field. "I just need a minute or two. You can go ahead." He stayed by me for a few more minutes.

"Are you sure you'll be okay?" Steve eyed me.

I nodded.

"Come straight in and see us if you need anything."

I nodded again. "Thanks." I put one knee up and rested my forehead on it. I still felt overheated and dizzy. Maybe I was coming down with the flu.

As I tried to blink the spots out of my eyes, a pair of large feet emerged into my field of vision. Was I seeing things? Slowly, I looked up. A sweaty Chris Morgan was in front of me. No. Not today. I lowered my eyes.

"Next time finish your running, bitch."

I didn't have the strength to even look back up at him, much less tell him to shut his trap. Fortunately, that was all he said and left.

I put a hand down to the cool grass. Only a few players remained, but I still didn't trust my legs enough to stand up. Jeremy was still there. I had a sense he was keeping an eye on me.

Finally, when I was the last player left, I pulled myself to my feet. Easy does it. My legs wobbled like Jell-O as I slowly walked off the field. Eventually I made it up the hill to the complex. As soon as I reached the door, I felt the vomit rising in my throat.

Still unsteady, I covered my mouth and moved as fast as possible to my locker room. I thrust open the door and made it to the sink just in time. I started to vomit uncontrollably. In between the retching, I stumbled into a stall. I held on to the sides of the toilet and tried to control the violent waves of nausea. My blotchy vision had turned into a tunnel and I collapsed onto the floor of the stall. Several minutes passed. My eyes fluttered slightly and I remember feeling the cool tile floor against my cheek. My head was fuzzy and my mouth tasted of sour bile. It took me a minute to get my bearings. I had blacked out. I lay on the ground for a few more minutes, then struggled up and rested my back against the wall. Finally I picked myself up. I staggered toward my locker, yanking out my bag and retrieving my cell phone. I leaned against my locker, prayed for service, and dialed home. I rarely got reception in the depths of the Dal Ward, but miraculously, my call went through.

"Hello?"

"Dad," I croaked, my voice hoarse from all the stomach acid that had run through my throat. "I'm sick. I'm coming home." I explained to him what happened while we were running and how I had gotten shaky and sick.

"Don't drive," he said. "We'll come up and get you."

"No, no, I'm okay. I want to get home. I'm going to leave now."

"Kate . . ." my father said.

"Dad, I'll be okay. I'm not seeing spots anymore. I think my body just gave out on me from the running. I don't feel great, but I can drive."

He was quiet for a moment. "Okay," he responded reluctantly. "But if you feel the slightest bit nauseous, pull over. Your mom or I will be there."

I promised to call when I was on the road, and I left my locker room. The hallways were dark. So much time had passed, there was no one left in the building. I hit the button for the elevator. As I waited, an eerie sensation fell over me like a cold blanket. The hall-ways I had walked through as a 16-year-old no longer gave me a sense of wonder and excitement. Instead, they brought feelings of fear and dread. Hastily, I decided not to wait for the elevator any longer. Even though my body was beaten to a pulp, I staggered as quickly as possible up the stairs and out to my car.

I probably shouldn't have driven that night, but I got home safely. As I pulled into the driveway, tears filled my eyes. My dream, CU, had quickly become a nightmare. When I turned the key to the house, my parents quickly came to meet me. Mom pulled me into a hug as my father looked me over.

"You don't look good," he said. "Your lips are as white as a sheet. Let's go check you over." I let Dad lead me to his home of-fice, where he pulled out a thermometer.

No temperature. Next he looked into my mouth.

"Kate, your throat is as red as a fire engine! Has it been sore?"

I nodded wearily, and he placed his hands underneath my chin to feel my glands.

Wincing, I instinctually yanked my head back. "That hurts," I mumbled hoarsely.

Dad nodded.

"I'm not surprised; your glands are huge. It could be strep, so let's get you started on antibiotics. How long have you been feeling bad?"

I shrugged. I was so exhausted that I couldn't think. It had felt like forever.

"I don't know . . . a week? Two? I thought I just had a cold that kept lingering."

Dad shook his head. "This is no cold, kiddo. Lie down; I want to check something."

I stretched out on the floor. He poked around on my stomach.

I groaned. I had retched so much that my stomach was sore to the touch. He moved to my abdomen.

"Agh!" I exclaimed. Dad had hit something that caused an uncomfortable twinge. "What is that?"

"I think it might be your spleen. It feels a little big, and that could be a sign for mono," he answered. My spleen? I didn't even know what my spleen did, let alone that it could hurt so much. Cringing, I sat up.

"Okay, let's get you into bed. I think it's best if you sleep in tomorrow. Can you do that?" Dad asked.

I nodded. I phoned Coach Hansburg and let him know I wouldn't be at study hall in the morning. Thank God the next day was Monday; that meant no practice, and all I had was lifting. The next day, I slept until midafternoon, more than 12 hours straight. My body was a little better after resting, but I still felt like I could sleep for the rest of the week. Dad had gotten me antibiotics and I got ready to head back to school.

"We'll see if the antibiotics help at all, but if they don't, I have a feeling you might have picked up a virus . . . plus I may want you checked for mono."

Great, I thought. Who knew how many germs I had been exposed to, between living in the dorms and sharing water bottles with 100 guys? I hoped the antibiotics would kick in and I would perk up. I made it back up to Boulder, went straight to the complex, and struggled through a brief weight workout. After it, I was totally wiped again. My body ached. My throat was on fire. I trudged up the stairs to the offices to see Coach Hansburg about making up my missed study hall.

"Coach?" I tapped on his cracked door. Coach Hansburg spun around his chair.

"Katie? Come in. You don't look so well."

I shook my head, which was beginning to ache as well. I told him I had started medicine and would hopefully be better soon.

"Why don't you go to the training room? Let's have our people look you over, too. We can talk about study hall later."

I agreed and trudged back down to the training room. I was *so* tired. After examining me in the training room, they arranged for me to see a doctor at the student health center the next morning. I hadn't eaten, and it was already 7 P.M., but I went back to my dorm and dropped into bed. The next day I went to the student health center, where a doctor again looked at my throat, my ears, and then poked around on me. She pressed on an area in my left abdomen and again I cringed. "It looks like your spleen might be enlarged. I think you might have mononucleosis—mono." She continued, "We're going to draw blood and I'll have them check for that, too."

"Okay," I said, thinking that I couldn't possibly have mono. Granted, I felt pretty bad, but I thought that mono left you bedridden. Two days passed as I felt worse and worse, especially my throat. I had skipped class both days and was taking a nap before practice when the phone rang. It was the doctor from the health center. The mono test had come back positive.

"Are you kidding?" I sat up in my bed.

"No; you've definitely got it. I recommend you go home as soon as possible. I'll call to let the training room know."

"Thank you. How long does this last?" I asked, knowing that mono took a while to get over.

"Well, you'll be out of most physical activity for at least three or four weeks since your spleen is enlarged. Even though you just kick, we still want to make sure that you don't take a chance and rupture it. We'll keep checking your spleen and see how you feel. We just have to let it run its course. And Katie, you have to rest."

The doctor went on to explain that I had probably been carrying the virus for a month or two and it had finally manifested itself. I closed my eyes. I was tired, but I felt frustrated at the fact that I was going to miss up to a month of football. I had been working so hard for the past few weeks. At least this explained why my running and lifting had been going downhill even though I was working harder than ever. After I got off with the doctor, I called Coach Embree to let him know.

"Keep me posted, but you take care of yourself—your health always comes first. Okay?" He said.

I thanked him. Coach Embree had always been so good to me.

I spent the next week at home, bedridden. My throat continued to swell. It hurt so badly that I couldn't swallow and had to keep a cup next to the bed to spit excess saliva into. I didn't have much of an appetite, and it was hard to eat anything solid. I drank as many milkshakes as possible, mixing in protein powder and weight gainers. It was October, and since June, Doc and I had managed to push my weight up by over 10 pounds since I started training. I was now just at 140 pounds and I was determined not lose it.

As I lay in bed, I had a lot of time to think—something I hadn't had much of since I'd started college. Images of some of the things guys on the team had done or said to me would float through my head. I had always blown them off so quickly so I could keep functioning. A discomforting and sad thought hit me—there was a part of me that was glad to be away from football. It was undeniable. I thought about it for a moment, but then turned quickly to the defense mechanism that I'd begun using as soon as I got to CU: Don't think about it; just keep going.

And I did.

Our schedule had us on the road for the next two games, so I didn't need to worry about suiting up. I still wasn't feeling well but thought I could at least practice at a slow pace. It took two full weeks to get even a little strength back.

When I finally went back to practice, it was in an orange-colored jersey. The orange color signified an injured player. I was under strict orders not to push too hard, and I wasn't allowed to lift for another week until my spleen was declared normal. My first day back, I decided some light stretching would be good while the kickers warmed up. Some of the other players were already down on the field as well. When I walked under the goalposts, a familiar voice called out to me.

"Oh, you're back, are you? Feeling all better?" It was the mocking tone of Chris Morgan, of course. Zac Colvin was next to him.

"Yes, I feel much better, and, thank you for asking," I answered.

"Well, that's too bad," Morgan said.

"What's too bad is that she didn't die," Colvin chortled. They snickered.

"Well, maybe next time," I responded.

"I hope so," Colvin said. He hoped I would die? What a jerk.

I walked away. Even though I knew they were idiots, the comments still stung.

As I started to stretch, a few of the other players and coaches walked by me. Their reactions were starkly different from Colvin's and Morgan's.

"Katie, hey, how are you feeling?" Coach McMahon, one of the assistant coaches, asked as he passed by.

"Much better, thanks," I replied.

"Glad to hear it," he said, and paused to give me a quick smile. I smiled back. He didn't know it, but with a few words Coach McMahon had eased the discomfort I felt after my encounter with Colvin and Morgan.

At the end of practice that day, the whole team gathered together as usual for post-practice comments or announcements from Barnett. When he was finished, he asked if anyone had anything to say. Jesse Warren, a defensive tackle I had always liked a lot, raised his hand.

"Katie's back!" Some of the guys cheered and one patted me on the back. Though I was blushing slightly, I smiled. Wow. It felt good to hear something positive from a teammate. Quite a contrast to the treatment I received from some of the others.

"Yes," Barnett said, almost begrudgingly. "Katie is back." My spirits dropped just as quickly as they had risen. I could read his face: It seemed as if he was saying, "Oh yeah, that girl kicker is back, now I have to deal with *that* whole situation again." I got the feeling he didn't particularly miss me when I was gone. Practice ended and I returned to my locker room with mixed feelings. There were some good guys on this team. Then there was a group who made my life a living hell. And then I had a head coach who just didn't seem to want me. I didn't know what to think.

The days moved forward slowly, and so did my health. While my fevers were gone and my throat had returned to a more normal size, I still fatigued extremely quickly. I was on the sidelines in my jersey when we played Oklahoma—there was no way I could have gone through even a small set of warm-ups. We won the game 38–24.

Our next two games were on the road, losing to sixth-ranked Kansas State, 20–14, and beating Baylor, 37–0. We then had an extra week off as we prepared for our next and final regular-season opponent, the Nebraska Cornhuskers. The game was the day after Thanksgiving and was our biggest contest of the year. The passion to beat the hated Huskers was hotter than even the CSU contest that opened the season. Nebraska came to Boulder ranked third in the nation, and it would make the season if we could pull off an upset. Nebraska took a sizable lead and held it through most of the game. We just couldn't seem to move the ball on the Nebraska defense, and by the time we entered the fourth quarter the game looked like it was settled. Suddenly Nebraska started making mistakes and we took advantage of them, erasing a 24-point deficit to send the game into overtime. Jeremy hit a clutch 49-yard field goal with less than a minute to play to tie things up. Fans were delirious as we took the field for sudden-death overtime. Nebraska got the ball first and couldn't put it in the end zone for a score. All we had to do was get the ball into field-goal range, have Jeremy kick it through, and the victory would be the biggest upset at CU in years. Jeremy Aldrich was probably the best kicker in CU history, and all he had to do to win the game was kick a 33-yard field goal. I held my breath as he lined up. The kick was up and . . . the refs were signaling no good. Jeremy missed the kick literally by inches, and we went on to lose 33–30. I felt terrible for him, even worse when some of our own players publicly criticized him for missing an "easy" kick. One guy went as far to say that Jeremy "choked," a quote that became a headline on the front page of the sports section. I couldn't believe that a teammate would say that about one of his own. And not to mention the fact that Jeremy had been the hero more times than not all season long. Yet no one remembered the dropped passes earlier in the Nebraska game, a fumble, missed tackle, or some other key mistake that would have prevented the need for an overtime kick in the first place. I knew Jeremy had to be hurting, yet he had the courage to go in front of the press after the game and say he was sorry and that these things happened while playing football. As for the head coach, Barnett didn't say much publicly in defense of one of his best players. While I was shocked over the reaction of some of my teammates and my coach, I found more respect for Jeremy. He conducted himself with dignity and kept things in perspective. Though I had learned much from Jeremy about kicking, I also learned a life lesson when I watched his graceful handling of a painful situation.

After the tough loss to Nebraska, we didn't know if our season was over. College football doesn't have a playoff system like pro football; all you can do is hope for an invitation to a bowl game. If you're invited, you get an extra game as well as a trip to some warm-weather spot for the holidays. If you're not invited, it's wait until next year; the season is done.

The minimum qualification to be eligible for a bowl is a winning record, so with a 6–5 record, we had just made the cut. But about a week after the Nebraska game the word came: We were going to Tucson. We'd be playing Boston College on New Year's Eve in the Insight.com Bowl.

8

Just When I Thought
It Couldn't Get Any Worse

I HAD MIXED FEELINGS about going to a bowl game. Of course, it was an achievement for the team to be invited and play on national TV. And the whole bowl experience is exciting, with the game only part of the festivities. The week leading up to the game is filled with luncheons, pep rallies, and team events.

Underneath these feelings, though, was a small part of me that had just wanted the season to be over. Mentally, I simply wanted to go home. The season had gone completely the opposite of the way I had expected, and I needed some time off to regroup. I had jumped back into my full schedule as quickly as possible after being sidelined with mono, and some of the symptoms were still dragging me down. Besides football, the end of the semester drew near, and I went through my first hell week of college finals. Somehow, despite everything, I managed to maintain good grades and finished on the Big 12 Conference's first-team student athlete honor roll.

Our bowl game was on December 31, 1999, so when the rest of the students went home for winter break, the football team stayed in Boulder for an extra couple of weeks of practice. We worked out until December 23 and then went home for a brief holiday with our families. Barnett wanted to begin practicing in Tucson as soon as possible, so we flew down to Arizona on Christmas night. Having only one full day at home and knowing I would be leaving the following night, it didn't really feel much like a normal Christmas.

The players who lived in Colorado would be meeting at either the airport in Denver, or up at CU, where buses would drive us to the chartered plane that would fly into Tucson. The airport was a long drive from Littleton, so I decided to go to Boulder. My parents drove me up to the dark and deserted campus after Christmas dinner. I didn't say much on the car ride up and couldn't shake off a feeling of dread.

Don't be ridiculous, I told myself. This is like a once-in-a-lifetime opportunity. It's exciting; it's going to be fun. In reality, though, all I wanted was to go home and be with my family, a place where I felt safe. My parents noticed that I wasn't my usual self.

"Kate . . . you okay?" Mom asked as we drove. "You're really quiet."

"Yeah," I lied. "I was just thinking how it doesn't feel much like Christmas . . . and I'm really tired."

The team was supposed to meet at the basketball arena and then catch buses to the airport. Dad unloaded my luggage and I said good-bye to my parents.

"Have fun, sweetie. We'll see you in a few days." My parents and the kids were going to drive down a day later. I hugged them both, and then trudged up the stairs to the arena.

Inside, there was a small smattering of people—maybe a dozen players, but mostly coaches, their families, and other CU personnel.

Everyone seemed to be in a jolly mood. As I went to plop on one of the sofas, I passed Coach Barnett.

"Katie . . . I'm surprised you're here," he said. What? Was I not supposed to be there?

"I thought you would have gone straight to the airport." Oh.

"Actually," I said, "Boulder is a closer dr—"

I didn't get a chance to finish my sentence. He had simply walked away. I knew the guy wasn't my biggest fan, but he couldn't even listen to me finish a sentence.

Feeling dejected, I sat down and waited for the buses to come. The flight to Tucson was fairly uneventful, but when we got off the plane, a large welcoming crew from the city greeted us like we were royalty. I had to admit, it was a pretty cool start to the week.

But the rest of the trip wound up being a mixed bag. We were practicing at a local high school, and the heat was nearly unbearable. Was it really December? The guys were given roommates, but since I was the lone female, I ended up with my own room. I was happy with the arrangement; it gave me a bit of an escape where I could take it easy. My relaxation was often short-lived. I was getting telephone calls at odd times throughout the week. Sometimes it would just be a hang-up call; at other time the calls were along the lines of "Katie, how 'bout me and you hook up and have a little fun." Sometimes I would recognize the voice; at other times I had no idea. I finally quit answering the phone and figured that would take care of it. That was, until one night early in the week when I was awakened by a bang on my door. I jolted up in bed. What was that? I waited for a second and then heard a bunch of muffled voices. Then another bang. Someone was banging on my door. Who could it be? I looked at the clock: it was nearly 3 A.M. We'd had an early curfew, so I didn't think it would be any of my teammates. I strained to hear. Instead of voices, though, I heard the handle of my door being jiggled. I froze, then grabbed the phone on the nightstand and hit the button for the front desk. I explained that there was a lot of noise outside my room; could they please send someone to check it out?

As I hung up, there was another series of thumps on my door. Then more voices. I was able to make out a few words.

"Katie . . . Katie," someone called.

"Dude, this might not be her room."

I struggled to hear more, but that was all I could make out. I thought I recognized one of those voices, but whose was it? I stayed sitting in bed, hugging my knees to my chest. Though that was the end of the noise, I found myself unable to settle down. I didn't sleep much that night.

The next morning, I went to the front desk to block my room number from being given out. After that, I had no more middle-of-the-night visitors and fewer calls. I still didn't feel like I could go to my coaches to tell them what was happening. I didn't know for sure which guys were calling and was still uneasy over some of the events that had occurred in the fall. I especially didn't want to go to Barnett over what was happening.

I could tell he was irritated with me through the week. Once again, it had to do with the media attention. I would be the first woman ever to suit up for a college bowl game, and the press wanted some background about my experience in Division I football. As in the press conference during the season, I knew Barnett felt like having to give quotes or take the time to talk about a walk-on placekicker was an extra "chore" he had to deal with. Nonetheless, I did the interviews, and tried to go about my business practicing without causing a distraction.

In fact, the week wasn't a total disaster. I had the chance to go out for food with several groups of teammates I got along with well, as well as to go through the bowl experience, getting bowl game souvenirs: shirts, hats, watches, even an Insight.com Bowl letter jacket, and going to pregame functions, such as a luncheon for both teams. As for the game itself, the best way to describe it would be anticlimactic. The bowl committee wasn't equipped to have a female player at the stadium, so I wound up changing into my uniform behind a chalkboard in the training room. The crowd wasn't very big and not really into the game. We beat Boston College in a 62–28 romp. Even though the crowd kept chanting my name to get into the game, Jeremy kicked all the extra points and I spent the game watching from the sidelines. I appreciated the support, but was a little uncomfortable hearing the chants—Mark and Derek were both ahead of me on the depth chart, and should have kicked before me.

I went out to dinner with my family after the game; afterward they dropped me off at the team hotel. I met up with Justin Bates, Pete Friedrich, Jake Jones, and a few other guys, and we basically rang in the New Year just hanging out. We went over to the parents' hotel, where Dad asked Justin to "keep an eye out for me" that night. Justin was a good guy I had played against in high school, so we had known each other for a few years and spent a lot of time busting each other about how bad each other's high school team was. We all then went back to the team hotel, where a bunch of the other players were hanging out swimming and sitting in the Jacuzzi. A number of women volleyball players from CU were there, and so were a few of the players' girlfriends. Even though it was a safe crowd and I was comfortable with my teammates who were there, I still wasn't totally at ease hanging out in my bikini with all the guys. I decided to wear my football shorts over my bikini bottoms. After hanging out for a while, I made it safely back to my dorm room, and the next day back to Colorado.

After the bowl game, I got to go home and spend the rest of my winter vacation there. For the first time in months, I had time to just sit and think. The fall season had brought me to a place I never expected to be. Anytime I thought about what had gone on, I would feel sick to my stomach. I turned to my tried and true defense mechanism that had allowed me to survive the season: block it out, shove it as far back as possible. For a short time it worked, and I was able to spend time relaxing and hanging out with my family. But as the time to return to school drew closer, I noticed I would wake each morning with more and more anxiety. Underneath it all, I knew it was because I didn't want to go back to football. I had made it through the season on autopilot, but after having time away from the horrendous atmosphere at CU, the thought of going back to it terrified me.

The night before I was supposed to return to Boulder, I broke down in tears. My parents were bewildered. They knew that the season hadn't gone well and that I'd had some problems with my kicking and a few teammates. Mom held me as I tried to explain to them what was going on. But I couldn't. I couldn't put into plain words what was bothering me. There were so many things; I didn't even know where to start. Finally Dad took me over to our church. Though it was eleven at night, my pastor, Father Ken, took the time to meet with me. With one look at my red eyes and tear-stained cheeks, he pulled me into his arms and held me for several seconds.

"Katie," he said, pulling back and looking me directly in the eyes, "whatever it is, you can and you will get through this." I nodded through my tears. We spent a few minutes together. He asked if I wanted to talk, but when I still couldn't find words, he simply sat silently, letting me cry while holding my hand.

"Thank you," I whispered to him. Father Ken simply gave me a soft smile and then got up. He went behind his desk and pulled out a small Bible. He opened it, pulled out a pen, scribbled, and then handed it to me. It was opened to James 1:2–4, which was underlined.

"Consider it pure joy, my brothers, whenever you face trials of many kinds, because you know that the testing of your faith develops perseverance. Perseverance must finish its work so that you may be mature and complete, not lacking anything."

"Whenever you feel down, I want you to open this passage, know that God is watching over you, and remember how much we all love you."

"Thank you so much." Now it was tears of gratitude flowing.

He nodded. "You know that you can come here if you need anything, day or night—it doesn't matter."

I gave him a big hug and met Dad in the hallway. I felt a little more at peace. I would be okay. It had been a rough past few months, but I still believed in my heart that I was meant to kick. As I lay in bed that night, I thanked God for blessing me with a strong family and a wonderful priest. I also asked that He would continue to guide me and give me the strength to face whatever would come my way.

It was a prayer I would repeat many, many times in the months ahead.

I drove back to Boulder the next day and began my new semester. I had moved into my new dorm room and was happy with the change. I was now close to some old friends from high school and liked my new roommate, Libby. I was relieved to be in a place where I wouldn't have random strangers being able to find out where I lived and it was fun hanging out with the girls who lived on the floor. The dorms were all coed but each floor was designated men's or women's. I was hoping to get a little more of a typical college experience, rather than the isolation and seclusion I'd had the semester before.

It was a fresh start. After getting real time to rest during winter vacation, I was finally feeling like I had kicked most of the residual mononucleosis. I tried to take a new approach to football—I was going to keep working as hard as I could, but I also was going to make a point to try to enjoy it more, no matter what was happening. The fall had been so negative, but I was going to focus on the positive. Just the plain act of kicking had always brought a tremendous sense of pleasure to me. I wanted to try to concentrate on getting that feeling back.

In mid-January, Dad had a quick meeting with Barnett at Dal Ward. Barnett had met Dad for the first time before the bowl game and asked if he wouldn't mind stopping by for a talk someday. Nothing important, just a chance to meet each other.

It was casual and pleasant, with Barnett asking if I was enjoying things and planning on continuing with the sport. "Of course," Dad said. "Why wouldn't she?"

"No reason; just wondering if things were going okay," replied Barnett. Was I feeling better and getting my strength back?

Dad said I was slowly feeling better and then asked if there were any problems he needed to know about. Barnett reassured him that there were none.

"How about the other players? Is she fitting in with the team?"

Everyone is settling in and getting used to a female on the team.

Dad then went on to ask about how Barnett felt about my kicking. I was struggling and worried about slow progress, especially with the mono.

Barnett launched into a long speech about how he knew the high-school-to-college adjustment was really hard for a kicker. He said no one he had coached in his long career had made the transition easily.

"I always give my placekickers two full years to get used to kicking off the ground without a tee. It takes time. She has time," Barnett said.

"Katie has no pressure from you? Nothing to worry about?" Dad asked.

"None. She's got nothing to worry about. Just keep working hard."

They shook hands and Dad thanked Barnett for his time. I was glad he met with Dad but was still unsure about where I stood with the man. His words didn't always seem to match his actions.

Winter workouts started as soon as we began classes. We went to the complex twice a day—first at 5:45 A.M. for our conditioning workout, then back in the afternoon after classes for a weight-lifting workout. Though I hated waking up so early in the morning, I liked our winter conditioning program. We worked out indoors in the field house. We were broken up by position groups and went through sets of stations. The stations were designed to work all the different muscle groups, as well as cardiovascular elements and agility. We jumped rope, did 20-yard shuttle runs, and jumped hurdles. I had brought a kicking net into the field house, and every day after we finished up our running, I would kick a ball over and over into the net. I had analyzed my form on tape for hours during the off-season and found that there were some inconsistencies in the way I would kick the ball. Each day I would pick one of those inconsistencies to work on and do all of my reps, focusing on that one aspect. I was getting stronger in the weight room and, true to his word, Doc Kreis had managed to put some pounds on me. Every day when we reported in our weight-lifting workout, we stepped on the scale. In January I had hit 150 pounds, 15 pounds more than I had ever weighed. By mid-March, at the end of winter conditioning, I peaked at 160 pounds. I couldn't believe it. I joked that I hadn't gained the "freshman 15," I had gained the "freshman 30." Except my freshman "15" hadn't come from pizza and beer, it had come from power cleans and gallons of protein shakes.

Even though I was working hard, there were consistent reminders of the fact that I was still in an uphill battle—and I never knew when something was going to try to knock me backward. One case was at the end of a winter weight-lifting contest.

It was a competition that took place after our two months of almost daily workouts. Two hundred twenty-five pounds were placed on the lifting bar, and each player did as many repetitions at that weight as possible while lying on the weight bench. We were divided into two groups: offensive players and kickers; defensive players and punters. Whichever group had more repetitions at the end was declared the winner. I knew I wasn't going to be much help to my group. Though my weight and strength has increased since I started at CU, I was still working on bench-pressing 125 pounds, let alone 225. It didn't matter though, it ended up being no contest. The defense quickly pulled ahead, and it seemed that almost all of their players could outlift ours. As the weight coaches were about to proclaim the defense as the winner, Barnett interrupted: "Wait a second—every single player must at least get under bar and give it a shot." He was referring to me and to a wide receiver who also hadn't hit 225 for his bench press.

What was the point of that? Was he trying to embarrass us? Motivate us? He knew I couldn't lift as much as any of the guys. Whatever, I thought, making my way over to the bench as the guys all yelled for me. Okay, this might be all right. I waited for Gavin, one of the weight coaches, to come over to spot me. As I got positioned on the bench, Zac Colvin pranced over before Gavin could get there. Colvin went through an exaggerated motion of pretending like he was going to spot me, but "accidentally" let the bar fall on my neck, knowing I would be stuck, if not hurt. As far as I was concerned, it wasn't funny. Laughter erupted from several players as I scrambled to sit back up and face him. Luckily, Gavin gave him a look and swatted him away. I was seething as I lay under the bar. This was a guy who had called me vile names and had spent the previous fall harassing me. I honestly didn't know if he meant to hurt me or just make me look stupid. As I lay on the weight bench, my mind replayed the incident of Colvin mocking me when I sang before the team at the beginning of the fall season. I pushed with all my might as Gavin helped me get the bar up. As soon as I placed it back in the rack, I looked up for Zac. Among the blur of the hundred guys gathered around, I couldn't see him. Just as well, I told myself. I was pissed off and had long ago learned not to show any emotion when things happened to me. The last guy got off the bench and we returned to the locker rooms. I sat in mine for a long time, thinking. Barnett was there; he had seen it. He was the one who had just called for me to get under the bench press. The entire team had seen it. Did everyone think it was funny? I was tired of having more than the usual hazing a new player might get. It seemed clear that most of this wasn't "hazing," and I wasn't a new player any longer.

Two of the kickers had graduated: Jeremy and Matt Altman. We had a new Jeremy, Jeremy Flores, a transfer from a junior college. He was slated to be the starter the next year and seemed to be a pretty nice guy. Once the weather got better, I quit using the net and moved to the goalposts outside. Spring practice was just around the corner, and I knew it was an important time for me. I had a season under my belt and was more comfortable with kicking off the ground. As the days went by, I felt myself returning to my old form.

Finally! I thought. I had put in literally hundreds of hours, and it was finally going to pay off. Formal spring practice would last about a month, culminating in a spring game, where the team gets divided in half and plays an intrasquad scrimmage.

The first day of spring practice went well for me. I kicked during a live drill, and my kicks were higher and had better rotation then ever before. A few hadn't gone as straight as I would have liked, but I was hitting the ball well and knew that with a little bit of tweaking, I'd be in good shape. A few of my teammates noticed the change in my kicking as well.

"Hey Katie, is that you?!" One of the O-linemen yelled to me as we finished the drill. Even Flores, who had been around for only a few months, could see the difference.

"What happened? You look like a brand-new kicker," he said to me, smiling.

"I think I finally got my rhythm back," I replied, smiling back. I continued to kick better, and it made me feel like I could handle anything else that came my way.

A few practices into the spring, I was out warming up when I saw Zac Colvin piddling around by the fence surrounding the field. What was he doing? There were only a handful of players; not even all of the kickers had made it out to warm up yet. Though it was a bright, sunny day, it had snowed the week before, and there were big piles of snow that had been bulldozed off the practice field. He was making snowballs. Immediately I knew where they were going to be headed—straight at my head. A few times before I had noticed that recently there seemed to be a lot of footballs flying by my head during warm-ups. At first I figured it was just errant balls that were being kicked and punted back and forth. More than once one of the kickers had gotten nailed in the face from a ball being kicked back and someone not yelling "Heads up!" in time. This was different, though. Balls weren't just flying out of the sky—the balls were lower and had a spiral to them. One day, I was in the middle of lining up for a kick when a ball zoomed right past the side of my head. I jumped back, stunned.

Looking up, I saw Zac Colvin across the fields. Was he throwing footballs at my head? No way, the guy was a jerk to me, but that was ridiculous. I had gone back to warming up and a few minutes later another football whizzed by. Startled again, I turned and looked. There was Zac, hands on his hips, laughing. He was using my head as a target. Unbelievable. It was one more thing I had to be on guard about. How could I totally focus on my kicking with footballs zooming at my head? That day I continued to warm up, but kept a subtle eye on Zac making his snowballs. Sure enough, I was right. He launched one, but to his surprise, I turned around and caught it. The snowball had a hard chunk of solid ice in the middle. I exploded.

"Why don't you grow up, Zac?!" I screamed across the field. I wasn't in the mood for his immature bullshit anymore. With my kicking improving, my confidence was starting to come back, and with it, my strength.

"Why don't you quit running and crying to people about what I do?" he yelled back.

What was he talking about? I still hadn't gone to the coaches or anyone else in the program about any of the harassment that had gone on.

"Just leave me ALONE!" I yelled.

Exasperated, I went back to warming up. Even though Zac had rattled me a bit, I still pulled out a decent performance that day. I was pleased with myself—I knew that the crap I had dealt with during the fall had taken a real mental toll on my kicking. Now my kicking was improving on a physical level, and it looked like I was regaining some of my mental prowess. That made me happier than anything. My mental game had always been the strongest component of my kicking, and I knew that if I got that back, there would be no stopping me.

By this point in the spring, football was better, Libby and I had become close friends as well as roommates, and I actually had some classes this semester that I really enjoyed. Finally, it seemed as though everything was starting to fall into place.

I had spoken too soon. The next day, I was thrown for a loop that I couldn't have ever anticipated. We didn't have practice that day, just a weight workout. I decided to do it before my morning classes, so I could take advantage of a free afternoon. Maybe Libby and I could crash out and watch a movie and order a pizza. It was just 8:00 A.M. on a beautiful Colorado day when I jumped into my truck to head back to the dorms. I usually gave rides to four other teammates who lived in the same dorm complex when we'd go lift, but since I'd gone in the morning, I was by myself. I had the window down and was humming to the song on the radio as I pulled up to a stop sign at the exit of the complex. As I waited to go, I happened to glance in my rearview mirror. There was an old white pickup truck behind me. I didn't think anything of it; it looked like the kind of pickup truck a lot of the CU maintenance workers drove. I'd seen them around campus before. I pulled out and the truck behind me quickly followed. Geez, he must be in a hurry, I thought. He was really on my tail. It was less than half a mile back to my dorm, and the truck followed me as I went into my parking lot. He must be doing work at the dorms, I thought.

As I circled around, the truck didn't pull into one of the spots reserved for maintenance. That's a bit strange, I thought. Something just seemed a little off. Thinking I was being paranoid, I decided I'd park in a different lot. The truck followed me. Okay, this is definitely weird, I thought. I parked in the closest spot to the dorm I could find and then started to haul butt toward the door. I shot a quick look over my shoulder. The man was getting out of his truck and starting behind me. I picked up my pace. I was about 20 yards away from the door. I glanced again. He had picked up his pace as well and seemed to be gaining on me. I made it to the door and quickly pushed through the first set. I could hear him behind me. I had my key out and quickly inserted it into the second door, then slammed it shut behind me. I heard him as he pulled on the handle. He couldn't get through. My heart had started to race. As I got farther into the hallway, I dared a slight peek around. There he was, outside the glass doors, staring at me. He was a complete stranger to me. I shot up the three flights of stairs and into my room. Libby was already in class. I locked the door behind me and sat on my bed. I felt a little shaken, but couldn't figure out if I was just being paranoid. I was always cautious by nature, but had become more so after my first round of media attention while in high school, when I'd had a few creepy experiences. I briefly thought of calling my parents, but I didn't want to alarm them. It could just be a bizarre accident, I reasoned. I left for class about an hour later and did a quick scan before I left. There was no sign of the guy. I kept my eyes open as I walked to class. No sign of him. Whew. Must have just been a fluke. I was a little tired from working out that morning, and sitting in a large lecture hall, I could feel my eyelids getting heavy. I kept blinking to try to get myself to stay awake. Class dragged on. At last it was over. Now I knew exactly how I was going to spend my free afternoon: taking a nap. As soon I stepped out into the plaza, though, my brain jarred me alive. It was him. The man from this morning. Was I sure? Yes, the mint green shirt, the sunglasses. I ducked back behind a wall and tried to get a look at him. He was just sitting in the plaza. Maybe it was a coincidence? I didn't know, but my gut told me to go out another way. I ducked back into the building and went out a door on the other side.

I walked as quickly as possible back to my dorm, constantly checking behind me. When I got back in, Libby was there. I told her about that morning and then seeing the guy after class. Weird, she agreed. Maybe something, maybe nothing. She had to go to class, but we decided we'd order in when she got back.

"You sure you're okay?" Lib asked. "I can skip class if you want."

"No, I'm fine. It was just weird. Let's order a pizza when you get back."

Libby took off, and I decided to call my parents. They were a little more concerned. Dad told me to keep my eyes open and pay attention to everyone around me. Then he told me to stay in a group.

"Even if it was just some strange coincidence, it's better to be safe," Dad said.

I agreed. I told my parents I'd call them before bed to check in later that night. I was able to rest a bit, and when Libby got back, we ordered in and kicked back for the night.

I called my parents, assured them everything was fine, and then called it an early night. Tomorrow was a full practice session, the third of the spring, and I wanted to make sure I had a good one.

The next morning I got up and went to class. I was still keeping my eyes open but not expecting to see anything. On my way there, I didn't. But on my way back, I did. It was him. I was positive; he had the same mint green shirt, sunglasses, and ball cap on. I suddenly felt chilled in the sunshine. Did he see me? I switched direction and headed to the stadium. I didn't know what to do. Three times seemed a little more than a coincidence.

I called Mom from the lobby.

"I saw him again. . . . I don't think this is an accident," I told her. She called Dad at work, who decided he would come up as soon as he could get off work. In the meantime, I was to stay in the football complex. I went up and talked to Coach Embree. I explained what happened yesterday and after class today. I told him that Dad was coming up. He looked troubled.

"Be careful. When you go down to practice today, make sure you walk with some of the guys. Keep me posted. If you see this guy again, it might be good to go to alert the campus police."

I nodded. Mom and I had discussed the same thing. I left his office and went downstairs to my locker room. I had some time to kill before practice. I sat down and leaned my head against my locker. This was the last thing I needed. I felt like I was finally turning the corner, and now this. I tried to unwind a bit. I could deal with this, whatever it turned out to be.

I dressed, and made sure to catch a few of my teammates as I walked down to the practice fields. As I left the building, I could feel myself tense. My eyes shot all around. There was no one there, but I still felt uptight. I tried to warm up the best I could, but my mind kept wandering. Focus, focus, I told myself. But I couldn't help glancing around every few moments. Practice started, and I managed to kick decently during our live drills. I then took myself through my usual workout drills, but kept looking up to the roped-off area where the reporters and other visitors stood during practice—I knew Dad should be getting there soon. I was going to retrieve a ball when I looked up again. I froze. Mint green behind the black tarp that lined our fences. Was I seeing something? No. The figure was moving along the side of the fence. It was him again. Even though there were tons of people around, I felt panicky. How long had he been out there? What was I supposed to do? I didn't know where Coach Embree was on the practice field, but I spotted Doc near the gates. I dropped the ball and made my way across the field to him.

Doc saw the look on my face and immediately took me aside from the group he was standing near.

"What's up, Katie?" he asked.

"There's been this guy . . . this man . . . I keep seeing." I didn't realize that I had started to tremble. "He just . . . I just saw him again, outside the fences." I nodded in the direction where I had seen him. I explained what happened the previous day.

Even when I was a child my determined spirit was evident.

Kicking a field goal against Highlands Ranch High School in 1999.

Being crowned
homecoming queen
in my pads.

Cleaned up: With high school
head coach Keith Mead at the
homecoming dance.

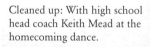

A warm-up kick at CU.

Top: Warming up with CU for the Insight.com Bowl in 1999. I became the first woman to dress for a bowl game when I suited up for that game.

Middle: With my brothers and sister the morning I left for Santa Barbara.

Bottom: Family Christmas photo 2002. From left to right: Dad, Jim, Joe, me, Kristen, Mom, and KJ.

Joe and I after one of his practices at the University of Oregon during the 2002 season. We were the first brother and sister to be playing Division I football concurrently.

With teammates Sydney Wiley, Kevin Walton, and Joel Paoli for the 2002 women's football clinic. I was showing off our pads, they were showing off some muscles.

GQ guys and the kicker in a red dress: All dressed up for senior pictures in 2003.

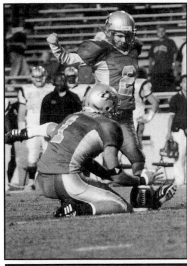

History made: Kicking my
first of two extra points.
(Photo by Matt Dunn)

Above: Waving to the
crowd after my first
extra point. The UNM
fans embraced me the
minute I arrived in
Albuquerque. (Photo by
Matt Dunn)

Bottom: A high five
from Coach Everett
Todd after scoring my
first point. (Photo by
Matt Dunn)

Top: Receiving an award for being the first woman to score in Division I at the 2003 Lou Groza Kicking Awards ceremony. (Courtesy of the Palm Beach County Sports Commission and Institute)

Middle: In a formal dress or in my pads, I'm always up for tossing the football.

Bottom: Teaching a group of female Lobo fans how to kick at UNM's annual women's football clinic. (Photo by David Benyack)

On the sidelines during a 2004 game. (Photo by Gary Stepic)

Coach Long in action. He is not only a great coach but a great man. (Photo by Gary Stepic)

With friends Val and Yvette after beating San Diego State 19–9 in 2004. (Photo by Gary Stepic)

Top: Postgame gathering with some of my teammates.

Middle: Cross training by pushing my pickup truck up the street.

Bottom: Speaking about sexual assault at the "It Happened To Alexa Foundation" 2005 annual fund-raiser.

"Have you told anyone about this yet?" Doc asked. I nodded.

"I talked to Coach Embree before practice, and my dad is on his way up now," I said.

Doc went into action. "All right. Practice will be over in about 15 minutes. You go back and stay near the guys. I'm going to send someone to look around the fences. As soon as the coaches let you go, come back over here." I returned to the kickers.

"Hey Katie, you okay?" Mike Twisselman, one of the punters, asked. I told him what was happening.

"Oh, man, that's creepy. Listen, if you need someone to walk you somewhere, don't be afraid to ask," he said. I thanked him and noticed that Dad had arrived. He was talking with Doc. Practice ended, and I made my way over to them.

Dad had a look of concern and anger on his face.

"Are you okay?" he asked me.

"A little shook up . . ." I admitted.

"I'm going to take you over to the police station as soon as you change." I nodded again.

I got into my street clothes and met Dad back upstairs.

Doc was with him. "I'll let Coach Embree know you saw this guy again at practice. You go take care of business, then see me in the morning. We'll make sure that this guy doesn't get near you," Doc growled.

"Thank you," I said, attempting a half smile.

Doc waved me off. "We'll make sure you're safe."

I could feel myself stiffen as I walked out of the building. Dad put his arm around me.

We took his truck over to the campus police station; we'd come back and pick mine up later. At the station, I met a detective and filed a complaint. They told me to stay on the lookout for the man and gave me a number to call if or when I saw him again. "If." Maybe he wouldn't come back around. I had a sinking suspicion that I hadn't seen the last of him.

Dad went home that night, and I spent the night tossing and turning. Who was this man? Why was he wearing the mint green shirt both days? Was it some kind of work attire? How did he know my schedule? I was sickened by the thought that he could have been hanging around and I had never noticed. *Why was he watching me?* Finally, I fell into an uneasy sleep. I overslept the next morning and was running late for class. As I sprinted across campus, I tried to keep my eyes open. I didn't see him. I made it though class and started to walk to the athletic complex. When I stepped out the door, my stomach lurched. He was there again, just casually sitting on a bench across from the building. Should I go to the police department? I made a quick decision. I was closer to the athletic complex; I would go there and call the police from there. I walked as quickly as I could, trying to keep an eye out for the man. I went straight through the weight room and into Doc's office. Shaking his head, he sat me down.

"You saw that rat again, didn't you."

"I need to call the police," I said shakily. Doc put his hand on my shoulder.

"Katie, we'll keep you safe. I don't know what this lunatic's story is, but he isn't going to get at you." He brought me the phone and I dug out the number I had been given last night. The detective told me to start keeping a log of when I saw him and to try to get a better look at him. At this point it was considered "suspicious activity," and they could question him if I saw him again. They'd have me come in and work with a sketch artist. I hung up and called my parents. Both were distressed; Dad was ready to drop everything and come up to Boulder. I told him I was okay, that I was with Doc and we would make sure I was as safe as possible. Doc had produced a small alarm and a miniature air horn.

"You keep this with you at all times. If he dares to get close to you, you push this thing as hard as you can. It'll damn near blow his ear off. In the meantime, I'll make sure we have guys who can be with you whenever you're going anywhere."

I talked to Coach Embree, then called Libby over at the dorm to have her pick me up. I didn't feel like walking anywhere, even if I wasn't alone. I skipped the rest of my classes that day and tried to catch up on rest. I didn't want to leave our dorm room.

I didn't see him again until I was getting ready to go to practice the next day. I was grabbing a PowerBar to eat along the way when I looked out the window. Was that him? Tentatively, I moved toward the window. Dozens of students were milling around, but there he was. He was sitting directly across from my dorm window. A strange sense of déjà vu came over me. I felt as though I had seen him in that exact spot before. Had he ever been? I dialed the police. It took a minute to get to the person I needed, and he said they'd dispatch someone immediately. I hung up, getting as close to the window as I dared. Could he see me? He had gotten up! I watched him as he moved across the grass and up the hill. He paused by the building across from me, leaning against the wall. Even though I was locked in my dorm room I didn't want to be alone. Libby was at class, so I called one of the girls who lived below us to come up. Classes had let out, and more and more students were filling the area. I tried to keep my eyes on him. In the sea of people, I lost him. Where were the police? The phone rang, and I jumped out of my skin. It was one of my teammates, letting me know that they were going over to practice, so I could walk with them. I shook my head. I had to wait for the police.

I realized I needed to tell Coach Embree I wasn't going to be there on time. I called over. He told me to take my time and come over when I could. The police finally got there and came up to my dorm room. I went through a series of questions with the officers again.

I had never seen him before this week. He had not tried to approach me. He did not look like a student, rather someone who was possibly 10 to 15 years older. Skinny build. Always had on a cap and sunglasses. Had anything else unusual been happening, such as random phone calls? Wait a sec. Yes, we'd had quite a few hang-ups in the past week, now that they mentioned it. My dorm phone number, as well as my address, were inaccessible to almost anyone, so I had thought we'd just had some wrong numbers. Now I wondered. Did he know my telephone number? And my dorm room number as well? He certainly was sitting directly across from our window. I was becoming agitated. Libby arrived back from class, alarmed at the officers in our room. He had been outside, I told her. Libby hugged me, then sat as the officers finished.

"We're going to type this up and put it in your case file. After practice tonight, we'd like to have you come by and do a composite sketch." Practice, right; I was supposed to be going to practice.

"Do you want me to drive you over?" Libby asked softly.

Before I could answer, the officer intervened. "We'll take her over now, just to be on the safe side. We'll also send an officer over to the fields to keep an eye out today."

I thanked Libby, gathered my stuff, and left with the officers. As we drove, I wondered if the man had seen the squad car. Did he know I was reporting him?

I thanked the officer who drove me over and said that I would return to the station as soon as practice was over. I realized I needed to call my family. As soon as I did, Dad decided to head straight up. Since most of the players were done with meetings and on the field, one of the managers waited with me until I was changed, then drove me down in one of the golf carts. I had an awful practice. I couldn't concentrate and wasn't hitting the ball like I had been recently. It's been a long day, I told myself. Give yourself a break. Practice wrapped up, and Dad was there. We headed to the police station. I sat with the sketch artist and tried to give the best description I could of the man I had seen. It was harder than I thought. Finally we came up with something that seemed to resemble him. The police gave me an alarm to keep with me. If he came near me, I was to hit the alarm, which would set off a high-pitched wail and connect me directly to police dispatch. It was bulky and heavy. Libby and I also changed our dorm phone number, just to be on the safe side.

Finally, as I left, the police made me an appointment over at the Student Health Center, to see a crisis counselor. "These things can impact you more than you realize," the woman officer said. Wearily, I nodded. I was exhausted.

The next few days were a nightmare. I was trying to maintain a normal schedule, but kept catching glimpses of the man wherever I went. He seemed to be able to be everywhere, but he also seemed to be able to disappear at the blink of an eye. The police never seemed to get there in enough time, but I hadn't wanted to hit the alarm unless he actually approached me. I was becoming unraveled. I couldn't sleep and was constantly paranoid that someone was behind me. We had a few more hang-up calls, and any time the phone rang, I would jump out of my skin. I started to skip classes, going only to football and anything that was vital. I would lie in bed at night with my head next to the giant alarm the police had given me.

My kicking had started to go down the tubes, but I couldn't focus no matter how hard I tried. I couldn't help but spend parts of practice searching the fences or looking for the nameless man. Dad had started skipping work and would literally sit outside my dorm or practice to keep an eye out.

It was one of the last days of practice before our spring game, and since we didn't have any room to work on the lower fields, the kickers and punters decided to go back up to the stadium to kick. We had started to kick when I noticed a figure lurking near the top of the stadium. I blinked. Were my eyes playing tricks on me? No. There a man was there. Maybe a stadium worker? He was walking into and out of the tunnels. I knew that walk. I scrambled off the sideline where I was working and motioned to my father, who was watching from his car. He jumped out.

"Dad, call the police. He's here." I motioned up into the stadium. "He's up in the tunnels." I had started to cry. I couldn't handle it anymore.

Dad dialed the police as we walked back down to the lower practice fields. I quickly found Coach Embree and told him that the man was back and I was heading back to the police. I was praying that they'd catch him this time.

"Call me if you need anything else. Don't worry about football now; do what you have to do. Be safe," Coach Embree said.

I nodded, then met Dad. The police had dispatched officers again, and I headed over to the crisis center. The counselor was good and able to calm me down a bit.

"Don't feel like you have to keep a brave face," she told me gently. "This is serious. This man is stalking you." Through my tears, I nodded. For the first time in weeks, I felt relatively out of harm's way. I was given a sleeping pill and went back to the dorms. Dad stayed in Boulder that night, and the sleeping pill did its job. I slept deep into the morning and then had to head back to the athletic complex. In the lobby I ran into Coach Barnett. I expected to pass him with a usual nod of the head, but he stopped me.

"I didn't know that you were having problems. Katie, you need to come see me. We can help with this stuff." He sounded exasperated. I felt a sting of irritation at his tone. I hadn't gone to talk to him, but I figured that Coach Embree or Doc had let him know. Barnett was not a figure I felt like I could get help from. We didn't speak regularly. He was unapproachable, and I knew that he didn't like me. I was just an "obligation" he had been stuck with. After the press conference in the fall, I was always trying to make sure I didn't cause any other kind of distraction. We agreed that we would meet later that day.

The meeting was short. Barnett sat down across from me and asked what had been going on. I was stunned at how little he knew. I explained what had been happening the past two weeks. I was working with the police. I had been keeping Coach Embree in the loop. Doc and a few of the equipment managers had been watching and helping out. Some of the guys knew and would make sure I wasn't walking alone. I watched his reaction as I talked. It looked like I was stressing him out. He ran his hand across his head. I distinctly got the feeling he was thinking that if I were a male player, he wouldn't have this problem. But since I was a woman, it was a different story, and now he had to deal with it.

"I've got the situation under control," I said. "I will be fine." Barnett offered nothing further. The meeting had lasted about a minute.

The next day was the spring intrasquad game. The police, as well as Doc, had arranged for security to be posted around the stadium. It was more than likely that the man would show up. The police also thought there was a decent possibility that he would approach me after the game, when we were having an autograph session. I was nervous, but hoped that maybe he would show up and that would be the end of this nightmare.

I woke up to a blizzard. Though it was late April, Colorado weather could be unpredictable. The game was a total whiteout; we even shortened our last two quarters, since no one could see. I couldn't make out my family in the stands, let alone try to see if the man was somewhere among the bundled figures. We were drenched and freezing, and it was decided that the autograph session would be in the field house. My family stayed close behind me, as well as a few plainclothes police officers. I signed autographs and smiled for pictures, all the while keeping an eye out for my stalker. There was no sign of him. The last of the fans trickled out, and I talked with an officer. No sign of him was probably a good sign. I went down to my locker room to change. Then I was going home with my family for the rest of the weekend. Mom drove my truck down, and I napped in the back. I finally felt a little bit of peace. I was getting out of Boulder, away from this man, and would be safe at home. I slept for most of the weekend. The past month had taken its toll. I had been fighting off a sore throat the past week. I was emotionally drained and sleep-deprived. What a year this has been, I thought. Luckily, the semester was drawing to a close. We had only a few weight workouts for football and a one-on-one meeting with Coach Barnett. I had half a week of classes to go, and then finals would start. After that, I would get a few weeks at home before having to come back for summer conditioning. I was looking forward to the time off.

On Sunday night I got ready to go back to Boulder. I had traded cars with Mom the week before, in an effort to throw off the stalker. I loaded my bag in, along with a big bag of food. Mom had baked up a sizable batch of treats for Libby and me to nibble on as we studied for our exams. She also gave me a jar of iced tea to keep in our minifridge. I put my alarm on the front seat next to me and said good-bye to my parents. I assured them I would be okay, I'd call as soon as I got in, and I would absolutely not walk in the dark alone. I drove up that night with a flicker of hope going through my body. The stalker hadn't shown up at the game. Maybe he had seen that the police were involved, gotten scared, and backed off. I hoped so. When I got up to Boulder, I drove into the parking lot. Crap. It was totally packed; I was going to have to go down to the lower lot, just as I did the first day I had encountered the stalker. I pushed the thought out of my mind and circled down to the lower lot. I pulled out my cell and dialed our dorm room. It rang and rang. Where was Libby? Maybe she was in the bathroom.

I found a spot in the lower lot and tried the room again. Still no answer. I called the girls who lived next door. No answer. I sighed, then dialed the guys below us. Okay, where was everyone? Frustrated, I sat there for a moment. I tried the room again. Nothing. There was no way I was walking by myself in the dark right now. Something was going on at the events center that was next to our dorms. Even though they weren't close, I could see people and hear voices. Maybe I should just walk in. No. I contemplated what to do. I would wait a few more minutes, then call my room again. In the meantime, I would gather up my stuff to carry. I had brought a large load of laundry that I'd done at home. I stepped out of the car and then opened up the back door. I thought I would move all of the snacks Mom had given me into my backpack. I had just grabbed the jar of iced tea when I heard a voice behind me.

"You looked cold on Saturday." My heart stopped. Slowly, I turned around. It was him.

"You looked like you needed someone to warm you up." He took a step closer. Terrified, I dropped the jar of iced tea and lunged toward the alarm on the front seat. Grabbing it, I hit the button with all my might. A loud, ear-splitting wail pierced the night. I opened my mouth to scream. A look of panic crossed his face. I threw myself back into the car and shut the door. He broke into a run. The police alarm was deafening. I fumbled to press the button that would silence it.

"Hello? Hello?" I could hear a woman's voice coming through the transmitter. Shaking, I reminded myself how to work the alarm so I could speak with the police.

"I'm here," I said.

"Okay, is this Katie and are you safe?"

"Yes and yes."

"Where are you?"

"Kittredge dorms. In the lower parking lot near Arnett Hall."

"I'm sending someone to you now. Did you see the man again?"

"Yes, he approached me this time. I hit the alarm immediately."

"Is the man still in your sight?"

"No . . . no. He ran," I answered, looking toward the path he'd run down.

"What direction?"

"Um . . . south, southeast? He ran underneath the bridge that leads to 30th Street." He could be anywhere, I thought.

"We've got people in that area. Hold on." I listened as the woman sent a description over the radio.

"Still there?"

"Yes," I answered.

"Can you remember anything specific about him tonight? Clothing? Any different?"

I closed my eyes and thought. "No sunglasses. Still had on a baseball cap. I think that his shirt was blue. A turquoise blue, with a pocket. Jeans."

"Okay, there should be a squad car there any second. I'm going to send out what you just told me and then we'll stay on until the car gets there."

"Okay." Again, I listened to her give a further description. Please let them pick him up, I prayed. Nothing yet. The squad car arrived and I unlocked my doors. Slowly, I stepped out.

"Katie?" The officer asked. I nodded. She introduced herself and noticed the broken glass at my feet.

"What happened? Can you take me through it out here so I can see where he came from and where he went? Then we'll do an official report."

I retold the story, telling her about not being able to get hold of anyone, then stepping out, dropping the iced tea, what he said, and finally, the direction in which he ran. She jotted a few notes and then said, "Let's get you up to your room. We can go over it there, unless you want to do it at the station." I shook my head and grabbed my backpack. We went to my dorm room and went over everything in detail until my brain was fried. In the middle of it, my cell phone rang. It was my parents. I was supposed to call as soon as I got to Boulder. I explained to them what had happened. "You are not staying up there alone tonight." Dad was on his way. I still didn't sleep that night. My mind was blurred with questions. How did he know I had been gone? Had he been hanging around the lot for hours? How did he recognize me in Mom's car? What would have happened if I didn't have the alarm? Would he be back?

* * *

I never saw the man again. But I never forgot him.

I managed to get through the next week. Football was laid back, and I had my individual meeting with Coach Barnett. It was the one time every player on the team came to his office to discuss the season and look at the season to come. This meeting was even shorter than my meeting about the stalker.

"How do you feel the spring went?" he asked me.

"Not as well as I would have liked. I was happy with the way things started, but then I started to struggle. Obviously, there were some outside factors affecting me." I paused. "You have not gotten to see me kick even half as well as I can. But I promise you, I will not stop working until you do."

Barnett looked at me.

"I don't have room for you in preseason camp," he said flat out. "You'll start the first day of school again."

I nodded my head. "That's fine. I'll be up here training again for the summer."

"Okay," Barnett said.

And that was that. My year and future discussed in 60 seconds or less.

I finished my finals and once again managed to squeeze out decent enough grades to end up on the first-team Big 12 athletic honor roll. What a first year of college, I thought. I looked forward to the next few weeks off. I would relax, recollect, and then begin anew. I had been through an awful lot in one year, I reflected. But I had survived. I would come back stronger and be ready to take the next step into my football journey.

Libby and I had decided to live together the following year and found a great apartment to share. I was looking forward to having our own place and glad that Libby would be my roommate again. We'd kept growing closer during the spring semester and had a lot of fun together. She was going to spend the summer back home in Wisconsin, but I would be back in Boulder pretty quickly to start summer conditioning and work, so we signed our lease to start in June. I was gong to spend a week at home for some down time, then start moving some of our stuff in. My plans got delayed, though, when I got a bad case of tonsillitis. My tonsils were covered in pus pockets and felt totally raw. Ugh, not now, I thought. I had finally seemed to get over the lingering effects of mononucleosis and wanted to go into summer workouts feeling well physically. I took some antibiotics and the throat cleared up.

It didn't last for long. As we started our summer conditioning, I kept getting more and more burning sore throats. The medicine would usually take care of the problem, but then it would come back a week later. I was irritated at the frequency of them and the fact that I was starting to feel tired again. I didn't want to take a chance of relapsing, so I took it easy, mostly just going to football and work.

Until one day, when my life changed forever in a matter of minutes.

9

The Night That Changed My Life Forever

EIGHT . . . NINE . . . TEN! Whew. The dumbbells clanged as I heaved them back into the rack and breathed a sigh of exhaustion. Thank God we had the next day off. My throat was beginning to feel raw again, and the last thing I needed was another bout of tonsillitis. My body hadn't felt 100 percent since I'd had mono.

I picked up my water bottle and began to walk across the weight room toward the massive windows that overlooked our game field. It was a sort of ritual for me; after every weight workout I'd gaze out at the field. The placid field always had a calming effect on me—the green grass, the black turf behind the south goalpost that boldly proclaimed "Colorado." The stillness in the air. It was beautiful.

I was walking toward the windows when I heard his voice.

"Hey."

I stopped and turned around. There he was, a few feet away, spotting another teammate on the bench press.

"Hang on," he said to his partner and walked over to me.

"What's up? You done?" he asked, wiping the sweat from his brow.

"Yeah," I said, nodding.

"What are you doing later? You wanna hang out or something?"

"Oh, I don't know . . ." I responded. "I still haven't been feeling that great. . . . I'm so tired."

"Come on . . . we can just chill. Ball game tonight."

I hesitated.

"It's an early game and we haven't hung out in forever. Come on, you'll be in bed early," he coaxed.

"Well . . . okay. Maybe," I relented.

"Great. You need to get out more. I'll call you when I'm done here." He gave me a goofy smile, then walked back to his bench.

I shook my head, smiling. Maybe he was right. All my life had consisted of in the past month was training, eating, and sleeping. My body felt so lethargic I never wanted to do anything else. Maybe I should get out, even if it was just to watch a game.

I stepped up to the window and stared out. There it was—the unblemished field, the stadium, and the sense of peace. *You'll be out there someday*, I told myself. *You are going to do this.* I laid my head on the cool glass and closed my eyes. For that moment, the serene look of the field made it into my body. *You're going to be okay. You'll make it.* I exhaled and opened my eyes.

Little did I know that that would be the last peaceful feeling I would have for a long time.

Hours later, my life changed forever.

* * *

I knocked twice.

"Come in, it's open," a voice called.

I turned the knob and stepped inside. The room was dark and small. I'd been there quite a few times before, to watch games, movies, or just hang out and shoot the breeze. He was one of my closer friends on the team, and we talked easily—and a lot. We discussed everything from football, movies, and school, to our families to religion. I considered him a confidant, a big-brother type—I was even able to talk to him about the harassment I faced from guys on the team and my kicking struggles. "You're a strong woman," he had told me. "Keep strong. Those guys are just morons."

He would often tease me or clown around, always trying to make me smile when he knew I was having a tough day at practice.

"Heeeeyy," he said, emerging from the darkness and giving me a squeeze around the waist.

"What'd I miss?" I asked, dropping my keys on the floor as I plopped onto the sofa.

"Nothing so far," he said, sitting down next to me. He was a little closer than usual, but I didn't really think much of it. The game wasn't very exciting, so we starting chitchatting about our workout that day and how hot it had been.

"You really should run in the morning session before it gets so hot," he said.

"Whatever. You know I can't get out of bed before ten!" I said with a laugh.

He slid his arm around me. "You are so pretty," he said.

What? That was strange for him to say. I looked at him.

"Really," he said. "You're beautiful." He began to kiss my neck.

"Hey!" I exclaimed. "What are you doing?" I was caught totally off guard. One of his hands was on my thigh, the other on my neck, pushing my face toward his. He started to kiss me. I flinched and jerked back. "Come on, babe . . ." he whispered. "You know you want me, too." What? No, I thought.

"You know how I feel about the whole teammate thing," I stammered.

"No one has to know." He was pushing me down with his forearm. "It's only our business."

He was on top of me, hand on my thigh.

"Stop!" I was starting to panic.

He ignored me and shoved his tongue into my mouth. One hand was on my shoulder; the other was feeling around under my skirt.

"I don't want to do this," I pleaded, trying to maneuver my body out from under his. I couldn't move. He outweighed me by more than a hundred pounds and was God knows how much stronger. I was stuck.

His hand was inside me. Oh, God, I thought.

"I don't, no," I tried to form words.

"Shhhh . . ." he said, shoving his finger onto my lips. "You're old enough for this now."

He propped himself over me and pulled down his shorts. He lowered himself back onto me and I feebly tried to get one of my arms to push on his shoulder. *Oh, my God.* I squeezed my eyes shut as he forced himself inside me. It hurt like hell for a minute, but then the feelings stopped. My body was limp and lifeless. I could vaguely feel his cheek rubbing against my own and could smell a mixture of his cologne and his sweat.

I felt like I had disconnected from my own body. I was watching this happen to someone else.

Suddenly a buzzing came from the other side of the room. The phone. His cell was ringing. He muttered something and pushed himself off me. For a moment I didn't move, then I blinked. Slowly I pulled myself up.

Completely disoriented, I stared at him as he picked up his cell phone and began to talk. I was paralyzed for a moment when suddenly my instincts came crashing in. Go! Run! Run as fast as you can! My body suddenly came to life. I grabbed my keys and bolted through the door, heaving for fresh air and ran outside. I hit the button to unlock my car and flung myself in. By now, I was shaking so violently I couldn't get my keys into the ignition the first few tries. *Go, go! Please please!* My brain kept screaming for my fingers to work. After what seemed like an eternity my truck started and I whipped the transmission into reverse. I stomped the pedal so hard I slammed into a light pole behind me, smashing my bumper. *Go, go!* I finally got the car into drive and peeled out of the parking lot.

I don't remember much of the drive home. My body was now going numb. I vaguely remember getting back to my apartment and fumbling to get the door unlocked. I was still shaking violently. Inside, I shut the door and automatically locked each of the three locks on my door. I turned on no lights but stumbled to the couch. I sat in the dark for hours trying to get something to make sense. Nothing did. Hours went by. Four, five, six? I don't know how many. Finally I went to the phone. Libby was back home in Wisconsin. Not knowing what I would say to her, I called her house. Her dad answered with a groggy hello. I'd lost sense of time and it was 2:30 in the morning there. I apologized for calling so late and asked if Libby was around. She was out. No, no, everything was fine, I assured her father. I apologized again for calling so late and hung up. After not being able to reach Libby, I began to totally shut down. I spent the night on the couch, drifting into and out of consciousness. Toward daybreak the questions began to float into and out of my head. What had happened to me? Where did this come from? What should I do? Was I . . . raped? No, my mind said. He's a good friend. He's your *teammate*. Rape is what happens to you when you walk alone at night and a stranger tackles you with a weapon. But I said no—that meant rape, didn't it? No, no, no. This had to be a mistake. This wasn't happening. It couldn't be.

When the sun came up, I was still in a daze, and began having horrible waves of nausea. I finally changed, mechanically taking off my clothes and shoving them deep into the hamper. I went back to the couch and had tears come to my eyes for the first time since it all happened. I just didn't know what to do. I felt disgusting and ashamed. I didn't want to tell my parents, let alone my coach. My thinking was inevitably blurred by the events that had been going on since I joined the team—groping, sexual and physical intimidation, harassment. No one seemed particularly bothered by that behavior. What would they think about what had happened now?

10

Cut Adrift

I TOLD NO ONE ABOUT THE RAPE. I knew what happened was wrong, but I didn't know who to turn to. I didn't even know what to say. I was scared, ashamed, and somehow felt responsible for the incident. I'd heard the term "date rape" but wasn't educated as to what it exactly entailed. I was also scared to death of what this guy would do to me if I told someone what had happened. After the other night, I had no idea what he could be capable of doing. Already tortured from the abuse that occurred during the year, I tried to convince myself that it wasn't a big deal. Though I still talked to my parents nearly every day, I couldn't bear to tell them. I knew it would hurt them, as well as my siblings. Plus, knowing how some of my teammates were treating me, and then the stalker, had sent Dad into ultraprotective mode. What would he do if I told him what had happened?

I knew the last place I would get any support was from my football coach. Barnett didn't want me around, was unapproachable, and frankly, I didn't trust him anyway. So instead, I shut down. Since it was the summer, most of my friends had left Boulder. I started to seclude myself, going into autopilot to get through the days.

It seemed like I didn't have a rope to grab on to, only a string. That string was football. It had always been a source of peace for me, and even though my first year at CU was terrible, I still had a fierce determination coming from somewhere deep inside to make it work.

Mentally, I was scraping the bottom of the barrel. My physical health was deteriorating as well. I thought I had recovered from the mononucleosis, but I had gone though the winter and spring with occasional bouts of severe sore throats. Now the episodes came more frequently and were worse. Antibiotics no longer worked as well as they did before. I had no energy, but had no alternative than to keep plugging along.

Summer training was "voluntary" in theory, but in fact we were supposed to be there. It was essentially the same as it was the year before: held off-campus at a practice field, there were four training sessions a day; we needed to attend only one. I knew the player who raped me was taking summer courses, so I would go to the workouts when he had class. I managed my schedule as well as I could so we wouldn't cross paths.

The workouts were also almost identical to the ones I did the summer before. A session started with stretching and warm-ups, then the agony of sprints. Sixteen sets of 80-yard sprints. A couple of sets of suicides—the spaced-out sprints, touch the ground, turn, and do it again—and again. Then 12 sets of shuttles where we'd sprint 25 yards 12 times for a total of 300 yards. Each week we'd do a little more and had to do it a little faster. However, I felt like I was going in the opposite direction—I was dragging more and going slower week by week. I had shut down emotionally; now my body was ready to shut down physically.

Even though I was feeling awful, I continued to push through workouts. Then, at a conditioning session in the last days of June, I started to warm up and then felt like I was going to pass out. It was like in the fall when I found out that I had mono. My throat was on fire and I had broken into a cold sweat. I got off the field and made my way to a bathroom. My knees buckled as I slid down to the floor. I was less than half a mile from my apartment, but I knew I couldn't drive then. After half an hour, I could finally stand again without fainting. I got some water from the sink and pulled myself together enough to get home.

I called Dad and started on yet another round of antibiotics. We decided I needed to see a specialist to find out what was wrong. The timing, though, was bad. Mom needed surgery on her neck to remove a lump, and I was more concerned about her. The day of her surgery was one of our harder days of running. At the end, we were doing long sets of suicides and I wasn't keeping up with the rest of the team. When we were finally done, the group gathered to end the session the way we always did.

I was feeling dizzy and nauseous, and wanted to get back to my apartment to call and find out how Mom was. As we stood there, one of my senior teammates spoke. He had never given me any problems and caught me completely off-guard with his words. Looking at me, he said, "Okay, the hypocrisy stops here. Katie, you are not keeping up with the group. You need to start coming to sessions twice a day or do something to improve."

I couldn't speak. I just looked at him and shook my head in disbelief. I got up and went around the boundaries of the field collecting the orange cones we used to mark off our running lanes.

A player from the women's volleyball team had been working out with us that day. She came up to me, insisting, "No, no, you did a good job. Way to go."

One of my other teammates came over and told me to keep my head up. "Katie, hang in there. It didn't look like you were going at full speed today but maybe you just had an off day. Don't worry about it."

"Yeah," I said softly. "I just didn't have a good day." I turned and walked away.

"Hypocrisy." The word stung. I walked back to my car, knowing that my teammate had been comparing me to a player who was so overweight that he had to do extra running sessions daily. He would try to train with us but be so far behind we'd go on and do other drills without him. That was why he was running twice a day, because he couldn't get a full workout in one session.

Completely fatigued, I struggled up the stairs to my apartment. Once inside, I finally broke. Tears came pouring out. It was the first time I had cried since the night of the rape. As much as possible, I finally let out some of the emotions I had been repressing. I was physically working harder than I ever had in my life, but I was moving backward, not forward. I was holding mountains of grief inside. For the first time in a long time, I let myself go—I called in sick to my summer job and spent the night resting. I was working in a part-time fund-raising job for the CU Foundation, calling alumni and alumnae for donations. During the worst summer of my life, I managed to raise $20,000 for the university.

I struggled through the rest of the summer workouts and was surprised when I received a letter from the football office in late July signed by Barnett. I was invited to camp in early August instead of being told to report for practice on the first day of school. When we had met in the spring, Barnett told me straight out that I wouldn't be going to camp. Due to NCAA rules, only 105 players can attend camp, and usually only the top two kickers go. It's an intense two weeks of workouts. Players live in a hotel, are up early for meetings, and then off to the field for the first of three daily practices.

I decided to call the football office to see if the letter was a mistake. It was. I was told only two kickers would be in camp, and I was to report for practice with the rest of the walk-ons the first day of school.

Like any player, I really wanted to go to camp, but I was looking forward to the time off. I needed it. As soon as summer conditioning stopped, my health crashed. Antibiotics weren't helping, and I was starting to run fevers nearly daily. I couldn't wait any longer—I had to get to the specialist.

I made an appointment with the doctor and spent all of my time sleeping. A week into camp, Mom got a call at home. It was Barnett's secretary. She said the coach needed to speak with me. Would I please return the call? Mom said yes and wondered to herself if I was being invited back to camp. It wasn't unheard of; sometimes a player would get injured and a space would open up.

I was less optimistic and wondered why he would be calling now. I was wary of Barnett, yet I knew I needed to return the call. Barnett was usually hard to reach, so I had no expectations of actually speaking with him.

I was put right through.

"Katie." His voice is distinctive.

"Yes," I said.

"Katie." The abruptness in his tone was evident. "I'm not sure if we're going to have room for you on the team this year. I brought a few new guys into camp, and in order for you to stay, you're going to need to come in for a tryout and outkick them."

Completely blindsided, it took me a few seconds to regain my composure. That was not what I expected to hear. I was sick and had to go to the doctor. With a fever of 103, there was no way I could kick a ball, let alone be in a kicking competition for a spot on the team. I told Barnett I couldn't do it right away, so we arranged to meet later in the week.

Slowly, I replaced the receiver. I stood in my kitchen, staring out the window. Tears filled my eyes. My dream of being a Buff had shattered to the floor. While it hurt, the tears streaming down my cheeks were also tears of relief. Deep inside, I knew it was the end of my time at CU. I didn't ever have to go back there. No more abuse. No more harassment. No more groping. No worries about running into my rapist. I wouldn't have to wake up every morning and worry every day what hell was in store at practice that afternoon. No more playing for a coach who didn't want me. Being sick, I couldn't go out and kick now. I took it as a sign from God. I would go somewhere else. This was not the right place for me, but I wouldn't give up my dream. My head was a jumbled mess of emotions.

Finally, I called Dad. He was seeing patients and answered on his cell. When I told him what had happened, he was stunned. When he had met with Barnett earlier in the year, Barnett had specifically assured him that I didn't need to worry about my spot on the roster. I was working hard, and Barnett said he always gave his kickers two seasons to make sure they were adjusted to the college game. I had heard the same spiel about my roster spot being safe, and even though I knew how college football worked, I had trusted my coach. A part of me wasn't happy about the way Barnett was handling the situation as well, but I couldn't deny that I wanted out. I had been living a nightmare for too long.

I called Mom next, and she was speechless. "Come home," she said. "At least for the night." My fever hadn't broken yet, and I knew I shouldn't drive and needed to rest. She asked if I wanted her to come up. I reassured her that I would be okay, and was going to lie back down.

I was too sick to drive so Dad came up to Boulder to get me for my doctor's appointment. Dr. Paul Dragul was a highly regarded ear, nose, and throat specialist. As soon as he looked in my throat he said, "These tonsils need to come out as soon as possible. I bet you've got an abscess that's been hiding somewhere back there since you had mono." That was an explanation for the sore throats, fevers, and fatigue I hadn't been able to kick. I had several tubes of blood drawn, and surgery was scheduled. I also was given a newer, more powerful antibiotic plus some cortisone to shrink the swelling in my throat. Dad got me back up to Boulder, and by the next morning I was feeling a little better. Not strong enough to kick, but at least I could make it up the stairs to my apartment without feeling like I was going to keel over.

Even though I felt like I should be resting, I still had to meet with Coach Barnett. During my first year at CU I had never spent more than five minutes in conversation with Gary Barnett. This meeting would be no different.

We sat across from each other in the same office I had sat with Coach Neuheisel years before. The view out on the field was still beautiful, but it was hard to believe how different everything else was since that time.

Barnett started the conversation saying he had brought in two extra kickers to camp. They had performed well and he wanted me to have a tryout against them. Tomorrow. For a moment, I wondered who these two "extra" kickers were, since I was told just a few weeks earlier that there would be only two kickers at camp. Just the first- and second-string guys; no "extras." I was also confused that my place on the team was now evaporating even though I was told to report for practice the first day of school. I explained to Barnett that I had been sick all summer and was scheduled to have my tonsils out. I had a fever right now. There was no way I could make my way onto a field. It made the whole process easier for Barnett. Since I couldn't compete, the new guys would stay on the team and I was off. Barnett said there was no option of a short-term medical leave and rejoining the team when I was healthy. I wasn't looking for that, though. What I wanted to talk about was the way this situation had been dealt with.

I was blunt. "You're leaving me in a really tough spot. I can't transfer. We are five days away from the start of school. I am going to lose eligibility because there's no time to look at, let alone start at, another program. What am I supposed to do?"

Barnett looked stunned. I think he expected me to wither away and just call it quits. He was momentarily silent.

"You care about this that much?"

Now it was I who was stunned. Did he even have to ask? I had made my intentions clear before I even got to CU. I loved football. I spent hour upon hour kicking after practice. Yet he was asking if I cared about it "that much"? I locked my eyes onto his and said simply, "Yes."

Barnett seemed to be at a loss for words. "I don't know what to tell you," he said.

But I already knew what I was going to tell him. "I think the best thing to do is get my release." After the meeting, I was going straight to the athletic director to get a formal release from the Athletic Department—the first step in transferring out of CU.

Once again, Barnett seemed caught off-guard. Transfer? Meet with the athletic director? The way he seemed to squirm in his chair told me this wasn't the way he thought this whole deal would play out. He knew about some of the harassment I had endured. Barnett had just finished his first season as head coach and was still in the process of solidifying his reputation. Even though I hadn't played during my first year, it would look bad if the truth came out about how things had gone for me under his leadership.

"Katie, I really don't know what to say." He looked distressed.

"Okay," I said, and excused myself from his office. As I left, I came to realize the complete disregard Barnett had for my life. I meant absolutely nothing to him.

I went directly from Barnett's office to make an appointment to see Dick Tharp, CU's athletic director. We met a few days later.

I thought about the first time I had seen Tharp. He was walking through one of our football practices early in my freshman year. He looked slightly familiar, but I wasn't sure who he was so I asked one of the other kickers. "That guy's the reason why you still got to be on the team after Coach Neuheisel left," I was told. Before I could ask him what he meant, we had been called in for a drill. Tharp knew me from my high school career at Chatfield. He knew the public support and excitement about my joining the team. He'd also read Barnett's comments that I was the best kicker he'd seen on tape out of all the potential walk-on candidates. Tharp was a lawyer as well as an athletic director.

Now we were discussing my future at CU. I had no future. I believe he had an idea of the harassment I'd gone through as well as the fact Barnett hadn't truly wanted me from day one. I told him how unhappy I was about my meeting with Barnett, especially getting the ax from the team at such a late date. If Barnett had been truthful with me several months before, I could have transferred.

"Oh, yeah, I understand. This has got to be hard." It seemed as though he wanted to put himself on my side. By the end of the meeting he said, "We really want the best for you. We'll give you your release and I'll personally write a letter of recommendation for wherever you want to go, talking about what a great student athlete you are."

Tharp then said, "Of course, we don't want to have a huge media mess about this falling-out." I got the unspoken message: If I wanted to get my release without a problem, I would keep quiet about my experience at CU. I knew it would be another media circus once it got out that I wouldn't be playing, and frankly, at this point, it was the last thing I wanted to deal with.

"I don't want a media mess either," I said.

It hit me that if I wanted to go to another school, I needed to make sure the information came out properly. I knew that if it was reported that I had problems at CU, other schools would certainly be more hesitant to take me on. I was stuck and had to think this out.

Tharp and I agreed to keep it simple and true: tell the press I was sick and having surgery. I would not play football at CU that fall. We also agreed that I'd cooperate with the sports information director about releasing the information to the media. Once again, keep it simple for now and then give more details after my surgery, if necessary.

I had always gotten along with Dave Plati, the head of media relations for the football department. He seemed to be one of the few people in the athletic department who recognized that my situation was different from that of anyone in the country, since I was the only female on a Division I football team. Plati never wanted to capitalize on it or exploit it, but just acknowledge that it was different. Quite a contrast to Barnett, who during my freshman year said, "I can't understand why I am having a press conference about a walk-on placekicker."

I went to Plati's office the night before the start of school for a quick meeting. I wasn't in the best mood to be dealing with a press release. I didn't feel well, and the next day was the official first day of practice for the entire team. It would be the first time in five years that I wouldn't be on a football field with a team. Plati and I brainstormed for a few hours about how we were going to release the news to the media.

Should I put out a statement or should CU? Should Barnett say something? The consensus was that he should not. In the end, we agreed one more time to just focus on the simple facts: a release that said I'd had repeated cases of severe tonsillitis, which required surgery. I would miss the 2000 season. No further details. It didn't sound like the kind of medical problem that would keep someone out for a season, but it was honest.

On August 30, a headline in the *Rocky Mountain News* said, "Hnida to Miss 2000 Season." The short story that followed said I had complications of tonsillitis and would be having surgery. I would rejoin the team in the spring.

Rejoin the team in the spring? Where did that come from? There was no way I wanted to stay at CU.

After my meetings with Tharp and Plati, I had my first chance to look in detail at the Division I football transfer rules. I now realized being released at such a late date wouldn't cost me one season; it would be two. The NCAA says a transferring player must attend the new school for at least one full year before being allowed to participate. I couldn't find a good program, transfer, and start that 12-month clock in less than a week. I would have to stay at CU, find the right fit at a new school, then transfer. It would be January at the earliest before I could enroll anywhere. I would miss this season and wouldn't finish my 12-month sitting-out time at the new school until a year from January. That meant next season was shot as well. Two years—no football. It was worse than I thought. It was also a breaking point for my parents. Aside from Dad's meeting with Coach Barnett after my fall season—at Barnett's suggestion—I had kept my parents from becoming involved with my dealings at CU. After all, I was an adult and felt I wanted to handle things on my own. However, by this time both Mom and Dad were bothered enough by the treatment I'd received that they wanted to speak with someone. I finally agreed to let Dad go up.

He met with Tharp a few days later. The first item on the agenda was my treatment from some of the players. Although I hadn't told my parents about the rape or other sexual intimidations, I did tell them over the course of the spring and summer about more of the troublesome things that had happened. I thought that with time I could eventually fix the situation, so I had talked Dad out of confronting anyone.

He knew it was too late to undo the past, but wanted some accountability from those in charge. My father told Tharp that the environment and culture of the football program needed change. Tharp only replied that he would "look into matters" and talk with Barnett.

Dad also spelled out what we now knew about my lost eligibility. He believed it was unfair for any player to get released from the team at the last minute, especially without warning. Tharp's attitude was clear: "Barnett is the head coach and can make any decision he wants. I can't intercede." Dad pressed him on the harassment, but Tharp brushed it off as something in the past. Bringing it up now would only hurt my chances to transfer.

"The main thing now is to take care of Katie. Can we get her to another school, do something? She can always try out for spring ball," Tharp said. Knowing that spring ball at CU was the last thing on earth I wanted, Dad just asked that I get my release and that it be kept quiet. Me not being on the team for the fall was one media mess. If it got out that I'd asked for my release, there was sure to be another one. Tharp assured Dad that nobody would be told about the release. "I promise. It's her release; only she can talk about it."

With that, Dad shook hands with Tharp and left.

I had my surgery on September 11, 2000, and all went well. Dr. Dragul had been right: at the back of my throat was an abscess that had been there since I'd had mono. It had never healed and had grown bigger in six months. It was no wonder I had been so sick. Considering that I was still trying to work out all that time, it was a small wonder that I hadn't completely collapsed.

Even though I was sore from the surgery, I finally felt like I could swallow, the chills and fevers went away, and my strength started to come back. Three days later, I felt even better. A letter came from the CU Athletics Compliance Office and simply said: "The University of Colorado grants release per NCAA Bylaw 13.1.1.1.3 to any institution to discuss transfer with Katie Hnida, sport–football."

I was now free to contact other schools and send audition tapes of my kicking. I had time to get healthy as well as start practicing on my own again. But I was still in a rut. I knew that wherever I transferred, I would be two seasons out of football.

Some reporters were suspicious about the news release explaining my withdrawal from the team. They called my parents asking for a statement but got only "She had surgery and is out for the season." They also tried to contact me, but I had no comment. All I wanted was to be left alone and have things die down.

Unfortunately, just as it began to simmer down, word somehow leaked out that I had asked for my release—a certain sign that I was going to go to another school. The media again went into a frenzy, calling me, my family, and the Athletic Department. No comment, no comment, no comment. Until they got to Barnett. He confirmed to the papers that I had asked for my release and then stated, "Yeah, I know that she asked for her release. I think she is going to the University of Washington." I had no clue where Barnett even got that idea. He had to be kidding.

There was no way I was going to Washington. There was an NCAA stipulation that prevented anyone from CU following Coach Neuheisel to Washington. Even if that hadn't been an NCAA rule, I would never have gone there and opened myself to accusations I wasn't good enough to play for anyone else. Neuheisel might be a good resource for advice about other schools and coaches, but that was it.

Barnett's comments fueled the rumors, and everyone now knew my breakup with CU wasn't a pretty one. I continued to refuse to comment, but the papers kept writing anyway.

A few mornings later, I picked up the *Denver Post* and flipped to the sports section. There was my picture. I cringed. A writer named Mark Kiszla had an article about why women shouldn't play football, and I was the perfect example. "Linebackers are from Mars, women athletes should be named Venus Williams. It's a bad idea for sports bras and shoulder pads to stand together in the same huddle. A football field is no place for the battle of the sexes."

I was never at war with men. I loved football. But to Kiszla, I was nothing more than "a poster girl for diversity on the CU squad." The more I read, the more upset I got.

"A blond in pigtails with an unreliable leg was a dilemma Barnett never sought. He inherited Hnida from predecessor Rick Neuheisel, a coach who never met a cute story that couldn't be exploited and blown up into a big headline."

Kiszla concluded that my dream had died. "Putting a woman in football cleats as a cheap publicity stunt is a dangerous game."

Another article called me a "nightmare for Coach Barnett" and a kicker "living in a world absent of reality." And yet another said the only reason I was leaving was to attend another school where my brother Joe was going to be playing football.

It was the first time in my life that I had ever had anything negative written about me. I tried not to let the words get me down, but it hurt more than I thought possible. No one knew about the harassment, the assaults, or the rape, and I was getting ripped to shreds.

How had the word leaked? Barnett. I was not happy about it and wanted to make sure nothing further was said. I went to see Tharp, Dad went to see Barnett. I had no desire to see Barnett myself. I trusted him about as far as I could throw him and had gotten nowhere with him in any meeting we'd ever had.

When I met with Tharp, I was furious. I thought we had agreed to keep things quiet, to avoid "the media mess." How was that possible if Barnett was talking, especially about things that weren't even true? Tharp reassured me over and over that it wouldn't happen again, that he would talk to Barnett and make sure of it. He knew I was angry and was no longer worried that I would talk to the media about my experience at CU, but Tharp was worried that I would think about a lawsuit. I shook my head. A lawsuit would solve nothing. All I wanted was to get on with my life and play football. That was all I had ever wanted in the first place.

Dad met with Barnett on October 23. The meeting started with a handshake and a few pleasantries and then got down to the issues. Dad barely knew where to start. He didn't just have questions about Barnett talking about my release, he had questions about everything. Dad started by asking why Barnett hadn't told me sooner that "there wasn't going to be room" for me this year and explained that I would now be missing two seasons of football instead of one.

"That's if she tries to go to a Division I school. She'll never do that, so it shouldn't be a problem. How about Western State College or some smaller school? There are no transfer limitations to drop down a level of competition or two," Barnett responded.

"She says she wants to play Division I."

"She never will. No team will take her now."

Dad shook his head, then asked why Barnett had told him that he gave he gave kickers two years to adjust when they had met last spring, why Barnett himself had told me I would be reporting the first day of classes again.

Barnett's answer was simple: "Things change."

That was it. He wouldn't elaborate. He just said things change. Dad then went on to a bigger issue—my treatment by certain players on the team. He asked about me being called a cunt and footballs being thrown at my head.

Barnett again answered simply: "That's just the way this guy is. I gave him a tongue lashing."

"So you knew things were going on?"

"He's from Texas. You've got to expect that."

Dad was taken aback. "So that makes it okay?"

"That's just the way it is."

"So basically you can curse, be abusive, throw stuff, and it's okay as long as you are from Texas?! And you know it just wasn't one guy."

Barnett was silent. Dad shook his head in disbelief and then asked a final question.

"What was the story with going to the papers about Katie's release? It was supposed to be her call about if and when she was going to talk about it."

"I just don't think it's a big deal."

And with that, Barnett stood up and walked out of his office.

11

Hope Is Spelled U-C-L-A

I TRIED TO LEARN HOW to be a regular, everyday college student. But I didn't want to be recognized, and I didn't want to answer questions. My long blond hair had become a trademark. The kicker with the ponytail. I hadn't done more than trim my hair for years, but one morning I cut off about eight inches. I wanted to make myself invisible.

That fall, I would go to class, go home to my apartment, do my homework, then repeat the routine, day after day. I completely secluded myself from everyone except Libby and I avoided every situation where I might run into football players. I spent long hours awake at night, missing football, but aching over everything I had gone through the year before. I wouldn't talk about it. All I wanted to do was get out of Boulder and start fresh. I was completely miserable. I was trying to make sense out of what had hap-

pened the year before, particularly the rape, but found nothing
but more pain. Even though I lived only 45 minutes away, I was
so busy with football my freshman year that I had rarely gone
home. Now I found myself going home more often, especially
when the football team would have a home game in Boulder. I felt
better when I was with my family, but I knew that I didn't belong
at home in Littleton anymore. I didn't feel like I belonged anywhere. Libby was my lifeline that semester. Though I didn't always
talk about it, I knew that she could sense the pain I was going
through. She knew a lot more than most people did about the harassment I underwent on the team but still not even close to the
extent. There would be days when I would want to spill my guts
out to her, but I would shut off. If I talked about it, it would make
it all real. Instead it was easier to ignore it and keep trying to think
about the future. I had to find a way back onto the field. I had
gotten my athletic release, but was stuck in the apartment lease
and didn't have anywhere to go. It took so long to get everything
squared away with CU and my health that I hadn't had time to
start looking at a new school. It being so late in the fall, I decided
that I would wait and see which schools would be looking for kickers after the 2000 season wrapped up. Then I would start sending
out tapes to prospective schools. I had never imagined my life
without football. After kicking my first ball at the age of 14, I just
expected that it would always be there. That fall, the football
movie *Remember the Titans* came out. Joe saw it first and loved it.
My parents then saw it and told me I had to go see it—not only
was it a great sports movie, but the coach's intense, football-crazed
young daughter in the film had reminded them of me when I was
younger. I went alone to a small theater in our neighborhood. I
bought a ticket and sat in the back row. It was a true story about a
high school football team that is integrated during a time of high
racial tensions. The movie hit me hard. During the opening
scenes, tears filled my eyes. I missed the game so much. I watched

the players on screen get pulled out of bed for an early-morning run and realized that as much as I had hated having to get up for early-morning conditioning, I actually *missed* it.

By second semester sophomore year, I made an effort to escape the isolation I had been in the first half of the year.

Libby and I went out a few times, occasionally to parties; sometimes we'd just hang out with friends. CU is a huge drinking school and is annually on the list of top party schools in America. I quickly realized that wasn't the life for me. Being an athlete for such a long time, I had never adapted to the party lifestyle. Sure, I liked to go out from time to time, but doing it all the time didn't do much for me. In fact, I think it just made me more unhappy.

For the first time in almost nine months, I started kicking. I kept a stash of footballs in the apartment, and some nights I'd go down to Potts Field, where we'd done our summer workouts. I wanted to kick without drawing any attention, so I kicked ball after ball into the darkness. When I was finished, I'd find the footballs and then start all over.

Although I hadn't been on the team, I continued to get fan mail. One letter turned out to be the one that gave me the final nudge to get back into the game—from a direction I hadn't even considered. It came from a junior college in California. While reading the letter, it hit me. I didn't have to sit out an extra season; I could attend a junior college, kick there, and then transfer to Division I. I talked to my parents, and we all agreed I should send out kicking tapes.

The responses were better than I expected. I made my first trip with Mom to see a college in Scottsdale, Arizona.

I knew there would be a dramatic difference between the junior college and a Division I school. None of the schools had facilities like I was used to in the Big 12 Conference at CU. In Scottsdale, the mascot was simply The Artichoke. Three guys from my high school were playing there and loved it. The coach seemed like a good guy, and the school made it clear that a small scholarship was available to me.

But when I got back to Colorado, I knew I needed to see more schools and make a well-thought-out decision. California had a lot of junior colleges with good football programs, so out went more tapes. Once again, great responses. I researched the schools and narrowed the list to four: Santa Barbara, Pasadena, San Jacinto, and Moorpark.

Dad and I set out together on the California college tour. The schools seemed small, but all of them had one thing in common: a love for their football programs. San Jacinto had a young, eager coach who liked his team to dress in all-black uniforms while playing in 100-degree temperatures. Pasadena had brand-new facilities. I got a great reception and a two-hour tour from the head coach. Moorpark was a junior college power that scored a lot of points every season, so I'd get lots of kicking there. Our last visit was Santa Barbara. But we had a totally unexpected detour.

I knew I wanted to go to a junior college, but as I was researching schools and then making audition tapes to send them, I had decided to send a tape to UCLA, too. Geographically, it was right in the middle of a bunch of the junior colleges I was looking at and I knew that UCLA's football program often took JC transfers. What the heck? I thought. I included a letter saying that I was going to play this year at a junior college and would be looking to transfer back to a Division I program. Maybe someone would look at it and keep an eye out for me. I figured it couldn't hurt.

Then, while Dad and I were in California, Mom got a call at home. It was Ron Carragher, UCLA's recruiting coordinator. He had looked at my tape and wanted to talk to me. Mom explained that I was actually in California at that moment, looking at schools. Carragher gave her his number and asked her to pass it on to me.

Dad and I had just returned from a long day of driving and looking at schools when Mom called. I immediately was on the phone to Coach Carragher. Could Dad and I stop for a visit tomorrow morning, by any chance? It was the only time and day that the coaches were going to be around that week. We were staying in the Huntington Beach area, and knowing the California traffic, we left extra early to get up to UCLA.

The day was tremendous. I met Coach Carragher and then sat down for a talk with Randy Taylor, UCLA's director of football operations. He told me about the program and asked me to keep in touch. Coach Carragher had watched my tape and thought it was good—there was a possibility they'd be interested in having me on the team. I briefly met the head coach, Bob Toledo, on my way out and he was very friendly. I was elated as I left the athletic complex and looked at the campus. UCLA. It was a huge school with a tradition of both academic and athletic excellence. The idea that a place like that would even be interested in me gave me the ray of hope I needed during that bleak time. I was now filled with a renewed faith that my dream was not dead. I could still make it happen—and I would.

On our way to Santa Barbara, we stopped by the Rose Bowl. It's where UCLA plays their home games and a place I had seen only on TV. It was a stunning stadium, one I hoped to play in someday.

We finally made it to Santa Barbara City College after our visit to UCLA. I felt a strong pull to the school immediately. The stadium is right on the ocean and is surrounded by palm trees. The coach, Carmen DiPoalo, was a laid-back and kind man who said the main reason to play football was to have fun. He had grown up in Santa Barbara, played college football at UCLA, then returned home to teach and coach.

No one knew my real reason for transferring. I only said that things hadn't worked out for me at CU after Coach Neuheisel left.

"It just wasn't the right fit," I said.

I came back to Colorado feeling more optimistic than I had in more than a year. I actually had choices for my future. The choice turned out to be Santa Barbara.

12

Santa Barbara

M Y DAD AND I loaded all my things into a U-Haul trailer and we were finally ready to head to Santa Barbara. Dad was going to drive out and help me get settled. The rest of the family came outside to see us off. Someone had unearthed an old license plate that said "California or Bust," and we stuck it up on the windshield for the drive. I couldn't wait to get going. I was ready for a new place, a new start in a place where I wouldn't be constantly reminded of the nightmares of my past. "Time to move on" became my mantra.

I also couldn't wait to get on the field again. A year away from football had felt like an eternity. A junior college seemed like it would be the best place to work on regaining my kicking form. I'd get lots of playing time and a place to practice to my heart's content. I would have fresh kicking tapes to send to schools and continue my quest to become the first Division I female football player.

The trip to Santa Barbara was almost 1,000 miles and gave me plenty of time to think. Anytime CU would pop into my mind, I would force it out quickly. That time in my life was over. Still, fleeting thoughts left me feeling unsettled. When we finally started to see the signs we were nearing Santa Barbara, I was thankful. A new chapter was about to begin. I had no idea that it was going to be another tough and painful journey.

My apartment wasn't going to be ready for another month, but Pat McPhee, the assistant athletic director, kindly offered me use of her extra bedroom for the time being. I moved a small suitcase into Pat's place and then moved the contents of the U-Haul into a storage unit. Since I was keeping the car, Dad flew back home the next day from the small Santa Barbara airport.

Saying good-bye to him was tough. He knew what I'd been through and hoped this new opportunity was going to be the right one. I stood there and watched him walk across the tarmac and board the small commuter plane. He could see me from the window of the airplane, and we waved to each other for as long as we could.

Dad said that for some reason he had a sinking feeling in the pit in his stomach. Even now he finds it hard to think back to the pain of that moment. The plane turned and taxied away. I finally headed back to my car. As I pulled onto the highway, the unsettled feeling washed over me again. It's normal, I told myself. After all, I was in a brand-new place and knew virtually no one.

The next few days went well. Pat was kind and welcoming. I drove around and explored the campus—it was much smaller than the huge university I had come from. The town itself was gorgeous—palm-tree-lined streets and a glittering ocean. I checked out the football stadium, which was just a few hundred yards from the ocean. I breathed in the thick, salty air, ready to be back in pads and a helmet. In just a few days, I finally would be. As I walked off the field, though, an uneasy feeling began to creep over me. I shook it off, just as I had shaken off any of the thoughts that had crept into my mind on the drive to Santa Barbara.

When I went to my first football meeting, it was déjà vu all over again. A room full of men . . . and me. The guys were pretty impressed that I'd come from a Division I school. That earned me some respect right off the bat. Most of them were from Santa Barbara and had played high school football locally.

After the meeting, four of us went to the field to kick some balls. As I stretched out, I kept getting waves of uneasiness. It was the same feeling I got when I had visited the field nights before. It was almost as if my body was trying to tell me something . . . but what? "Just start kicking," I told myself. "You're just nervous." As soon as I started kicking, I would fall into my rhythm and relax. I got up and went to start kicking. Something wasn't right. My kicks were missing the pop they usually carried after I hit them. Work through it, I told myself.

As I went to pick up a ball, I felt a strange pang. Suddenly my heart began to race and my hands felt sticky. A football flying at my head. Hands reaching toward me, trying to grab me. The dark corners of the Dal Ward basement. My stalker coming toward me in the darkness, shattering glass from the jar I dropped. Oh, my God. I couldn't move. *He* was there. I could feel the weight of his body and the damp skin pressed against me. Pushing my shoulder down, putting his hand to my mouth to shush me. Moving slowly up the inside of my thighs. For a moment I thought I was going to start screaming.

"Katie? You okay?" One of the other kickers was standing next to me. "You don't look very good."

I mumbled something about not feeling well and left the field. I made it up to the women's locker room and crashed onto the bench. My head fell into my hands. Images from my time at CU were exploding in my head. It was like a movie flashing between scenes. In psychological terms, I was suffering my first flashback. My mind was spinning, out of control. I felt as though I was actually back at CU. "Deep breaths," I told myself. Gradually I was able to slow my breathing and then my heartbeat. I walked to the sink and splashed water on my face. How did that happen? The turf of football fields was supposed to be a place where I could find peace . . . and safety. Safety. The words hung in the air. The football field, once my safe place, my escape, my heart's home, was no longer a place of peace for me. How could that happen? My heart began to ache. I knew what had happened. CU had happened. The football field had become a place where I had been harassed, abused, and accosted. God, no. The memories were too much for my head to handle. I was a football player. I had come to Santa Barbara to play football. I was not going to let what had happened in my past control what was going on now. CU was over. *Time to move on.*

I gathered my things and drove back to Pat's house. I would be okay. Today was a fluke. Yet, as I passed the football field on my way back, a sharp pang had struck inside me.

"Katie? Is that you?" Pat heard me at the door. "Are you okay?" I stepped inside. Pat was looking at me with concern in her eyes. "One of the boys said you didn't feel well. Are you sick?" she asked.

"No . . . I . . ." I paused. "I just had a bad day . . . bad kicking." I found myself at a loss for words.

I couldn't tell her what had really happened.

"You don't look very good. Do you need to see a doctor?" Pat asked. I shook my head.

"No, I'll be okay. Tomorrow will be better," I said. "Thank you, though. I'm just going to go rest now."

I walked down the hall and shut my door. I called my parents and talked to them briefly. They could tell I wasn't doing well, but I told them the same thing I told Pat: it had just been a bad day. It would be better tomorrow. I was going to bed. My parents told me to hang in there and reluctantly got off the phone with me. I knew that they sensed I hadn't told them what was really going on. I stretched out on the bed in the semidarkness, trying to clear my head. Though I'd spent a hellish year in Boulder, I had never experienced anything like the flashback. I had always been able to keep my emotions in control. Today I couldn't. I had no control over the images in my head. And for the first time in my life, I didn't want to set foot on a football field.

The thought brought tears to my eyes. I tried to fight it off, but the emotions were too strong. I curled up in bed and cried. It was one of the first times I had cried about everything that had happened to me. At some point, between tears and exhaustion, I fell asleep.

The next day I woke up with a feeling of dread. It was our first official football practice. I still didn't want to go back on the field. The doorway to my return to football was wide open. All I had to do was walk through. I knew the NCAA rules that said once I took a single step onto that field I was committed to stay—or else I would not be eligible to go straight back to Division I. I drove to the school not knowing what I should do. I got to the school and went to my locker room. I changed into my workout clothes, then carried my helmet and cleats outside. I sat on the steps, preparing to lace up my shoes, when I got hit again. Suddenly I was back at CU, lacing my cleats for a summer conditioning practice. There he was. My rapist, walking through the gates. I had wanted to run. This time I did. One unlaced cleat on, the other in my hand, I got off the steps and half ran into my locker room. My mind was once again being flooded with images. DAMN IT! GET YOURSELF BACK OUT THERE! I screamed at myself. YOU *NEVER* BACKED DOWN BEFORE! I threw the cleat in my hand across the room, in disgust and anger with myself. As the shoe clanged against a locker, I realized the truth. Walking back onto the field wasn't the courageous thing. The courageous thing to do would be to face the events that haunted me. I had been running from them ever since they had happened. I spent the next few hours in the locker room in agony. I was coming to the realization that I needed to deal with what I'd gone through. But I didn't like it. Why now? I was supposed to be back playing football, going to school, reclaiming my life. Instead, was I going to journey into the deepest, darkest corners of my being? I couldn't do that now, I would lose yet *another* season of football. But if I didn't take care of this now, when would I? No time was exactly convenient to deal with issues as deep as these. And at the same time, I recognized another fact: If I didn't work through these matters, I probably would never be the football player I wanted to be, let alone the person. That thought was the sinker. I wasn't going to go on the field and be half a kicker, and I sure as hell wasn't going to live my life as half a person, running away from my past. That wasn't how I was raised. Wearily, I recalled the mantra I had been repeating. *Time to move on.* It turned out that moving on would actually mean going back in time so I could move forward.

But could I really walk away from football?

Finally I changed back into my street clothes and went outside into the highest stands of the stadium. Practice had long been over. I sat down and gazed out at the ocean. I couldn't believe I was about to do this. How was I ever going to explain this to my parents? I reached into my bag, dialed home, and closed my eyes. After two rings, Dad answered.

"Kate! How'd everything go?" he asked, expecting to hear good news about the first day of practice. Instead, he got the words he least expected to hear.

"Dad, I can't do this." Tears had begun to fall, and I couldn't get any other words out.

"Can't do what?"

"Football." My heart felt like it was being squeezed.

He was silent for a moment. "What's going on?"

"I can't go onto the field." I choked on my words. "I just can't."

"Why? What's going on?"

"I can't explain it, I just can't. I'm so sorry." I kept repeating that over and over. Dad would ask me questions, and all I could do was apologize and say to him, "I can't explain it, I just can't."

He was stunned. So was Mom, who'd picked up the extension a few moments earlier. I felt awful. They had spent time and money, helping me to visit schools, find and pay for an apartment, move to Santa Barbara, and now, just as the season was officially under way, I was bowing out for no apparent reason.

Finally, through my tears, I managed to get out the letters "CU."

"CU?" My parents were aware that it had been rough at CU, but still didn't know the full extent of what had occurred while I was there.

"Kate? CU? What happened?" Closing my eyes, I shook my head. I couldn't tell them yet.

"Kate? Kate, sweetie, are you there?"

"It was bad. Worse than I told you." That was the best I could get out.

Both of my parents were silent again.

"I'm sorry." I started to weep.

"Kate, honey, it's okay. It's okay," Mom said.

That night was the darkest of my life. Though I had been through some horrendous nights before, this was the worst. I'd never felt so lost. I couldn't believe that I was actually walking away from football by choice. Were my playing days over? Did I just throw away my dream? Then there were the mountains of memories I had pushed as far into the recesses of my brain as possible. As scary as the thought of no football was, the idea of confronting my past was terrifying. Would it be too much for me? Would I be able to work through it? On top of it all, I felt like I had let my family down, and everyone who had supported me and my dreams. I might have slept a few hours that night. I don't remember. All I remember is that I felt like my world, the world I had been struggling to hold together for the past few years, had finally collapsed. Even during the hell at Colorado, I had somehow managed to keep it together.

As I lay in bed, not bothering to wipe away the constant flow of tears, another image from the past entered my mind. This one, however, wasn't bad. I was remembering the darkness that had covered the field after a game in high school. In the darkness of the room in Santa Barbara, I could see Coach Mead before me. "No matter how dark the night gets, the sun will always rise." It would. And so would I. His words, spoken four years earlier, a lifetime and almost 1,000 miles away from where I was now, were my lone thought of comfort that night.

The next morning I spoke with my parents again. They had gotten over the shock of my news last night, and Dad talked to me first.

"Your mom and I love you. Whatever you want or need to do is fine with us. Your happiness and health are the most important things. If you need to come home, come home. If you want to play football, play football. If you don't, don't. We're here to support you, no matter what." They were exactly the words I needed to hear. I thanked God for my parents' unconditional love. With their support, I knew that no matter what I faced in the next few months, I would be okay.

Dad also had gotten in touch with Maggie, a sports psychologist I had seen before I left Boulder. We did a phone session later that day. She probed further into my experience at CU in a gentle way. I told her a little bit more about the harassment I endured. Toward the end of the call, Maggie said that considering my emotional state, maybe walking onto a football field at this time in my life was the very last thing I should be doing. The words brought me relief. Even though I'd barely told Maggie the tip of the iceberg, she let me know that it was okay to feel bad. Though it was small, a burden had been lifted from me.

That night I talked with Pat and Carmen. I felt terrible—both of them had shown me incredible kindness and hospitality since I'd been in town. Now here I was, telling them I couldn't play football, but not able to tell them why. Both of them felt that the problem was my disappointment in my kicking. They were confident that my game would improve as I trained and played with the team. Their reasoning was completely logical. I was rusty, and they knew I had been frustrated with my performance the first day.

Carmen told me to take time, that if I wanted to come out for the team in a few weeks, I was welcome. I thanked him, but inside I knew I couldn't. Pat suggested that I see a school counselor and helped get me an appointment. It was a place to start.

I was emotionally exhausted and worn down from the past 24 hours. I was scared of what I was about to do, yet I knew I had to do it. Ironically, on that day, somehow I knew I would kick again. I would still achieve my dream. I just had another bridge to cross to get there.

I knew that returning to Colorado wasn't an option. I needed to be in a place where no one knew me, where I could think and be alone. So I decided to stay in Santa Barbara and stick it out with school. The next few months were difficult, even though I knew I had made the right decision. I started seeing the counselor at the school and slowly began to talk about my life. I wasn't ready to talk about the extent of the harassment I had endured, nor the rape. But I was able to finally admit to myself that I had been raped. *Rape.* To me, it was the vilest four-letter word on the planet. And although I had admitted to myself that I was a rape victim, I was still plagued with shame, fear, and self-blame. I had been the All-American girl. Homecoming queen, honor rolls, the number one teen most likely to change the world. The one nicknamed "Golden Girl" by the papers. "Rape victim" didn't seem like it belonged under any of those identities. How would people react? I had been raped by someone I knew. I had gone into his apartment willingly. I felt like I should have known.

I was in a deep depression. I was tired all the time, yet I could rarely sleep. Instead, I'd stay up all night, agonizing over incidents that had happened during my years at CU. Or on the rare occasion I did fall asleep, I'd wake at 4 A.M. and not be able to fall back asleep. I would skip classes constantly and just lie in bed. I didn't have any motivation to go out, to do anything besides going to therapy. I would let the phone ring and let e-mails go unanswered. I just didn't care.

I was allowed only a limited number of sessions with the school counselor, so she referred me to a psychologist, and in turn, a psychiatrist. I started on antidepressants and tried to continue with the counseling. I went through a number of visits to psychologists but didn't find someone I felt completely comfortable with. Still, the school counselor and a few more talks with Maggie had opened me up and I was letting the pain come.

The antidepressants helped, too. They were by no means an instant fix, but they allowed me to keep my head above water, and in turn, continue to find the strength to go onward.

Going onward came in baby steps. The first one was going back to Littleton. I flew back a few times to see my brother Joe play. By now he was a senior at Chatfield and captain of a team that was nationally ranked and would go on to win the state championship. He had been through two reconstructive surgeries on his shoulder, and I knew that that season he was playing through some intense pain. Though my pain had been different, I could relate. Watching him push through game after game gave me hope and motivation to push on myself.

I needed to watch Joe play, but a more subtle reason for being home was to lean on him. I was finally coming to the point where I was ready to talk about the rape, and I knew he was who I could tell. Steady, practical, he's the one who always keeps his cool. Joe was the one in my family who could center me when I became too emotional about things. Joe knew how crazy the two years at CU had been. Though I knew telling him I had been raped would hurt him, I also knew he was strong enough to handle it.

After Joe's games, we'd usually eat a truckload of food, sit in the Jacuzzi, and talk or just mess around. One night, when we were out picking up food, I was finally ready.

The truck came to a stoplight.

"Joe," I said, "I need to tell you something."

He was quiet, but looked across the truck at me.

"When I was at CU, I told you that a lot of bad stuff happened."

Still silent.

"I haven't talked about it all yet. I was raped."

I had finally said it out loud. The words that had haunted me for more than a year. Joe was motionless and still silent.

Then he said, "I'm sorry, Kate." He paused. "Is there anything I can do?"

"Not right now," I said. "But please don't tell Mom and Dad."

The light changed and we moved on. Joe was very, very quiet, but the silence felt safe.

We got our food, and when we got out of the car, Joe put his hand on my arm and gently squeezed it. It was his way of telling me that he'd be there for me whenever I needed him. And he was. He patiently waited as I started to fill in the blanks. I became more comfortable. I trusted him completely and knew that he would not tell anyone until I was ready. Having Joe know brought a tremendous relief—I was no longer alone with my secret.

I went back to Santa Barbara and tried to finish the semester. Even with all the missed classes, my courses were easy enough that I had stayed on track. There were more long days and nights, but I was trudging through. December arrived, and there was a bracing chill in the usually mild Santa Barbara air. I was getting ready for finals and counting down the days until I went home for Christmas. I was typing a long English paper when my phone rang one night. It was a friend from Colorado.

"Hey," I said. "How are you?" He mumbled a response and a red flag went up in my body.

"What's going on? Is something the matter?" I asked tentatively.

There was a pause. "There are some girls . . . some girls say they were raped at CU by some football players."

I closed my eyes. *Dear God, no.*

I hung up quickly and sat staring blankly at the computer screen. I felt numb for a moment, then jolted up by waves of nausea. Scrambling, I ran to the bathroom and threw up.

I stayed up for most of the night, in a dissociated fog much like the one I had after my own rape. Thoughts of my own assault as well as questions filled my mind. Was it true? A rumor? Who were the players?

It wasn't a rumor. The next day, the Colorado papers carried the story. Several women said they were raped at party attended by CU football recruits on December 7. I read the story online and then called my parents. They had seen it as well.

Dad and I talked for a long time. We decided that he'd send an e-mail to the chancellor at CU. The chancellor, Richard Byyny, and a university regent, Maureen Ediger, had said that any allegations of sexual assault would be vigorously investigated by the university, the Athletic Department, and the football program. I was wary about the football program claiming they would "vigorously investigate," and the e-mail Dad wrote reflected that feeling.

It said, in part, "I hope your faith and trust in the head football coach and the Athletic Department to investigate this situation of alleged sexual misconduct is not misplaced. You may recall my daughter Katie Hnida, who was a member of the 1999 football team. Katie endured a year's worth of harassment: verbal, sexual, and physical. But to give you an example of how this was handled, take my meeting with Coach Barnett in fall 2000 when I complained about a player calling my daughter the 'c' word for the female genital opening. The reply from Coach Barnett regarding that player—'he's from Texas so you've got to expect that.'" The e-mail concluded by saying that the athletic director was also aware of the situation and no action had been taken.

The chancellor responded a few days later, on December 15. It was a fairly vanilla reply, which thanked Dad for his concerns and said they would be taken seriously.

We never heard from the chancellor again.

But in the days and weeks after the news reports and the e-mail, I felt helpless and guilty. A tape kept playing through my head, "What if you'd come forward? Would that have prevented these girls from being raped?" Logically, I knew there wasn't a connection. But the self-blame so prevalent in rape victims was tearing at my heart.

Therapy would eventually teach me that the blame belonged to the rapist, not to me. But I had yet to tell anyone except Joe about the rape.

That changed when I went home for Christmas that year. Over break, I got together with an old friend, Yvette. Yvette and I had known each other for years through church and school. We'd always been friends, but didn't become especially close until our college years. We'd gone out for coffee and caught up on each other's lives. We left Starbucks and were in front of her house before it even came up. Every time we went out, we'd end up sitting in the car in front of one of our houses and talking for another hour or two. This time was no different. Somehow the story about the other women at CU found its way into our conversation. I was silent for a moment, then my own story came tumbling out. Yvette listened quietly as I told her nearly everything I could remember about my rape. When I was finished, she reached over and hugged me. "Oh, Kate, I am so sorry." Her eyes were filled with tears. "That is so horrible, so wrong. . . . What can I do?"

I smiled at her. "You've done enough just by listening. Thank you." It was true. Yvette's reaction to my story let me know again that my feelings were valid, that it was okay to feel bad. We stayed talking for a while longer, and then I finally left to go home. More weight was lifted off my shoulders, and I had another person I could talk to about the rape.

With all the football games being played over the break, the athlete inside me began to stir. Aside from all the pain I had gone through that semester, I had simply missed the game. As I was feeling stronger, my desire to get back into the game intensified as well. Then the feelings became an intense hunger, an ache to be back where I belonged. I was willing to do whatever it was going to take to get back on the field.

When I returned to Santa Barbara, it was with renewed determination. I knew the road ahead was long, but I decided I could continue taking those baby steps toward my dream.

I started going to the football field at night. I'd take my cleats, a few balls, and hop the fence into the stadium. I'd start at extra-point range and kick 10 balls through the uprights. Then I'd chase them and begin again. Move back. Ten more. Move back. Kick and chase. Again and again. It drew out emotions, and I let them come. I dealt with them as they came. I kicked through anger, through hurt, through fear, and through frustration. It didn't matter the emotion, I just kept kicking. Some nights were lonely, some nights were frustrating, but I wouldn't stop.

I went at night because I didn't want to draw attention to myself. It was rough enough for me just to walk onto the field. I didn't want to talk to people or answer questions. A kicker with a long blond ponytail always brought stares and questions. When I needed to take a break I'd walk across the street to the ocean and stare at the waves. I knew in my bones that this dream was going to be mine again. I'd have some rotten kicks, but then ka-ching!! I'd get the rush, the euphoria, and the ecstasy of a perfect kick. Then I'd try to grab on to that and do it again. Somewhere inside it was all still there. I just needed to find it again, or rather, let it find *me* again.

While I poured my heart into my kicking at night, by day I pressed on with school. With more energy and momentum pushing me forward, academics in the second semester were even easier.

I got a job. My apartment in Santa Barbara wasn't exactly cheap, so money was on the tight side. I dressed up as the Statue of Liberty and danced alongside the main street of Santa Barbara as an advertisement for a tax company. Another step forward. One that gave me permission to goof around and get paid as well.

The Statue of Liberty job also introduced me to a woman who became a lifeline for me. Her name was Billie Purcell. She was 59 years old and a former Statue of Liberty who had to take a desk job when she broke her ankle on duty. She knew who I was, which was a little unusual. Though I'd received national attention while at CU, I had pretty much been able to remain anonymous in Santa Barbara. We were a funny match, a short, gray-haired grandma and a tall, blond college girl, but we hit it off. Billie was as spunky as she was kind and took me into her home and her heart. Often she'd invite me to her place for dinner after work. She loved to hear any stories I had about football. Billie had been one of the first few women to work in a fire department during her younger years, so she understood what it was like to be around all men all the time. We traded some pretty good stories. Billie had five children, and after her husband left, she raised them on her own. She was an incredible woman. Though I knew I could talk to her about anything, I didn't confide too much in her about the trauma of CU. Billie later told me that she sensed something had happened there, but never wanted to push me.

I also started to volunteer again. It was a part of my life that I missed, so when I saw a sign on campus asking for college students to mentor elementary school kids, I jumped. I soon became a mentor to a fifth-grade girl named Yuni. She was very shy at first, but opened up to me as time went on. I would come to her school once a week and we'd spend a few hours together. Sometimes I'd help her with her homework, sometimes we'd get ice cream. Either way, we had fun together. Spending time with Yuni ended up being very healing for me. Not only was I doing something worthwhile, but also her sweet spirit reminded me of the good in the world. We kept in touch long after I left Santa Barbara. Another bright spot came when Val flew out to visit. She came out over the third anniversary of the Columbine shootings, and we spent the day visiting Hollywood and Beverly Hills. It was good to have some fun, and to see how strong Val had remained after all she'd gone through was good for me. It gave me renewed hope.

13

80 Tapes Later

B Y THIS POINT, I knew I was ready to start finding a Division I school to kick at. There were still some very rough days, but I had come a long way. I had a feeling that my next step in healing was getting back on the field.

Joe came out to Santa Barbara over his spring break and brought a camcorder to get some fresh kicking video. We put that video together with my high school highlights and shipped them to dozens of schools—all Division I schools. I had worked too hard to start compromising, and my dream was still ready to be claimed: No woman had yet played or scored in a Division I game.

When the responses began to come in, I couldn't believe it. I was hearing from big schools with big-name programs: Ohio State, Oklahoma, Auburn, University of California at Berkeley, and Louisiana State. Ironically, the first response came from the University of New Mexico. It was a smaller school that I knew was on its way up. But other than that, I didn't know much about it, except that it didn't play in one of the "elite" Division I conferences such as the Big 10 or the Big 12. The UNM Lobos played in the Mountain West Conference, a newly formed "midmajor" conference that was smaller but still had as members some traditionally strong football schools such as Brigham Young University and the University of Utah.

Dad and I made some phone calls, narrowed the list to four schools, and hit the road.

First stop: Cal-Berkeley. I met with Dave Unger, the special teams coach. He said that they'd love to have me join the team as a walk-on kicker, and he reviewed their program with me. We watched a bit of film of the placekickers already on the team. As we were talking, Jeff Tedford, the head coach, came by. Coach Unger introduced me and told him I was the woman interested in placekicking for the team. Coach Tedford smiled, shook my hand, and sat down.

"Well, honey, have you ever worn a football helmet before?" he asked me kindly.

I stared at him. "Yeah . . ." I said slowly.

Unger scrambled and explained that I had played through high school and then at Colorado. Apparently when Unger ran the idea by Tedford of a woman wanting to kick for the team, Tedford thought I was a soccer player wanting to give football a try. He apologized, but I told him there was no need. That was the way it had been with the few women who had kicked at the college level. Most were soccer players. The only other female I knew of who was an actual full-time football player had played for a junior college.

I liked the program at Cal, but there was a catch. Because it was late in the spring and I hadn't even applied, I couldn't be admitted to the university in time for the fall. I did get accepted, but for the spring semester—one full year away. I couldn't wait that long and miss another season.

So it was on to the next stop: Albuquerque, New Mexico. We flew in at night, and as soon as we stepped off the plane, I felt like I had stepped into an oven. I wondered how hot it got during the day underneath a football helmet.

As we drove in from the airport, Dad and I stopped at the football stadium, which was nearby. It was lit up and beautiful. It wasn't as big as Folsom in Boulder or Cal's stadium, but it was nice. I could play here, I thought, gazing across the green grass.

However, the next day got off to a rocky start. When I went into the football office and asked to see Jeff Conway, their special teams coach, the secretary looked at me rudely. "Do you have an appointment?" she asked curtly.

"Yes. Katie Hnida," I said, nodding politely. She picked up the receiver and buzzed back to Coach Conway's office.

"Some girl says she has an appointment with you, Ka–" The woman looked back up at me, covering the mouthpiece. "What was your name again?"

"Katie Hnida."

"A Katie Hnida," she finished. "Okay." She hung up the receiver. "Sit down. He's coming."

"Thank you," I said. Boy, she was a friendly one. I returned to the couch where Dad sat.

"Very nice lady," I whispered. Dad shook his head; he'd heard the whole thing.

Coach Conway appeared and took us back to his office. It had huge glass windows that looked out onto the stadium. Darn, it was a pretty sight. It looked just as good today as it did last night. We had a good talk, I got a tour of the campus, and then I had a chance to go out and watch the kickers work out. When they were done, I told Coach Conway that I was confident I could compete with his kickers. He said he had a roster spot for me; all I had to do was say yes. The head coach, Rocky Long, was out of town, but Coach Conway promised to have him call me the following week. Though

Coach Conway said Coach Long was fine about having a woman on the team, I wanted to talk with him myself. After my experience with head coaches, I wasn't taking any chances.

Exactly one week later, I was back in Santa Barbara napping when the ring of the phone jarred me awake. Sleepily, I rolled over to turn the ringer off. Then I caught the area code on the caller ID: 505. New Mexico. I fumbled to pick up the receiver.

"Hello?" I said, blinking the sleep out of my eyes.

"Katie?" A gruff voice came across the line.

"Yes?"

"This is Coach Long at New Mexico. Coach Conway told me you wanted to speak with me."

"Hi. Yes, thank you for calling," I bumbled, my brain still off in dreamland.

"What can I do for you?" Well, he didn't waste time.

"Ah, well, I am looking at coming to play for New Mexico and I know that Coach Conway said you were fine with having a woman join the team, but I just wanted to make sure there weren't any problems . . . with that." I was struggling to sit up in bed. Nice, Kate, way to sound intelligent, I thought.

"Of course not. What kind of problems would there be?" he barked back. That woke me up. Dear God, I was bumbling like an idiot and this guy was scary as hell.

"Well . . ." I started. It was not the time to give a laundry list of my experiences at my former university. "The media can be a bit much."

Coach Long was blunt. "There'll be no problem. We'll just tell them that you'll talk to them when you want to. Then when you're not talking to them, you're not talking to them. That's it. You're off-limits." Okay. Took care of that one.

"Really, I just want to make sure that you're comfortable with this situation, I know it's a little different," I explained.

"It's fine. There will be no problems. Okay?" Coach Long boomed. Okey-dokey. I wasn't going to disagree with him.

"Okay. Great. Thank you for calling," I said.

"You're welcome. Anything else?" he asked.

"No, I think we got it," I said. "Thanks again for calling, I know you must be extremely busy."

"It's fine. Have a nice day. Good-bye." Click. I stared at the phone. Wow. That guy was one tough man. What was he like when he went on a recruiting trip and had to schmooze parents and players that New Mexico was the best place to play football?

I returned to my nap. Well, I don't think I'm going there, I thought. Yawning, I realized that though Rocky Long was gruff, he was blunt and no-nonsense . . . and that was very important to me. Hmmm . . . who knows? I drifted back off.

It was time to go to one of the meccas of college football, Ohio State University. *The* Ohio State University. This was the ultimate recruiting trip. They had a full two-day itinerary and I was welcomed like I was some big-shot superstar. Before I came out, I'd been asked what I wanted to study. When I arrived in Columbus, a full academic packet had been prepared for me in my areas of interest, explaining the departments and the advisers. The campus was traditional and I liked the atmosphere.

But I was knocked over when we went to the stadium. It was . . . huge. I couldn't believe my eyes when we reached the locker room and saw a locker with my name on it. There was also a helmet and a Buckeye jersey waiting for me with the name HNIDA printed on it. The jersey was number 2, the number that carried me through my high school years and even CU.

"Put it on," the recruiting coach, John Hill, said.

I did and looked in the mirror. *Wow.* Then we went back onto the field. I imagined myself knocking balls through the uprights in front of 102,000 screaming fans. I loved it.

The rest of the day we toured the weight rooms, indoor practice bubble, and meeting rooms. They had the most impressive athletic facilities I had ever seen. I met a few coaches and shot the breeze with them in a film room. They were friendly and seemed totally fine with the fact that I was female. The next day I met with academic advisors and took a look at some apartment complexes in town. They'd even taken the time to make me a list of popular places for students.

After my tortured first semester in Santa Barbara, when I'd been forced to confront that I might have to quit football altogether, this was an affirmation of an incredible magnitude. Colorado didn't want me but Ohio State University did. I loved the school, but I didn't want to say yes right away, since I had one more trip to go.

I'd been back in Santa Barbara for only a few days when I picked up the receiver and called Coach Hill and said, "You've got yourself a kicker." He said, "All right!" I put down a deposit on an apartment and set plans in motion. I was pumped.

A week later, I got a call from Jim Tressel, the head coach, who left a long message on my answering machine. He said that Coach Hill wasn't aware that he was planning to bring in another kicker, from the Southeastern Conference. There would be too many kickers. All recruited in the same week. He ended his message by saying, "I'm just not sure if we're going to have room for you."

I was blindsided. I called him back and found he was out of town. I called Coach Hill and he said he had no idea what was going on. He promised to call me back the following day, and when he did, he said when he'd first talked to the head coach everything had been totally fine. I believed him. There was absolutely no reason for him to lead me on.

I finally spoke with Coach Tressel over the phone. He was kind and reiterated what he'd said in the message. I'd really been thrown for a loop because I still didn't know exactly what had happened. My best guess was that a lot of wires were crossed and I was caught in the middle.

After the debacle of Ohio State, I went to visit Auburn in Alabama, my final recruiting visit. It was completely different from any other visit, mainly because it was in the Deep South. In the Bible Belt, football is right up there next to God. The Auburn Tigers were another big-name team, and I was excited to be invited to visit. I had academic meetings and then met with the kicking coach, Eddie Gran, and the head coach, Tommy Tuberville.

The atmosphere was positive, and both coaches were encouraging. I spent more than two hours with Coach Gran, then an extra hour with Coach Tuberville. It was important for me—especially after Ohio State—to make clear what my intentions were. If I came to Auburn, it was to be a player. My motivation was a love for football, pure and simple. I had no interest in media attention. After looking at my tape, Gran said he felt I could help the team. They already had a solid first-team kicker, Damon Duvall, who actually was an All-American. But they were looking for someone who could fill a backup role for at least a season and then push for the starting job after Duvall graduated. When he joined the meeting, Tuberville was positive as well. We finished our talks, then some of the "Tigerette" girls took me to lunch and to see the stadium. I'm not sure how they felt but I sensed both confusion and excitement. They were used to taking around 295-pound recruits, and here I was, this little blond female placekicker. All in all, they were great, as were the people in the town of Auburn. When Dad and I went to look at apartments or to go out to eat, people were incredibly excited that I was thinking about going to school there and playing football.

But once again, a seemingly perfect situation went imperfect quickly. Although my grades were good, the admissions office didn't think I could be admitted in time for the season. There were other recruits who still needed special academic attention—"blue-chippers," high school superstars who could step in and help the team right away. I felt that same sense of strangeness. Our meetings had gone so well, and then—an abrupt about-face. I even wondered if the schools wanted me, then changed their minds after somehow finding out about my problems at CU. It all seemed so strange, but then again, there had to be a reason. I thought about New Mexico. It was the smallest of all of the schools but the one with the coach who drove a pickup truck and only knew how to speak bluntly.

Hoping I wasn't too late, I called New Mexico and told both Coach Long and Coach Conway I wanted to come. They seemed genuinely excited: "Heck, yeah. Camp starts in two weeks. See you then."

By that time I was more relieved than overly excited. I was glad that a decision had been made. New Mexico had not been my first choice. But it was a Division I school, and that was ultimately what was most important. Like so much in my life, the journey to New Mexico had been one of unexpected detours and strange turns. And sometimes those strange turns are actually fate. Turns out, my fate was to be at the University of New Mexico.

14

Is This Heaven?
No, It's Albuquerque

WHEN I ARRIVED IN ALBUQUERQUE for the start of rookie camp in late July 2002, it had been two years since I'd kicked with a team. Part of me was excited to be starting over again. But there also were some serious butterflies. I had chosen the University of New Mexico, and this is where I would play out the rest of my college career. No more eligibility, no more transfers. I had rolled the dice on UNM.

From the office staff to the trainers to the equipment managers, everyone I'd met with the Lobos so far had been supportive and welcoming. But now came the most important part: I would find out how the players felt about having a woman on the team.

There were about 30 of us at rookie camp, mainly freshmen but also some guys who had transferred from junior college or other

Division I schools. No matter who we were, we were all newcomers to the program and these few days would help us to get acclimated.

Anyone who's lived through it will tell you that camp basically sucks. It's like boot camp, but with football and bed checks. You spend all your time on the field or in meetings, with a little time set aside to eat and sleep. We were staying in dorm rooms without air conditioning. In Albuquerque, the heat hits triple digits on the summer days, and the nights were still in the eighties. It was impossible to get comfortable in the heat and on the teeny dorm beds. It made sleep hard to come by, even though my body would be tired to the bone every night.

The first day of camp was easy. We started by going over the basic NCAA materials and rules. We met all the coaches, toured the facilities, and got acquainted with our new teammates. After my experiences at CU, I wasn't sure how I would be received. Some of the guys didn't know how to act, but a number of them were friendly up front. I realized that a lot of them were just as nervous as I was. I never thought of these big, rough-and-tough guys getting nervous, but I realized that a lot of them were away from home for the first time and also nervous about performing well on the field. This realization allowed me to relax and open up a little more. We were all in the same boat. As far as being a woman on the team was concerned, the more relaxed I was, the more relaxed the guys were. There wasn't a single negative comment uttered or look given. It was an immensely different reception than I had gotten at CU. I was relieved. Now I'd have to wait and see what happened when we hit the field—and see how the returning veteran players would react when they reported the following week. All in all, I counted day one of rookie camp as a success. I trudged back to my small dorm room and sweated myself to a fitful sleep.

The next morning brought the long lines and long grinds of physicals. No one likes them because it's a snail's pace of a process, especially with so many players. You wait, fill out forms, wait, get poked and prodded, wait some more, fill out a few more forms, get some blood taken. It seems like it just keeps going and going.

I was sitting in a group of rookies waiting for a blood pressure check when I noticed one of the guys, a big O-lineman named Marty, looking at me. "So, you've played football before?" he asked.

I nodded my head.

"Man, though, this is college ball. It's going to be a lot different than high school," he said, shaking his head at me.

"Yeah, it is." I looked at him. "I've already played college football. I'm a transfer from the University of Colorado." Even though no one had given me any problems, my guard was up.

A quiet "Oh" came out of his mouth. Then he looked back up at me. "Well, dang, girl, you got it going on!" A few of the other guys sitting with us chuckled. I did, too, and smiled at Marty.

After physicals, it was time to finally hit the fields. After a quick team pep talk, we separated into groups. There were six kickers and punters at rookie camp. All were freshmen except me. With three veteran kickers coming in next week, there was a lot of pressure on us to perform. Only one of the six of us would go to regular camp the next week. I know each of us felt the heat to make each kick perfect. I wish I could say I kicked perfectly. But I struggled badly that day. Memories of CU were in the back of my mind. I had known that they were going to be there and was able to keep them relatively under control. Inevitably, though, they had some effect on my kicking. Aside from the memories, I just didn't seem to have it that day. With all the sets of eyes glued on me from all sections of the practice fields, I was frustrated. It didn't matter that none of the other kickers lit up the field that day; I just knew I hadn't kicked *anywhere* close to my best. Luckily, I was blessed that I still had a fire deep inside that wouldn't let me quit. I didn't understand God's plan, but I knew I was supposed to be out there and would continue to work as hard as I could.

When I looked around the practice fields after kicking that day,

I could see a handful of fans standing around and others parked in lawn chairs under the shade trees. There was an open, welcoming atmosphere toward fans. Everyone and anyone was welcome, even the media.

As usual, I just wanted to kick footballs and not attract any undue attention. Coach Long and I had talked, agreed we'd do one media day and that would be it. Coach Long told reporters they could talk to me at rookie camp, but that would be it until after I did something newsworthy—such as getting into a game. It seemed like a good way to handle it—Coach Long had a good understanding of the media in Albuquerque. My interviews went well; they were all questions I had answered dozens of times before except for one new one: why I had left CU. I just said that there had been a coaching change and it didn't turn out to be the right fit for me. "Do you think New Mexico is going to be the right fit for you?" one of the reporters asked.

I thought of the past day and how different everything was. "Yes," I said, "I do." I meant it. The next day, I covered the sports pages. It was a little weird to be back in the spotlight again. I scanned a few of the articles. One from the *Albuquerque Journal* had a decent number of quotes from Coach Long.

"I wasn't impressed with any of [the kickers] following Thursday's practice . . . of course, I'm pretty hard on kickers. I didn't think Katie looked out of place. She looked like she belonged," I read.

Wow. Even after a rough day of kicking, he said that? It was more of an affirmation I'd ever had from any coach at CU. Coach Long also told the reporter that when he watched my kicking tape, he didn't even notice that I was a woman, despite my long, blond ponytail. I had to laugh. Was he serious? I was always getting teased about *not* looking anything like a football player. Did he think I was some skinny guy with really long hair? I smiled to myself. I could tell I was going to like Coach Long. He was gruff, but there was something about the way he carried himself. He had a very strong presence.

By the end of rookie camp, my kicking began to improve slightly. I felt comfortable with the other players—more comfortable after only days than I'd ever felt at CU.

Earlier in camp one of the first guys I met was an offensive lineman from Texas named Rob Turner. I liked him immediately. Even though he had no idea what I'd been through, before camp ended he said to me, "If anyone *ever* gives you any trouble, you come talk to me." I thanked him. As it turned out, Rob wasn't the only one. His offer was often repeated by different players in different times and places at UNM. But more important, I never had to take anyone up on it. Ever.

I felt like I was finally on more solid ground. On the last night of camp, I got ice pops and passed them out to the other players in the dorm. We all just hung out and talked in the hallway, gobbling down rapidly melting Popsicles and shooting the breeze. The only way to describe it was "comfortable," a feeling I hadn't had in a football environment since high school. In fact, I might have already been starting to feel more comfortable than in high school.

Since I didn't go to preseason camp with the returning players, I had two extra weeks in Albuquerque before school started and I was to report for practice. The two weeks were a blessing; I was able to settle into my apartment, as well as have some time to explore the campus and the city.

On the first day of school, I went to my classes in the morning, but my mind was preoccupied with practice later that afternoon. Even though I had been through rookie camp, I was still really nervous. My kicking hadn't been great and I was about to meet another 70 guys. I kept reminding myself that there was a noticeable difference in the overall atmosphere of the UNM football program.

After my last class, I drove to the athletic complex. UNM's stadium and practice facilities were about a mile off the university grounds, unlike CU, where they had been right on campus. I pulled my truck into the lot, said a quick prayer, and headed inside. My first stop was in the equipment room to pick up my workout clothes. When I was at rookie camp, I had met our head equipment managers, Rudy Garcia and Jacque May. Both of them were very friendly and made me feel comfortable immediately. The equipment room was right next to the football locker room and tons of guys were coming in and out. I was just starting to feel a little intimidated when Tali Ena walked out. Tali was a quarterback who'd been at rookie camp with me. He was a transfer from Washington State and we'd connected easily.

"Hey Katie," he said, as he squeezed one arm around my shoulders. "Good to see you again."

"You too," I said, smiling at him. "How's it been going?"

"Not too bad," Tali replied.

Rudy was at the door of the equipment room.

"Hey guys. Katie, I think Jacque already put your stuff for today in your locker room. Let me check." He turned as Jacque appeared from around the corner.

"Yeah, I stuck your gear on the bench in your locker room. I gave you the smallest stuff I could find, but it's still big. I'll start to order smaller stuff for you," she said.

"Thank you," I said. I was touched at the fact that Jacque had gone out of her way. "I really appreciate it a lot."

"It's no big deal. Let us know if you need anything," Jacque said matter-of-factly. Rudy was nodding.

"If you ever need anything—anything at all—come talk to us," he said. I sensed he was talking about more than just towels or helmets. I smiled at him, thankful that he already seemed to genuinely care about me. I could feel a sense of security inside me that I'd never experienced when at CU.

I said thank you once more and then went across the hall to the training room, where my locker room was located. When I walked into the room, a bright red number 2 jersey was lying with a T-shirt and a pair of shorts. My shoulder pads, helmet, and other gear were already in the locker I'd used for camp. I got dressed and pulled my hair back into a low ponytail. Here we go again, I thought. Closing my eyes, I said a quick prayer and headed out the door. When I got outside, there were a few guys sitting on the steps, putting on their cleats. I saw Wes Zunker, who was our starting kicker, and Kenny Byrd, a freshman kicker. Kenny had never played football before, but had been a soccer player and found he could kick footballs as well. I wandered over to them to say hi. I put my cleats on and the three of us headed out to the practice fields. The practices at UNM were similar to the setup at CU. The kickers and punters would come out early to warm up and then the first few blocks of practice were set aside for kicking and punting drills. Then we were on our own for the rest of practice.

I did my standard warm-up and stretching, and then started kicking. I still wasn't kicking great, but I was looking a heck of a lot better than I did during rookie camp. There were a lot of us, I mused, as I looked around. Besides Kenny, Wes, and I, there was another kicker, Matt Goldstein. Then we had a full stable of punters— Tyler Gaus, a freshman who would claim the starting spot, Stephen Lemrond, Trey Padilla, and Matt Berkovich. Martin Lovato, a deep snapper, would also usually spend most of practice with us.

The horn blew and my first official practice as a Lobo began. Overall, the day was decent. I got to work with the guys who would be my holders and watch how the live drills were run. I spent a lot of the first day observing my new coaches and teammates. All of the coaches seemed very hands on as they worked with the players. Coach Long seemed to be everywhere.

Being back out on the field felt good, but inevitably invoked memories of CU, even stronger than during rookie camp. No matter what I was doing or how hard I would concentrate, there was a constant background static in my mind. I had accepted that it was there and decided I would have to take it day by day.

As the days went by, I settled into a life in New Mexico. I got to know many of my new teammates quickly and found I got along with them well. On the second day of school, I was walking across campus when I ran into Rob, the lineman who'd told me to come to him if I had any problems with anyone. He was with a few other guys from the team. We talked for a minute and then all headed our own ways. When Rob found out we were going in the same direction, he scooped me up and gave me a piggyback ride to my next class. That ride was indicative of the way most of my teammates were with me, and I could feel myself dropping part of the guard I had brought with me from CU.

I had not only been accepted by my new teammates, but also fell into my own special role on the team. The guys embraced the uniqueness of having a female on the team. They took care of me and I took care of them. One day I had baked cookies and brought some of the extras over to our practice. The guys dove in and devoured them before I could even set the plate down. The next day, I had teammates coming up to me in the weight room, wanting to know where the cookies were.

"What?" I asked.

"I heard you made some really good cookies and I didn't get any. Where'd they go?" one player asked.

"You guys ate them all!" I said.

"Will you make some more?"

I agreed and thus took on an additional job—team chef. I didn't mind. I loved to cook and suddenly had 100 mouths to try new recipes on. The cookies I baked led to banana bread and brownies for road trips, cakes for birthdays, and even homemade chicken soup when someone was sick. I realized that most of the guys didn't get much homemade food, so I started cooking dinners and having different teammates over to eat during Monday Night Football and other games.

I also found a home in the equipment room with Jacque and Rudy. I'd often go in before or after practice, sit, and watch ESPN and just shoot the breeze with them. UNM had many people who played vital roles in the football program—from our equipment workers to the training room staff to the weight coaches. It was clear that everyone was valued and appreciated for what they did. It truly felt like we were one big family.

There was a huge emphasis on strength training at New Mexico. We lifted weights as a team—something we didn't do at CU or in high school. When I first heard about it, I thought the idea was nuts. How could 120 guys squeeze into a room and lift weights at the same time? I imagined utter pandemonium. It turned out to be exactly the opposite—it was organized and disciplined. A bond came from lifting together as well—it was an important part of the team's mentality. I worked as hard as everyone, and not only reached, but also passed the goals set for me by the strength and conditioning coaches. The guys were all in lifting groups, but since the weight I used was a lot lighter, I lifted alone. That didn't mean I was alone, though. My teammates were always nearby, asking if I needed a spot or giving a shout of encouragement. One of my first days, I was between sets when I saw a gray head pop up doing a power clean. I laughed. Through the years, I had seen some teammates do some nutty things with their hair, but never had I seen anyone do a gray dye job. I took a step over to see which one of my teammates it was. My mouth dropped open. It was no teammate, it was Coach Long! He had jumped in on a set with a few of the guys. I was stunned. I knew the man was built like a rock, but he was 50-some years old! Over the course of the season, Coach Long would always be in there working out with us. He was in tremendous shape. I couldn't get over it. Coach was stronger than a lot of the guys on the team, guys who were 30 years younger. No one could ever complain about a workout being too hard, not if our own coach could skip in and do it with us. It was only one of the ways that Coach Long led by example. The team was a direct reflection of his personality: hard work, unselfishness, and humility. We were known as a "blue-collar" team. Nothing fancy, no prima donnas—just smash-mouth football. We were built to be tough and relentless. Win or lose, we were going to physically drive the opposing team into the turf. I loved it and was proud to be a member of this team. Coach Long constantly stressed the importance of our characters—both on and off the field. He once put it this way—most of us wouldn't go on to the NFL, but every one of us would go out in the world. He wanted us to be good men and "a woman."

Everything seemed close to perfect. Classes were going well, my teammates were better than I ever hoped, I was getting into the best shape of my life. But I was still struggling in one of the most crucial areas—my kicking. Somewhere along the way in the horrendous journey at CU, I felt as if I had lost my natural ability to kick.

I was determined to do whatever it took to get my kicking back. There were nights when I would stay out after practice to keep kicking. If I wasn't kicking, I'd be working on my steps or doing sit-ups to strengthen my core muscles. Anything I thought would help, I did.

I talked with my position coach, Jeff Conway, and told him I wasn't kicking as well as I knew I could. I told him I was aware that the kicker he was seeing on the field was not the one he'd seen on videotape. Without pressing me for any explanation, Coach Conway suggested I see the sports psychologist that worked with the athletic department. "Dr. Bill," as I called him, was a retired psychologist and lifelong Lobo supporter.

I knew I had to finally talk in depth about the abuse I had gone through and the rape itself. I had repressed so many emotions for too long. I still found it difficult to even use the word "rape" in a sentence about myself. And now that I felt I was in a safe place, I felt I could finally let some of those emotions seep out. When I met with Dr. Bill, I realized just talking to someone about some of the things that had happened was a tremendous help. We decided we'd continue to meet regularly. In addition to working on the ramifications from my abuse, he gave me some breathing and relaxation techniques I could use on the field. Yet talking about everything turned out to be a double-edged sword. On one hand, it was incredibly healing to get things off my chest. On the other hand, going through the memories in depth brought up new emotions and was incredibly painful. I was finally able to tell my parents details of what I had endured and eventually about the rape itself. It was immensely hard on them, but they supported me with every step I took to heal.

Coach Conway and I also sat down together to compare my high school kicking tape with a tape of what I was doing now in New Mexico. What we saw on the videotape made it clear how much my style had changed.

In high school I opened up my hips and threw my arms out when I made contact with the ball. My kicking motion looked fluid and effortless.

But on the tape from New Mexico, I was hunched over and clenched, looking as though I was literally trying to protect my body. I was afraid to open myself to kick the ball. And with a more closed technique, I couldn't generate the same height and power in my kicks that I had in the past.

As much as seeing the tape helped, it also made me realize how much I had lost. Some nights I would stay up watching old film of myself kicking in high school, wondering how to get that form back. I knew I had to quit worrying about it so much and just let it come. My kicking had always been an innate part of me.

One of my favorite movies is *The Legend of Bagger Vance*. It's the fictional story of a golfer, Rannulph Junah, who has an amazing natural ability to hit a golf ball, as well as tremendous love of the sport. But after going through the horrors of war, he loses his ability to play golf, or what he called his "authentic swing." I could relate. Everything I'd gone through had caused me to lose my "authentic kick" and I had to get it back in some way, somehow. I watched the movie over and over.

The season got under way and I dressed for our first home game against Weber State on August 31, 2002. It was the first time I had been on the sideline of a game since the Insight.com Bowl with Colorado in 1999. We won the game against Weber State, but then as the season went on, we became more and more inconsistent. We dropped to 2–4 after a 49–0 loss to Texas Tech midway through the season. The game stung, not only because we lost, but also the way we lost: a shut-out on national television. But somehow that nightmare of a game didn't ruin our season. Even with our starting quarterback, Casey Kelly, out with a broken arm, we pulled out a win against UNLV the next weekend. That game showed the true character of our team. And over the next few weeks, our character was revealed even further. We played Utah State on October 19. I didn't make the trip and since the game wasn't televised, I was stuck listening to it on the radio. It was a wild game that was close the whole way, but with 25 seconds left, we scored a touchdown to put us ahead 38–31. It looked as if the game was wrapped up, but Utah State's offense drove down the field and scored a Hail Mary touchdown as time expired. The game went into overtime and Utah State had the ball first. They scored a touchdown to give them a 45–38 lead. Now it was our turn with the ball. Casey threw for a touchdown, now all we needed was for Kenny to tack on the extra point, and we'd keep on playing into a second overtime.

I listened as Kenny lined up for the kick.

"The ball is up and the extra point is . . . no good!" The announcer sounded as shocked as I was. Kenny had missed wide right by an inch. Wide right.

I remembered those words well. They were the same words that were repeated over and over at CU when we lost to Nebraska after Jeremy Aldrich's kick had sailed to the right. But this time around, there was a crucial difference: the reaction of the team. I listened as the announcer described Kenny falling to his knees in despair after the kick was signaled no good. But when Kenny went down, Claude Terrell, a 330-pound offensive lineman, came back and picked him up, literally and figuratively. Claude walked the length of the field to the visiting locker room, keeping his arm around Kenny, supporting him the whole way. It was a totally different reaction than at CU, where a teammate said that Jeremy "choked." Again I was reminded how strikingly different the programs were. At UNM, we really were a team. No one held Kenny personally responsible for the loss. After Utah State, we won four of our last five games. That was enough to give us a second-place finish in the conference.

15

"Let Katie Take the First Kick"

WE ENDED OUR SEASON with a win against Wyoming, giving us a 5–2 record in the conference and a 7–6 record overall. We finished second in the Mountain West Conference and it looked like a bowl was almost certain.

A week or so later, it was official—we were invited to play in the 2002 Las Vegas Bowl against UCLA on Christmas Day. It was ironic that we would be playing the first Division I team that had looked at me after I had left Colorado.

There was an incredible excitement in the air as we prepared for the game. It was only the second time in 41 years that UNM had been invited to a bowl game. School wrapped up; the team stayed to practice in Albuquerque for a few extra days and then went home for a quick visit with our families. We flew to Vegas four days before the game to begin practices and the bowl festivities.

The time leading up to the game was a blast. The bowl committee had put together a great week of events for us—the team went to see the Blue Man Group perform, had a day at the ESPN Zone, and had a pep rally. I hung out with my teammates at night, going out to dinner and seeing all the famed Vegas hot spots. Even though I had been to a bowl game when I was at Colorado, this was a completely different experience.

One of the best days was when four of my teammates and I went to visit a local children's hospital. We wore Santa hats and handed out little Lobo footballs to the kids. I was struck by the fact that while we were down in Vegas having a good time and getting to play football, these kids were going to be stuck spending their Christmas in the hospital. Some of my favorite memories from that trip are remembering what it was like to watch a kid's face light up with a bright smile. A few of the kids couldn't believe that I was really a football player. A young boy with cancer kept giggling and telling me I was lying, that I was really a cheerleader in disguise.

"No, I promise. I'm a kicker!" I kept saying. He didn't believe me until a few of my teammates came in and confirmed to him that I was in fact a real player on the team.

"Watch the game on TV!" I told him. "I'm the one with the ponytail hanging out of the helmet. Number 2." He kept giggling and smiling at me. Finally, I said good-bye, giving him a little kiss on the top of his bald head and an extra football. When I walked out of the room, I could feel an ache in my heart. This kid couldn't be more than seven or eight years old. I was leaving to go kick footballs and this little boy was confined to a hospital bed. As my eyes started to tear up, I rejoined my teammates. Daniel Kegler, one of the guys who had told the little boy that I was a football player, saw my tears and put his arm around me. He was shaking his head.

"It's not fair, is it?"

"No, it's not . . ." I said, leaning into his arm for a moment. "Thanks, Keg." I wiped away my tears and we headed to practice.

In the days leading up to the game, I had a gut feeling that I might have a shot at getting into the game. I was getting more and more live repetitions during practice. Coach Long was his typical business-as-usual self, but I could sense that he was watching me a little closer.

Instead of a trimmed tree and wrapped presents, Christmas morning that year consisted of a quick breakfast, chapel, and pregame meetings. Then we were off to the UNLV stadium for our 1:30 P.M. start. I changed that day in the makeshift locker room that Jacque and Rudy had put together for me by stacking up crates and covering them with a green tarp. They even stuck my nameplate on it. It was the best improvised locker room I'd ever had.

As usual, the kickers warmed up first. I felt like I was hitting the ball pretty well. We had gone to the sideline to stretch out and wait as the rest of the team went through pregame drills. Coach Long walked by; I assumed he was on his way to go watch the linebackers, but instead he stopped in front of us.

"Kenny," he said to our starting kicker, "let Katie take the first kick." My eyes flew wide open. I managed to stammer out a "thank you" to Coach, who was gone in an instant.

The other kickers congratulated me as I stood there trying to make sure I wasn't dreaming. I was going to get into the game? After all these years, the moment I had been preparing for and dreaming of was actually here? I immediately turned to the stands.

My entire family was there, even Joe, who had a bowl game with Oregon in Seattle a few days later.

They had gotten there early to watch me warm up. I motioned to Dad to come down to the fence near the sideline.

"I get the first kick!" I told him breathlessly. Dad's face broke into a grin.

"Go get it kiddo," he said, squeezing my hand. My adrenaline was starting to race. Calm down, calm down, I told myself. But this was it! The day was finally here! I saw Roger, our team chaplain, over by the water coolers and went to ask him to pray with me. On my way, I passed Jacque.

"I'm going to kick!" I whispered to her.

"Congratulations!" she said, her eyes lighting up. I grinned. I was so excited that I could barely breathe.

Calm down, I told myself again. Warm-ups finished, we had a quick time-out for a TV commercial, and then the game was under way. Kenny kicked off to UCLA. Their offense began a slow march down the field. I was trying to stay warm and stretched out when I saw the ball flying through the air. Desmar Black, one of our corner-backs, jumped in front of the UCLA receiver and intercepted the ball. I watched as he ran the ball 55 yards back for a touchdown. The crowd roared. For a moment I just stood there in shock. "You're up!" I thought. "Go!" I ran onto the field, my teammates slapping my shoulder pads and wishing me luck on the way out. It was all happening so fast. I quickly marked my spot and measured out my steps. The ball was snapped, I began my approach. I felt the instep of my foot connect with the ball cleanly. It was going to go straight. Just as my head came up, I saw a giant hand reach high above the line and hit the ball. The football spiraled toward the left sideline. I stood there in shock as the refs signaled no good. The kick had been blocked. "No," I thought. "That couldn't have just happened." I'd never had a kick blocked like that in my entire life.

I stood there in a daze for a moment, still staring at where the ball had been hit, before realizing I needed to get off the field. When I got to the sidelines, I went straight to Coach Conway.

"I timed you at about 1.4 seconds, so you were a bit slow. If you go again, just make sure you take off a little quicker." He tapped me on the helmet and I nodded my head.

The realization of what had just happened hit me. I felt as if I had been punched in the stomach. My teammates were around, telling me to keep my head up and that it was okay.

"Hey, it happens," Wes told me, shrugging. He was right, it did happen even to the best kickers. But it was not supposed to happen then, not on the kick I had literally spent years preparing for. Not in a moment that was supposed to make history. Knowing that it happened to all kickers didn't make me feel better. Neither did finding out later that the player who blocked it, Brandon Chillar, had a huge vertical jump and had blocked a number of kicks in his career. I was completely crushed and spent the rest of the game trying to hold myself together. My teammates kept telling me not to worry about it, but I was worried we were going to end up in a tight game—what if my blocked point was the difference maker between a win and a loss? As it turned out, it wasn't. UCLA ended up beating us 27–13. After the game, all I wanted to do was hide behind my tarp-covered crates. But instead, I had to go do the rounds of interviews. Coach Long, Casey Kelly, our quarterback, and I sat up at the press table. They asked a few questions on the game in general, and then quickly turned their attention to me. I answered all their questions, explaining that I felt I had hit the ball clean, that yes, I was disappointed, but no, I would not stop after that season, that my goal was not just to be the first woman to play Division I football, but to score. Furthermore, I reiterated that I played because I loved the game; it had nothing to do with making history. After I was finished, they turned their microphones to Coach Long. I cringed inside at the first question: "Do you regret putting Katie in the game?"

In his usual no-nonsense, bold tone, he answered, "No. I made the decision to let Katie kick the first extra point. And it was a great decision." I was stunned as he went on.

"Katie has been a vital part of our team all year, and I felt she deserved the opportunity to play."

Casey further came to my defense, saying that I worked hard, deserved to be on the team, and had "a great leg." Nothing had made the aching any better until now—my head coach and teammate coming to back me up. Why was I surprised? I had forgotten where I was. I was at New Mexico, where we were a team with an unspoken but unshakable bond. The entire program functioned as a unit, and we were there to back each other up, no matter what happened.

When I returned to my little space to change, Rudy grabbed me and held me for a second. "You are going to be okay, sweetheart," he told me. I nodded as I caught a tear rolling down my cheek. This one wasn't for the disappointment of missing the kick though—it was a tear of gratitude that I was with New Mexico. Silently, I thanked God for bringing me there. For an instant, my thoughts shifted back to the little boy who had cancer in the hospital. It gave me the perspective I needed during that moment. Yes, I was disappointed. But I also realized just how incredibly blessed I was.

That night, my family took me back to the hotel. They knew how crushed I was, but also understood that nothing could undo the events of the day and that I needed to work through my feelings. After lots of hugs, Kristen and I went back to my room. We stayed up for a while and caught a bit of *SportsCenter*. Watching myself on TV was surreal. I felt as if I was moving in a dream—no way did I just get in for the first time and have my extra point blocked. But there it was, the clip of my kick that would replay over and over that night on TV, as well as over in my mind for months to come. It was just a blind hand batting wildly at the ball. Three inches in either direction and the player would have missed the ball completely. But he didn't miss it; and I had learned long ago that football was a game of inches. We turned off the TV and stayed up talking. That night, I told her about the rape. She listened quietly and hugged me when I was done.

I assured her that I was okay, I was finally getting the help that I needed, and there was no better place for me to be than New Mexico. We talked for a long time about how much I loved the program, my teammates and my coaches.

The next more I awoke to more media madness. It seemed as if every news outlet in America wanted a comment. The pain was still fresh from the blocked kick, but I knew the best thing to do was to talk to the media, not hide. There were certainly going to be questions about whether this meant a woman should be on the football field and I wanted to be there to answer them. I ended up doing all three of the national morning shows, *Good Morning America,* the *Today* show, and the *Early Show.* That meant getting up at 4:00 A.M. so I could be on live on the East Coast. I was exhausted, but went through the interviews as positively as I could. Many people just seemed excited about the fact that I had gotten into the game—one of my coaches pointed out to me later "It still was history, Katie," but since the point had been blocked, it didn't feel like it to me. I was thankful to be with my family after that; we went up to Seattle for Joe's bowl game and then came home and celebrated a late Christmas. We watched the remaining bowl games together. The last match-up was for the National Championship and was between Ohio State and Miami. OSU won it all. Nine months ago I thought I was going to be a Buckeye, I mused. As I watched the confetti pour onto the field, I was glad I wasn't. I had found a home and a family in the Lobos, and my heart was going to bleed cherry and silver for the rest of my life. I knew I was exactly where I was meant to be. I also knew that I would get over the blocked kick. I was going to come back and still reach my goal. This was simply one more hurdle thrown in my way.

The next morning I found myself restless in the early hours of the morning. It had hit me that this was the first day toward my next season. By 5:15 A.M., I was downstairs on the treadmill. I was pounding away so hard that I woke my parents. Dad stumbled down the stairs.

"Kate, it's 5:25 in the morning. What the hell are you doing?"

I gasped for air.

"New football season starts today, Dad. I've got to get ready to go."

16

Rainbow Connection

AFTER WINTER BREAK I returned to New Mexico. I had quit the "what ifs," but no matter how hard I tried to forget, the blocked kick would replay over and over inside my head. Aside from my family, I don't think that anyone knew how hard it was for me deal with the missed kick. I had never set out to be a pioneer, but like it or not, I was. And after the miss I hated that I was being used as a reason why women shouldn't play football.

Our winter conditioning program ran six days a week from the end of January until mid-March, when we began formal spring practices. I threw myself into off-season training, again pushing myself to work harder than I ever had in my life. Even though the workouts were grueling, the athlete in me loved the intensity. Without having the worry of keeping our bodies ready for games, we were able to lift more and run harder.

I also loved training as a team. As in the fall, I was my own lifting group, but was never alone. The guys were always there, tugging my ponytail, offering encouragement, and even going as far as to blame their farts on me. Long ago I knew I had been fully accepted as a part of the team. But when we got into bodily functions, I knew I truly had become "one of the guys."

With 100-plus guys sweating in a weight room, there can be some funky smells. I was around it so much that my nose became immune to the stenches that filled the air. There were times, though, when someone would let out some unbelievably foul-smelling gas. In the hot and stuffy weight room, the smell would be incredibly magnified.

It didn't matter where I was in the weight room; anytime someone would groan, "Who farted?!" one of the guys would answer slyly, "It was Katie." Then they'd all go on to tease me, "Ew, Katie, come on!" "Katie, quit farting."

Even the shy guys on the team got into the habit of blaming me and the joke never got old through all the years I was on the team.

I would always respond the same way. "I don't know what you guys are talking about. I'm a girl, so my farts smell like flowers."

As "one of the guys" I got used to their farts, burps, and spitting. But they had to get used to something uniquely female: my period. Every month I would go through a few days where I would be a little grouchy, cranky, and not in the mood to joke around as usual.

"What's the matter?" my teammates would ask.

"PMS," I would grumble.

It was funny. Some of the guys couldn't even say the word "period." They'd freak out and keep their distance for a few days. Others would react by asking me if I wanted any chocolate or if I needed a heating pad from the training room. I was comfortable enough to bring the heating pad up into team meetings if I needed it. When my period came, I'd often wear my hair up in two buns. Some of the guys jokingly called them my "devil horns" or my "Princess Leia" look. Either way, they all knew what it meant: "Dude, be extra nice to Katie today—it's that time of the month."

In such a good environment, I felt like everything was falling into place. When I first arrived at New Mexico I weighed around 145 pounds, but as I worked out, I dropped back to what seemed to be my natural weight, 130 pounds. Even though I was now lighter, I was also stronger than I had ever been in my life. I was getting close to being able to bench-press the "big wheels"—the 45-pound plates on either side of the bar.

School was good as well. I decided on a double major in psychology and history and was able to maintain a 3.92 GPA despite my busy sports schedule. Outside of school I was involved with the community—I would speak at local schools and do community service events with guys from my team, whether it was helping set up "Race for the Cure" or playing with kids at a charity fund-raiser. I became involved with Big Brothers and Big Sisters of Albuquerque and had a "little sister" that I would do activities with a few times a month.

My kicking was slowly starting to come around. I still wasn't where I wanted to be, but I could tell I had made progress during our spring practice season. We had our 15 practices and then the annual Cherry-Silver intrasquad scrimmage. I was on the Cherry team and kicked our first two extra points—both clean hits that were right down the middle.

Mentally, I was finding a little more peace with the events from CU. I finally began to understand that nothing that had happened to me had been my fault.

Summer conditioning flew by and before I could bat an eye-lash, it was time for preseason camp. Not rookie camp like the year before, but two weeks of intense practices for the upcoming season. We stayed at a hotel close to the school and lived football morning, noon, and night. Literally. Some days we were on the field for three separate practices. Any time not spent on the field was spent in meetings or in the weight room. It was hot, and the days were long and exhausting. While I was at camp, Joe was in the process of moving down to Albuquerque. He had reinjured his shoulder playing at Oregon the year before and was now facing his third shoulder surgery if he wanted to keep playing. As hard as it was, Joe decided it was time to hang up his cleats. He didn't want to stay at Oregon without football, so Joe decided to transfer to UNM for a year to keep up with school while he contemplated what he wanted to do. We moved into a two-bedroom apartment and I was looking forward to having Joe around. Little did I know how much I would end up needing him in the time ahead.

Camp was winding down when I did an interview with a writer for the *Albuquerque Tribune*. It was a set of fairly routine preseason questions: how did I feel about the season ahead, what were my goals, etc. I was talking about how much I loved the program and my teammates at UNM when the writer asked me if I liked it better here than at CU. Yes, I said. He then asked why.

I answered that I was treated better down in New Mexico, that my teammates could handle the fact that I was both feminine and a football player. Knowing that I didn't want to go into any more detail about my CU experiences, I stopped there. The reporter pressed me for more, but I said that I didn't want to talk about it. He then moved on to another question and I thought that was the end of it.

Actually, it was just the beginning. The next day I got a call from our media director, Greg Remington. He told me that the reporter from the *Tribune* had spoken to Barnett up in Boulder and wanted to interview me again. What? Greg had to be kidding. Barnett was usually impossible to reach, especially at a busy time like the preseason. Plus, I didn't think he would want to comment on me. When I called the reporter back, I learned I was completely wrong. Barnett, in fact, had a lot to say about me. Among other things, Barnett called me a "media fiasco" and "a distraction" to the team when I was at Colorado. When the reporter told me that Barnett had said he only knew of one case where a player harassed me, I finally responded.

"That's impossible! I endured an entire season of harassment. I had footballs thrown at my head, I was called names that are unrepeatable . . . I was treated like a piece of meat there." I quickly shut my mouth, knowing that I shouldn't have said a word. "Look, a lot of very painful things happened to me at CU that I'm not comfortable talking to the media about."

I had no further comment. It didn't matter, though, I had given a response and Barnett had said enough for the reporter to put together a story. I knew it wouldn't be good.

The next day while I was at practice, the story ran in the *Tribune*. It was titled "Kicked Around" and essentially compared my experiences at UNM to CU. By the time practice ended, the Associated Press had a reporter ready and waiting to ask me questions about my time at Colorado. I declined all comments and fled inside the locker room and then back to my apartment as quickly as possible. Even though I wouldn't talk further, the story quickly became national news. It was the first time I had publicly said anything about my time at Colorado and it was a mess. I was lying down to try to take a nap when Coach Conway called.

"Katie, we have to talk. We are getting all these calls for Coach Long asking what's happening here, what happened at CU, to please make comments about you," he said.

I choked up on the phone. I knew I had to tell Coach Conway and Coach Long about all the things that had happened to me at CU, but I couldn't get the words out.

"Coach . . . some very bad things happened, I can't, I don't . . ." I started, then stopped. I told him I'd call him back. I called Dad. Crying, I told him I needed to tell my coaches about CU, including the rape, but couldn't bear to. I was so afraid that they were going to be upset with me for causing a distraction—the last thing I'd ever wanted to do. After listening, Dad told me he would call Coach Conway and fill him in on some of the details. I gave him the number, then sat and waited. Ten minutes felt like a decade. The phone finally rang again. It was Coach Conway.

The first words out of his mouth were, "Are you okay?"

"Yeah, hanging in there," I said. "Just a little taken aback at all of this."

Coach Conway went on to tell me he'd had no idea how bad things had been for me at CU and that he was very sorry. He told me he would tell Coach Long about what happened, but no one else. The next day I would come in and talk with Coach Long. In the meantime, though, he told me not to worry, they'd handle everything.

"Thank you," I managed to say. Even though everyone had treated me so well at UNM, I was still surprised at his words.

I met with Coach Conway the next day before going in to see Coach Long. Again, all he wanted to know was if I was okay. I assured him that I was. He wanted to know if I'd experienced any harassment at New Mexico, and I assured him I had not.

When we finished, I met with Coach Long alone in his office.

The first words out of his mouth were, "Are you doing okay?" I smiled and said that I was. He, too, asked if anyone had ever given me trouble.

"No," I answered honestly. "Not a single one." He told me that he would keep me from having contact with any other reporters and to let him know if I needed anything else. I thanked him and then apologized.

"I'm really sorry this came out right now. I didn't mean to cause a distraction, especially right before the season starts," I said, shaking my head.

Coach Long cut in. "I've been in this business for a long time and I know that no matter what you say to the media, it can be misconstrued and go in different directions from the way you've imagined. Sometimes they catch you off guard and you say something you wish you hadn't—but hey—it happens."

I went out to practice that day with mixed feelings. On one hand, I was glad that Coach Long and Coach Conway knew the truth. I was also thankful for the way they responded to the situation and how concerned they were about me. On the other hand, now that some parts of my CU experience had come out in the media I felt more vulnerable. I knew that the whole story would be told at some point, but I always felt it would be on my terms and when I was ready to tell it. A few of my teammates had seen the article before practice, but no one brought it up. I didn't know what to do when we finished for the day so I went and sat in the stadium, where I would often go when I needed quiet time to think. I went to our sideline and sat against the back wall. I stared at the field. The realization began to sink in: this is never going to go away.

I finally understood that as much as I wanted the horrors of CU to disappear, they would be part of me forever. The abuse would always be there and so would the rape.

Damien, one of the equipment managers, saw me in the stadium and came out to check on me. I told him I was okay, just a little shaken from all that had gone on. He told me to let him know if there was ever anything he could do to help. Then he gave me a big hug. I thanked him, and then thanked God for the umpteenth time for placing me at New Mexico.

It was only two weeks later that the season started. Our first game was on August 30, 2003, against Southwest Texas State. It had been raining all day, but when we went out to warm up, a small patch of sky cleared. I stopped in my tracks. In the patch of sky were two rainbows. For a few years, rainbows held a special meaning for me.

During one of my lowest points at CU, I had been driving home in a rainstorm to Littleton and bawling my eyes out along the way. When I went around a corner, I gasped. A huge rainbow had come into view. It was the first time I had ever seen a full rainbow and the sight of it stopped my tears. It was so beautiful that people were pulling off the highway to take pictures of it. I pulled over as well. I happened to have a disposable camera in the glove box, so I snapped a few shots and prayed that they would come out. I stayed for a moment or two, just staring at the glowing colors that seemed to be bursting across the sky. I thought of an old saying, something about if you wanted to see rainbows, you had to get through the rain first. My body filled with hope and in an instant, I felt more peaceful. I took it to be a sign from God. Fortunately, the quality of the pictures of the sky that day turned out perfectly. I had an 8x10 picture of that rainbow framed in my room. It served as a reminder that hope was always there.

When I saw the double rainbow the night of our first game, I knew it had to be a sign. It had been an emotional few weeks since the article about my harassment at CU had come out. I thanked God and then went on with my warm-ups. Later that night, I became the first woman to score in a Division I football game. With 5:05 left in the fourth quarter, I entered the game after Hank Baskett caught a touchdown pass thrown by Tali Ena. I knocked my first point through, then with 1:21 left, Danny Ramirez ran the ball in for another touchdown and I kicked my second extra point. As I contentedly gazed into the black night sky and the game clock wound down, my eyes traveled over to the spot where the rainbows had been. It hit me—two rainbows, two points! I smiled inside. I wasn't the only one who noticed, though. My family, who knew about the first rainbow as well, spotted the rainbows—and took a picture. The double rainbow shot now hangs next to the first one on my wall.

The 2003 season started well and continued that way through the fall. We went on to have another successful year, finishing with an 8–4 record. For the first time in 57 years, UNM was invited to back-to-back bowl games. We learned at Thanksgiving we would be headed back to the Las Vegas Bowl, this year to play Oregon State. The game would be played on Christmas Eve. But as Charles Dickens wrote, "It was the best of times, it was the worst of times." The season was successful and I was happier than ever to be at New Mexico. Yet at the same time, I was becoming increasingly troubled over the memories of what had happened to me in Boulder.

In December, I was invited to the Lou Groza Awards in Florida. The Groza trophy is given to the top placekicker in the country and at the ceremony I would be getting a special award for being the first female to kick in a Division I football game. It was a huge honor. After the Groza event came the ESPN College Football Awards. There I got a chance to meet the top players from all across the country who would be honored for being the best at their respective positions.

After a few days of awards and fun in Florida, it was time to head back to Albuquerque to get ready for our bowl game. But through the weeks of December before the bowl, my attention kept being drawn back to Boulder. More and more controversy was coming out about the football program at CU. A lawsuit had been filed against the university by one of the women who'd claimed she'd been raped at a recruiting party.

After my harassment had been made public, I had decided to meet with the Boulder district attorney, Mary Keenan, over my fall break. During the meeting, I told her the details of my rape and the name of the player who raped me. I didn't want to press charges at that time, but felt that I wanted to talk to law enforcement about what had happened to me and know what my options were. She told me to think things over and that we would meet again. It had been a good meeting, but also a painful one.

We returned to the Las Vegas Bowl. The trip was much like the one the year before. We ended up losing to Oregon State 55–14. It provided a temporary distraction from what was going on in Boulder and in my head. I felt like events were beginning to snowball and I didn't know exactly where I was going to fit into it all.

17

Coming Forward

I RETURNED TO NEW MEXICO after winter break in 2004 with two things to focus on: finishing up my courses to graduate and petitioning the NCAA for my sixth year of eligibility. But I was becoming more disturbed about reports from Boulder about alleged rapes of students by football players and recruits.

The first lawsuit against the university had been filed in 2002. Then, on December 10, 2003, a second woman, Jane Doe, filed suit. A third woman, Monique Gillaspie, came forward in the second week of January 2004, alleging she was sexually assaulted by two football players.

CU went into a full denial mode. They saw no basis for lawsuits, saying the party issue had been "dealt with two years ago" and that an investigation by the university police was complete.

Becoming more and more agitated as time went on, I decided I should meet with the Boulder district attorney again. I felt I had to do something, but what? Should I press charges? Come forward with my story? Just remain silent and let events play out?

Mary Keenan—now Mary Keenan Lacy—was once again straightforward about what I would face in all the scenarios. She thought I should still forge ahead but admitted it would be tough because it was an acquaintance rape. At best, she thought I had a 50–50 chance of a conviction if I prosecuted and that even if convicted, my rapist wouldn't be likely to go to prison. The 50–50 odds Mary had given me were much higher than what they usually were in an acquaintance rape trial. Despite a lack of physical evidence, Mary still thought we could put together a strong case. I couldn't understand how a rapist could be convicted and not have to spend a day in jail. I had always expected that anyone who was convicted of rape would automatically go to jail. But the rape laws were not as strong as I assumed them to be.

Mary knew who my rapist was, and since talking with her in the fall, she had investigated where he was and what he was doing. With pros and cons to each option, Mary explained that the decision was entirely mine. But I knew she could tell I was suffering a great deal over the situation, what I had endured while at CU, and hearing that other women were also suffering. The meeting lasted 90 long minutes.

I went home from the second meeting with Mary and thought hard. I didn't know what to do. Pressing charges was an option but a scary one. I knew the trial would be a nightmare. I would have to relive the rape itself and confront my rapist. I was still scared to death of him. If he was capable of rape, what else was he capable of? I had watched the other women involved in the civil case get dragged through the mud. I didn't doubt that the same thing would happen to me. I was also still in school, on my way to graduating, and petitioning the NCAA for an extra year of eligibility since I had lost so much time from the mono. I had no idea how pressing charges would affect either of these. If I did press charges and the case moved forward quickly, I could easily have to drop out of school. And of course, the media attention would be out of control. When thinking about all of this, I was not only thinking of myself but of my family as well. They would inevitably be affected by my decision; and Dad had just received army orders to go to Iraq. The thought that I had at best a 50–50 shot at a conviction and the fact that my rapist would probably not go to jail if he was found guilty played over and over in my mind. I decided to research rape trials to try to find any other information that might be useful in my decision. After talking with Mary, I learned as much as I could about what usually happens when a woman decides to press charges.

One case in particular stood out. A female student at a university on the East Coast had been raped early in her freshman year. She had gotten up to get a drink of water in the bathroom in the middle of the night when a man jumped out of the shower, held a knife to her throat, and raped her. He had broken into the women's dorm and waited until someone appeared. She was the first one to enter the bathroom. Fortunately, the man was caught right away as he ran from the dorm. But even though he had been apprehended, the woman's nightmare was far from over. It should have been an open-and-shut case. Instead, it took 18 months for the case even to go to trial. During that time, the rapist's legal team used a myriad of delays and harassing tactics to break the victim and her family. She spent hours in depositions and on the witness stand as defense attorneys tried to turn the blame to her for what happened. She was accused of being promiscuous and the defense team even accused that the rape was actually consensual sex, though the rapist used a knife. The man was eventually convicted, but learning about that case, and others like it, scared me to death. I was living in hell, but I couldn't imagine going through something like that and knowing my rapist might not even be convicted.

I continued to agonize over what to do.

Meanwhile, things continued to develop further up at CU. Gary Barnett publicly called Mary Keenan Lacy a liar about statements she had made under oath about the football program's using sex and alcohol to lure recruits. Information came out that football players hired strippers to entertain recruits.

In light of all the events, the university's president, Elizabeth Hoffman, promised to put together an "independent" commission to investigate CU's recruiting practices. I was stunned when I read comments by one of the newly appointed cochairs of the commission, Joyce Lawrence. She questioned why women would put themselves in a situation where they might be assaulted. Lawrence also insinuated that victims of sexual assault could be believed only when they take action right away, not if they waited to come forward. Her comments were painful to hear, and it was clear to me that the commission was being led by someone who knew little about violence against women.

Even if I didn't press charges at this point, I knew I had to speak up. I was literally sickened by the lies and denials coming from the university. My situation was different from those of the women who were suing, yet I didn't want to see them get stonewalled and smeared.

I had zero desire for a lawsuit or money. No amount of money would ever take away the pain of what had happened. What I wanted was to make sure that changes were truly going to be made in the culture at CU and that no other women would have to experience anything like I did. There were too many of us already. Aside from the three women involved in the lawsuit and me, a total of eight other women would come forward to describe how they had been raped or sexually assaulted by CU players or recruits. And I knew there were likely more, scared and suffering in silence.

I told my parents that I thought I was ready to speak up. I knew that the way I did it was going to be key in telling my story. I also knew just who to call—Rick Reilly. Rick and I had kept in sporadic touch after he had done his first article on me back in high school. He was an incredibly skilled writer and more important, I trusted him with my story. I also knew that *Sports Illustrated* was a well-trusted, credible publication—I believed they would print the story only if they believed it was true. I called Rick and told him there was some stuff I wanted to talk to him about. At first I could only tell him bits and pieces of the harassment and abuse. I could tell he couldn't believe what he was hearing.

"You're kidding. You're kidding. No way."

Then I told him I had been raped.

Dead silence on the other end of the line for a few moments.

"Are you okay? Do your parents know?"

I told him I was hanging in there and that my parents backed my decision to come forward 100 percent.

"When can I interview you? Are you at home? New Mexico?"

"I'm in school now down in Albuquerque."

We agreed on a time for him to fly down to New Mexico, but when I hung up the receiver, I started to get cold feet. There was no one perfect way to do this. I didn't want to hurt my former teammates, the ones who had been good to me. I didn't want a media circus and cause distractions for my current teammates.

I had gone to see Coach Long earlier to seek his guidance. I told him that I felt I had to speak up now and I thought I had found the best way to do it. But I also wanted to make sure I wasn't going to cause problems at UNM as well. I had been told by the NCAA that my chances of being granted the extra year looked good, but technically, I wasn't on the team since we were waiting for the request to go through. Either way, though, it was important to me to make sure that I talked to Coach Long about the situation. He told me to do whatever I had to do and that he and everyone in the program would support me in whatever decision I made. I thanked him and went to meet with Greg Remington to talk about the media. Obviously, it would be big news when the story broke. Greg and I decided that after doing the interview with Rick, we'd sit down together and write a statement to be released when the article came out. I would have no comment aside from that.

I was scared, but I knew I was making the right decision. Rick would be arriving the next morning.

I went down to let Rick into the entrance of my building. I saw him through the glass doors as I came around the corner. I flashed back to the first interview we'd done together. For a brief moment I was struck with a feeling of pain for the girl I had been during that first interview—a carefree 17-year-old who had such big dreams ahead of her. She had no idea of how her world was going to change so quickly. I shook the thought out of my head. Not now. Now I was 23 and had grown up in every sense of the word. Now I was a woman, a woman who knew it was time to tell the secrets she had been hiding for so long. I took a deep breath and opened the door.

Rick hadn't changed much. He looked the same and carried himself with the same zip I had always known. I, on the other hand, had changed in ways I didn't know were possible. It had been six years since our first meeting. I'd had enough life experiences in that time that those six years could have been 50.

We sat at my kitchen table, and Rick pulled out his laptop. My body was in turmoil from all the feelings racing through it. A part of me wanted to tell Rick I had changed my mind and go hide under my covers. Another part of my body was screaming at me "Don't go there! You know that thinking about those years rips you apart!" Yet underneath it all was stillness in my heart. The core of my being told me gently but firmly that I was doing the right thing.

Swallowing, I began my story: "It started the first day of practice."

The interview was hard. I had long ago learned to veil my feelings from the outside world, and I could feel myself doing it as I spoke. I had told pieces of the story before, but never from the beginning to the end.

It was terrifying. I would pause to gather strength to say the next words. I would pause because, even after all this time, some of the things that happened to me still shocked me. Slowly, though, I was becoming numb. By the end of our conversation, I had been transformed into a listless, detached form of myself. The story would soon be out for the world to see.

I went in to see Greg the day after I completed the interview. One of my teammates, Kyle Coulter, drove me over to Greg's office after class. Kyle was a history major as well, we'd had many classes together, and I trusted him a lot. He was the first of my teammates whom I told that I'd been raped while at CU. I sat down with Greg and we prepared a statement that was short and covered the major points.

(PRESS RELEASE—UNM) The recent allegations into the football program at the University of Colorado have caused me to come forward with details of my own experiences at CU. They occurred several years ago while I was enrolled at the school and was a member of the football team.

To this day, I am dealing with the repercussions suffered from my short time at CU. I will have to deal with it for the rest of my life.

Making this information public was not an easy decision. It has been extremely difficult for me, my family, and those closest to me, but it has also helped me. I did this because I hope no one else will have to deal with the horrors I've endured over the past few years.

I want to emphasize that a large number of my Colorado teammates during the fall of 1999 were good people. However, there were a select few whose actions toward me changed my life forever.

Being at the University of New Mexico the past 18 months and getting on the field again has really been a blessing. More than anything else, it has helped in my healing process. I have been able to play a game I love so much and also be part of a team that is like a family.

I have not had a single problem with any of my teammates at UNM. I have not received any special treatment, nor did I request any. That's a credit to the type of program that Coach (Rocky) Long is running at New Mexico.

Currently, my primary goals are to complete my education at the University of New Mexico and, hopefully, obtain a sixth year of eligibility from the NCAA. Since I'm not officially on the team anymore, I'm training on my own while awaiting word from the NCAA regarding the appeal I submitted last Friday (Feb. 13).

I was not at the University of Colorado in the fall of 2001, so I cannot comment about the current allegations being made. However, I felt that my information is pertinent to the investigation being conducted. I have been in contact with Boulder (Colo.) County law enforcement authorities, but I do not expect to file any charges at this time.

The next few days were long as I waited for the story to come out. I was still going to classes and working out at the football complex, but my mind was preoccupied. Dad had left for Fort Benning in Georgia and was in Iraq by February 14. Yvette, one of my closest friends, had made plans to take off work and come down to give me extra support after the story ran. The article came out on February 17, 2004.

Rick had done a good job. The article was factual, complete, and backed by solid research. He detailed how I was cornered my first day of practice at CU, then went on to describe how a few players had exposed themselves and how one rubbed his erect penis against me. The description of the rape was painful to read.

Reilly had talked to Barnett, who said, "None of the players wanted her on the team. Basically we were doing her a favor." Barnett also said he never heard about anyone treating me wrong—a statement that made no sense at all.

Justin Bates, a CU teammate, was quoted, "She endured more abuse than one person should have to bear."

The column was on target—and it caused me to become one as well. The CU Athletic Department called a press conference the day the article hit the news. CU had known it was coming, since Rick had called several days before for Barnett's comments. During the press conference, Barnett was sprayed with questions. With each one, he became more and more angry until he finally blew up.

"It's obvious that Katie was not very good. She was awful," he said. "Katie was not only a girl, she was terrible, okay? There's no other way to say it."

Joe and I watched the press conference together. As soon as the words came out of his mouth, we looked at each other. Did Barnett really say that? I just shook my head. It was a heck of a thing to say, but frankly, that was the Barnett I knew.

Barnett later backtracked and said the statement was taken out of context; that it was right in the middle of a long series of difficult questions. He said that what he was actually trying to express was support for me and how much he had wanted things to "work out" for me at CU. His actions, however, contradicted that explanation.

Barnett started the day on the attack. In an e-mail sent at 8:31 A.M. to athletic director Richard Tharp, he wrote, "How aggressive shoould [sic] I be re; Katie . . . sexual conquests by her etc."

"Sexual conquests" by me? What was he talking about? It became obvious to me that he was going to try to smear me, which was what had happened to the other women who had come forward. It was the first in a series of attacks on my reputation and my character.

I knew I had done the right thing. Immediately after my story broke, another woman came forward saying that she, too, had been raped by a football player. She was working in the CU athletic department in 2001 when the assault occurred. But she first went to her boss, who then went to Barnett. The woman said Barnett told her "he would back his player 100 percent if she took this forward in the criminal process." She was intimidated by Barnett but still went to the police and filed a report. The police report became public the day after my article was published. CU officials were stunned—they knew nothing about the case—yet Barnett's only comment was, "I believe there are inaccuracies in the police report."

Barnett was suspended by President Hoffman on February 18 for his comments regarding me and the second woman at the press conference the day before. The suspension didn't quiet the storm; it was more gasoline on the fire. With my coming forward and the events that followed, the story of CU's problems went from simple local interest to national front-page news.

The first to react publicly was the governor of Colorado, Bill Owens. He agreed with the suspension and demanded more answers from the university. The majority of CU regents seemed to agree with the decision as well.

Players from the 1999 team made statements in the local and national media.

One player, James Weingard, told the *Denver Post* that he saw one player throw footballs at my head, including one time when a ball actually hit me while I was warming up. Weingard said that same player constantly verbally abused me, and that others would then follow his lead. In other news articles, several players confirmed I was the object of verbal and physical abuse, including the footballs being thrown.

The media had confirmation that footballs had been thrown at me and that the thrower was abusive in other ways.

Other players said they had heard of problems but hadn't personally witnessed them. I wasn't totally surprised by that. A lot of the harassment, particularly the sexual encounters, had occurred when I had been alone. On the other hand, there were often people around when I was verbally harassed. Then there was a small group of players who said that nothing had happened to me and I shouldn't have been on the field in the first place. A few of my former teammates spoke on national television about me and their opinions differed. Ryan Johanningmeier, who was a senior offensive lineman when I was on the team, went on *Good Morning America*. He said that while he hadn't personally witnessed any of the things I'd said happened, he said that "there is no excuse for individual or individuals" who had done things to me. Johanningmeier was one of the men on the CU team who had treated me with respect and as a teammate. As an 18-year-old girl, I had looked up to him as one of the best leaders on the team.

Quarterback Mike Moschetti took a different approach. On ESPN, he publicly called me a "liar" and said that all these rape allegations were just a "witch hunt" by "these women's organizations and, you know, feminists."

I hadn't seen the Moschetti interview, but one of my teammates had. Months later, my teammate told me to say the word and he'd go pummel "that short guy."

I told him thanks, but it really wasn't necessary. My New Mexico teammates' support was enough. Coach Long had told the team during a meeting just before the article came out that they were not to comment to the press. They were relentlessly pursued by media, though, and after hearing the story and some of the attacks on me, players spoke out anyway.

They told the press that I was their teammate and their friend who had their unconditional support throughout this. No problems like those at Colorado would ever happen at UNM since Coach Long set a standard to follow. One of my teammates who'd graduated the year before said what happened to me was "a tragedy" and that I carried myself with a lot of class. Another player even told reporters about how I brought him chicken soup when he was sick.

The guys didn't just support me in the media. As soon as the article came out, I had a slew of messages on my cell phone, which I had turned off because of all the reporters calling.

"Katie, you don't have to call me back, I just wanted to tell you that I think you're a great person." "Katie, we love you, hang in there." "Katie, I'm praying for you, call me if you need to talk."

Confined to my apartment for days because the media attention was so out of control, messages like those helped me through the days, as did Joe and Yvette. We holed up and tried to keep things as normal as we could. It was impossible, though. While my professors responded well to the situation and helped me out, I was missing so many classes that I had to take incompletes in two of my courses. My grades in the others began to plummet.

Back home in Colorado, my family was stuck listening to a story that now dominated local headlines, newscasts, and conversations on the street. Mom had to deal with TV trucks parked outside our house and the doorbell ringing every few minutes with someone just wanting a brief "comment." The phone rang with appeals for information as well as offers of money, movie deals, and vacations if she would only grant an interview or, even better, get me to agree to an interview.

It seemed the vast majority of people were horrified by my story and Barnett's reaction. Many were loyal CU football fans and alums who were embarrassed by the actions of their coach and university.

Yet a small minority had a different opinion and weren't afraid to make a lot of noise. On one of the CU football Internet chat boards I was called a liar, a slut, a glory seeker, and seemingly every curse word ever invented. One fan even said I "should have the shit beat out of" me.

The diehards couldn't understand how I could have been raped yet not reported it. I had to be lying. I was trying to get back at Barnett because he'd cut me from the team two years before. There was no rape, no abuse, and no assaults.

A writer from the *Rocky Mountain News,* Tina Griego, came to my defense. She admitted that she had been raped and it took 20 years before she could tell anyone. Tina went on to explain the shame and stigma of rape; that it's a word that you can't even say aloud. And even if you simply think of the word "rape," you are attacked again. She knew exactly how other victims and I felt as well as how we would suffer the rest of our lives.

But that didn't mean all women were understanding. Although I was the first female to play at a Division I school, there were a couple of other women who had recently played football at smaller colleges. Ashley Martin had kicked at Jacksonville State in Alabama and told the *Atlanta Journal-Constitution* how bad she felt about what had happened to me. But another female kicker blasted me in the same article. Tonya Butler had played junior college football and now kicked at Western Alabama.

"When you think of female kickers, what you think of now is Katie Hnida, Heather Sue Mercer," Butler said, the latter referring to the woman who'd sued Duke University for sexual discrimination. "They all bring negativity to it. I just want to kick . . . I keep my mouth shut and let my kicking do the talking," she said.

Ironically, all I had ever wanted to do was kick, too, but unfortunately that wasn't what had happened at CU. A lot of very negative things had happened to me. Should I have just kept it a secret forever and make believe nothing had happened? I didn't think so. Plus, I had found a very positive place to continue kicking and had gone on to achieve one of my goals.

Rumors started to swirl out of Boulder. I was blindsided when a reporter called one night to ask about "topless lap dances" I had given my CU teammates. *What?* It took me a second to regain my composure. I asked the reporter where he'd heard that story. He wouldn't give me the name of the source, but was going to investigate the story fully. Go right ahead, I told him. That was the most ridiculous thing I'd ever heard. The reporter called back a few days later, saying he couldn't find anyone who would say that I had done anything like that. Nonetheless, I was disgusted that someone had even started a rumor so horrid.

Barnett kept busy during his suspension by making the rounds on the talk shows. On each, Barnett tried to explain how misunderstood he was as a person and a coach. He told Larry King, "I care about Katie, and I've always stood by my players and I'm standing by Katie now."

Funny, he never contacted me after the press conference. I didn't realize I had his support.

Barnett later appeared on *Real Sports* on HBO. By that time, the e-mail about how aggressive he should be about my so-called sexual conquests had become public and Barnett was again on the hot seat.

"It depends on how you read into that. *Discreet* is maybe another word I should have used in there . . . if I knew this was going to be a nationwide e-mail."

He added, "The best way to get this all healed faster, quicker, better, is to get me reinstated."

Fortunately for me, I got good news regarding my own reinstatement from the NCAA. On March 26, they approved my petition for an extra year of eligibility. The NCAA was very clear why they granted me a waiver—it was solely due to losing two seasons of eligibility because of illness. Mono had sidelined me most of my freshmen season and I wasn't medically cleared to play my sophomore year because of the complications of tonsillitis and surgery. The NCAA specifically stated no other factors were considered in granting me the extra year—meaning that my mistreatment at CU was not the reason for my extra year of eligibility.

It was the first piece of good news that I'd had in a while. It was good to get back onto the field and be with my teammates, but I was still struggling to concentrate in my classes, both because I was constantly stared at and because though the media had died down, new things would still come popping out of the woodwork.

The latest had to do with the e-mail Dad had sent to chancellor Richard Byyny in 2001. It had detailed my abuse at CU and warned that the athletic department might not be capable of investigating itself. In a January 2004 deposition, Byyny said he didn't remember receiving the e-mail. After he was later shown a copy of the e-mail from my father, he amended his deposition testimony to read, "I do not have a specific recollection, but I have seen the e-mail exchange."

How did Byyny forget about the e-mail? He promised to investigate thoroughly and he did send an e-mail to Barnett.

Barnett wrote to Byyny, "Dick, just to quickly respond to Dave Hnida's email: I would be more than happy to give you all the details of Katie's experience here. Furthermore, I would be happy to discuss my meeting with Dave and how he has taken a statement out of context to jab at us. Dave has no idea of the consequences handed out because these are private matters. This is a BS move by Dave. He is upset we are not recruiting his son."

Richard Byyny had a response that wasn't exactly investigative: "OK. Dick."

Byyny evidently didn't want to know the details of my experiences since he never looked into it any further, and the issue disappeared into the void of cyberspace. I never heard a word from Byyny, which showed me that my problems at the school had been blown off. Furthermore, the e-mail from Barnett was ridiculous. Dad was upset that they weren't recruiting Joe? Right, like Joe wanted to go play football at CU after I'd had such a great experience there.

I was being pressured to testify before the independent investigative commission that had been formed by CU president Hoffman. I didn't want to for several reasons: It had no subpoena power, and there was no confidentiality protection. When complete, the commission would only issue recommendations.

However, the governor of Colorado had asked the attorney general to act as special prosecutor to investigate CU and convene a grand jury. This was a task force that had legal powers as well as the ability to keep testimony confidential. I was asked to meet with them to provide information on my experiences at CU, including the rape. I readily agreed to come speak with them. The attorney general flew me to Colorado, and I met with a group of prosecutors on April 19. I told them everything that had happened, including the details of my rape and the issues I was dealing with about pressing charges in that case. The prosecutors told me I could take my time before making a decision—because of the grand jury, my statute of limitations was extended to 10 years. I was glad that more in law enforcement now knew the details of my case.

Despite the fact that I didn't go before the independent commission, I was interested in the testimony of someone who did. Megan Rogers was the equipment manager I had shared a locker room with at CU. We would make small talk, but other than that we didn't share very much. I had always had the distinct impression that she'd never cared for me. Yet when she went before the independent commission, she said she knew me well and noticed nothing unusual about my behavior during the season. And if something bad had happened, she would have known or I would have told her. Not only was that wrong, but her testimony was different from what she had said when interviewed by the *Rocky Mountain News* on February 18. At that time she had said she knew I had been verbally and physically abused and that some of the guys were "weirded out" when I joined the team. I was getting frustrated and tired of all the different accounts and accusations coming out of

Boulder. Megan had gone as far as to say to the commission that if something had happened to me, then I must have been a "good actress" because I hid it so well.

The commission issued their final report on May 17. In part, the commission felt that sex and alcohol were used as recruiting tools for football recruits. They blamed officials for failing to keep an eye on the recruiting process. Barnett was said to be resistant to change, with an "unproductive, defensive attitude." The president, chancellor, and athletic director were not doing a good job. Certain things were unacceptable and changes needed to be made, but the commission could only make recommendations. It was all up to the regents of the university to make the changes needed to clean things up.

The regents accepted the report, met in private, and then publicly announced that no one would be replaced. The consensus opinion was summed up by Regent Gail Schwartz, who said, "Giddy up!" It was time to move on. The commission was not happy that no solid action seemed to come out of their report and recommendations.

The members said they had felt as though the report would at least be a starting point to implement changes. With the way it turned out, I was glad that I had made the choice not to testify before that committee.

Barnett's supporters viewed the report as vindication. Jerry Rutledge, Barnett's friend on the Board of Regents, angered many victims' rights advocates when the report was released. He asked the parents of football players in the audience to stand up and be applauded, stating, "No one has suffered more than you."

On May 27, Gary Barnett was reinstated as head coach. Evidently I was still on his mind when he went on ESPN soon after and said, "Give us a name. Charge somebody. Show us. Who is it?"

After all that had happened, there was no way I was going to tell Gary Barnett who had raped me. I had already gone to the people who could possibly help me: the Boulder County district attorney and the grand jury committee made up of Colorado law enforcement officials.

And even though Barnett was publicly expressing how much he wanted to help me, his personal attorney took a different route. John Rodman was interviewed by the *Chicago Sun-Times* on June 4.

In that interview, Rodman said, "it has been documented that at the 1999–2000 Insight.com Bowl, Hnida took her top off at the team hotel."

There was no documentation. In fact, when Rick Reilly researched the article for *Sports Illustrated,* Barnett told him the "hot-tub" story. Reilly then asked numerous players to confirm the story. None could. And the newspaper reporter who had been told the same story could not confirm it either.

For the first time, I actually did consider filing a lawsuit. I didn't feel I could continue to be attacked and have my name slandered. But a lawsuit on my part turned out to be unnecessary. In the same interview, Rodman made other questionable accusations that drew the attention of the attorneys representing the women suing CU. They took action, so I didn't need to.

While all this was playing out in the public eye, I was going through my own private hell. I was reliving the rape every day. I started having flashbacks like the ones in Santa Barbara. But they were coming more frequently and with an intensity that I had never experienced. I was having nightmares and getting migraine headaches on a constant basis. The wounds that had finally started to heal over had been ripped back open.

I knew I needed to get help, so I started to see a therapist who specialized in the area of sexual assault. We met once, sometimes twice, a week. The sessions were often excruciating, but they helped me get through the day-to-day suffering and helped me stay on the path to healing.

18

Terms of Endearment

I TRIED TO SPEND the summer getting ready for the last season of my college career. Even though things had gone poorly in Colorado and nothing had changed, I concentrated on moving forward. All I wanted was to practice my kicking and spend time with my New Mexico teammates in summer workouts.

Then came yet one more bomb.

CU president Betsy Hoffman had given testimony in a deposition early in June, and on the 15th, her testimony was released to the public. The deposition was for the case of the women suing the university, but I was also one of the topics of discussion. Specifically, Hoffman was asked if being called a "cunt" was sexual harassment. At first she answered that it wasn't really her place to determine whether or not it was sexual harassment.

The attorney then asked her if "cunt" was a "filthy, vile, offensive term."

"That word is . . . yeah. I mean, it's a swear word," she answered.

But Hoffman then went on to say that the meaning of the word "cunt" actually depended on the context in which it was used. She was then asked if there were possibly any polite context where it might be used.

"Yes, I've actually heard it used as a term of endearment."

Was she kidding? Hoffman had heard the word "cunt" used as a term of endearment? When the papers ran the story, the word was considered offensive enough that they didn't even use the term "cunt"–they simply referred to it as the "c-word."

University officials immediately went into damage control. A spokesperson defended Hoffman, saying she is a medieval scholar and knew that centuries ago, the word "cunt" was a compliment. Geoffrey Chaucer used the term in a positive way in his classic 12th-century book *The Canterbury Tales.*

The player who called me the term was definitely not quoting Chaucer and we were living in an enlightened 21st century, or at least I thought we were.

Actually, I felt sorry for Hoffman. I don't believe she meant to be offensive when she said the word "cunt" could be a compliment. I think she got flustered under all the questioning and had something come out a very wrong way.

After being reinstated, Barnett worked hard to clear his name and reestablish his reputation. He refused to allow reporters to use the word "scandal" when referring to the events of the previous years. He even said that all of the things that did happen caused a lot of pain to him and his family. Nothing about the women who had come forward and been victimized.

All I could do was try to get ready for my final year of football and continue to make it day by day.

I was now a "sixth-year senior," and my role on the team had evolved since I started at UNM. I wasn't aware exactly how much until we were in a team meeting before the season began.

Coach Long had just finished talking about the upcoming schedule and how we couldn't be ignored if we won the big games—we had some opponents from the "bigger" conferences that year—when I raised my hand. He looked over at me.

"Yes, Katie?"

"Would it be okay if I said something?" I couldn't believe I'd had the guts to ask if I could address the team. Rarely did anyone except Coach Long say anything during these meetings.

"Go ahead."

I turned and faced the bulk of my teammates.

"Most of you guys know that I got to go to the college football awards last year in Florida. While it was great, when I was getting introduced to people, half the time they'd say I was from New Mexico State or if they got New Mexico right, they would be asking me what our mascot was." I paused. "Even though we've hit two bowl games in a row, people still don't know how great this program is. Coach Long is right; this year we've got a schedule that can change that. We gotta go out and *beat the living shit* out of—"

I got no further.

As soon as the guys heard the intensity of my tone and a curse word come out of my mouth, they started going nuts, cheering, clapping, and thumping on their chairs.

"Yeah, KATIE!"

"Whoo-hoo!"

A few of the coaches were chuckling. Even Coach Long was smiling.

"Katie, we don't use language like that around here," he joked.

I smiled—even after three years, the coaches would be in the middle of yelling, say a curse word, and then apologize to me.

I had spent the rest of the summer training as hard as I ever had.

That year, we brought back an old New Mexico training tradition . . . running sand hills. On scorching hot days, we'd pack into cars and drive out to the sand hills in the desert just outside the city. They were deceptively tall hills consisting of nothing but loose sand. We'd do short sprints and plyometrics for the first part of the workout, and then we'd end by running up the full hill once or twice. It was a steep 60 yards up, but felt more like a few miles. In a full sprint, you made it up about 20 yards before your legs gave out because of all the work you had to do to keep from sliding backward. After you do lose your footing, you're on your hands and knees crawling, sliding, grasping for fistfuls of sand, and gasping for air to get up the rest of the hill. They were some of the hardest workouts we'd ever done, but I absolutely loved them. A part of me craved being able to push my body so far. Yet I found that running the sand hills was as much a mental workout as it was physical. I couldn't lift as much in the weight room or run gassers as fast as the guys, but I could give them a good fight running a steep sand hill. It was an incredible bonding experience and there was nothing as sweet as the view when you made it to the top of the sand hill.

I went through my 2004 season making sure to enjoy every moment of it. It was healing to be out on the field, still kicking, after everything I'd gone through the previous spring. It was even more healing to be surrounded by the guys—my guys—for one more season. We finished the regular season at 7–4, ending with a trip to the Emerald Bowl in San Francisco. My last college game was a wet and muddy one against Navy, which we lost 34–19.

I finished my career at UNM with three winning seasons and three straight bowl trips.

We had another all-conference season in 2004 and I didn't see the field my final year. A lot of people have asked me if I regretted the extra season since I didn't get to play. My answer often surprised them: not for a second. In my college career, I did miss being the starting kicker. I had come out of high school truly believing that I would go to a Division I program and work my way up to being the starting kicker. Instead, my life took a few unexpected turns that severly affected my kicking. But I always knew that Division I was where I wanted to be. I didn't fulfill my expectations, but in the end what I got was so much more.

It was the bond that I shared with my teammates and the feeling of being an integral part of the team and program. And more than that, it truly was about the love of the game. There aren't that many people who get the chance to compete at the highest level of college football. I am forever blessed that I got to be one of the few.

I wasn't the starting kicker at UNM, but that doesn't mean I won't ever get a shot somewhere else in the future.

Epilogue

It Ain't Over Until the Skinny Girl Kicks

I T IS NOW MAY 2006. I am back at home in Littleton for Jimmy's graduation from high school. I turned 25 last week, and the last of the Hnida kids is graduating. As I look over the pages for this book, it's hard for me to believe that so much time has gone by, how many things happened during that time.

The CU scandal has continued to evolve. The lawsuit that ignited the whole fire was dismissed in April 2005. The women's lawyers are in the process of appealing to a higher court system. Though the case hasn't and may never go to trial, many changes have taken place. Most of the key players in the scandal are no longer in their positions at the university.

Richard "Dick" Tharp resigned under pressure as the CU athletic director on November 22, 2004. He was given an early retirement package. Shortly after, Chancellor Richard Byyny resigned from his position as well. He is now working at the University of Colorado's Hospital Center for Health Policy. At the end of June 2005, Betsy Hoffman submitted her resignation as president. She moved to the University of Colorado at Denver and is teaching public affairs.

The last to go was Gary Barnett. He was fired from his head coaching position on December 8, 2005, after losing his last two games with a combined score of 100–6. Barnett was paid three million dollars to buy out the remaining two years of his contract. CU replaced Barnett with Dan Hawkins, previously head coach at Boise State, as the new head coach. Ironically, while coaching in 1997 at a small college in Oregon, Hawkins became the first coach in history to use a female in a college football game, when Liz Heaston kicked two extra points for Willamette University.

I've not had any personal contact with Gary Barnett since the fall of 2000.

I continue to keep in touch with a large number of my teammates from the University of New Mexico and occasionally catch myself smiling out of the blue when a random memory pops into my head. No matter where I go or what I do, a piece of my heart will always remain with the people of Albuquerque, and an even bigger part will always be with the more than 200 men I was privileged enough to call teammates over the course of three years. A number of my former teammates are now playing at the professional level. It has been exciting to watch them and the UNM program progress.

Rocky Long is in his ninth season as head coach. He is the winningest coach in New Mexico history.

The community of Littleton had continued to grow. It seems as though everywhere I look, there is a new building. Ground is being broken next month for a permanent memorial site for the Columbine tragedy. More than eight years after the shooting, Frank

DeAngelis remains the principal of Columbine High School. He is a pillar of strength and of hope to all those in our community.

I am still close with Coach Mead. He is not the head coach of the football team any longer, but is now the principal of Chatfield Senior High. I can't think of a better man for the job.

About a year ago I started to speak publicly on a regular basis. Often I talk about rape or violence against women. At other times I work as a motivational speaker.

In addition to speaking, I work with nonprofit organizations, including Voices and Faces and RAINN (Rape, Abuse, and Incest National Network), two tremendous groups to combat sexual assault, and as an athlete ambassador for Right to Play, which is dedicated to bringing the joy and positive aspects of sports to children in Third World countries.

Not a day goes by that I don't think about what happened to me at CU. Though my rape was more than six years ago, I am still healing from it. Some counselors and sexual assault survivors say that you can never completely heal, just lessen the scar. While I know that I was forever changed by what happened to me, I continue to work toward lessening the scar each day. I have traveled the roads of fear, self-blame, and intense pain—some days I still do. There are still bad days, but they are becoming less and less frequent. I urge other victims of assault not to suffer in silence. Help is out there and even though it can be scary to reach for, it's worth it. I have healed a great deal in knowing that I am not alone in what happened to me, nor in the way I feel about it.

I was worried that going public might hurt the chances of other females being able to play football. I was supposed to be breaking down walls, not creating them. My fear was dismissed when I read the statistics: In 1997, there were 779 females playing on high school football teams across the country. In 2005, that number reached 2,759.

I never intentionally set out to break a barrier; I was simply following a dream. But as I followed that dream, there were many obstacles that blocked my way. There were times when it would have been easier to simply back down from those obstacles: the ones at CU, at Santa Barbara, or even at UNM, when I had my first extra point blocked. But I realized that I had to reach deep inside and keep going to reach my dream. I know that doing things that are important or significant seldom come easy. I owed it to myself and to those who believed in me. I wasn't going to let anyone take away something that was in my heart.

I was blessed to have tremendous support come in different forms—from the love of my family, my friends, as well as the unwavering strength of my faith in God. Those things, along with a dogged determination, allowed me to keep going, no matter how rough things got.

When I made history, I didn't do it alone. I had countless people who touched my life at various points along the way and they all were with me on the field that night.

And I'm not done dreaming—or doing—just quite yet. The possibilities seem endless. I plan to keep writing, speaking, and trying to make a difference in the world. Football? We'll see. I know I've never reached my full potential as a kicker.

So in the meantime, I'm still pushing trucks up streets and chasing after footballs I kicked on the practice field. I'm not sure where I might end up, but wherever it is, I know what I'll be doing: *still kicking*.

Katie Hnida, 2006

Acknowledgments

How do you ever say thank you to the people who make your life what it is? Even after writing close to a hundred thousand words, I still can't find ones strong enough to express my gratitude.

First, thanks goes to Laura Palmer for advisement and support through the writing process. You pushed me to be the best writer I could be and produce a manuscript that I was proud of.

Bob Barnett, your guidance has been impeccable and is only matched by your kindness. You are one in a million.

The staff at Scribner was incredible. Many thanks to Bill Drennan, Katie Rizzo, Lisa Erwin, Davina Mock, Katy Sprinkel, John Fulbrook, and Suzanne Balaban for making all different aspects of this book come together at warp speed.

Beth Wareham, my mama bear and cooker of cheese dip, is my editor extraordinaire. Thank you for believing in me the whole way through.

Jill Vogel, you have a heart of gold in a world of silver. Thank you for walking me through every step of the journey, especially at the end of the road! You don't know how special you really are.

Kate Bittman, you're my "itty bitty" but my big publicist. I'm grateful for all the work you put into this project. I love you.

My experience in New Mexico couldn't have been as great as it was without the following people: Dave Binder, Mark Paulsen, Aaron Day, Joaquin Chavez (and Holmes), Bill Fishburn, Lee Argubright, Bob Schenck, Don Forrester, Sylvia Lopez, Mike Hart, Andy Schultz, and Gary Stepic. A million thank-yous to all.

Celia Valencia, my sweet abuela, thank you for your tender love and care day in and day out. I miss you.

Rudy Garcia, you gave me a home away from home and always kept an extra eye out. You are the best.

Jacque May kept me sane and even ordered me football clothes that fit. Thank you for being there for everything.

Greg Remington, your salary should have increased tenfold for handling my media. Thank you for your assistance through all the ups and downs.

Janice Ruggiero and Kaari Zamora in UNM compliance got me the sixth year of eligibility that gave me the privilege to spend another season at New Mexico. Thanks to you both for the work that made that happen. Dr. Barbara Brown, if God puts angels on earth, you are surely one of them.

Father Ken Leone and Father Michael Pavlakovich, my love and thanks to you for the true support and care through the years. And, Father Ken, thanks for the Starburst!

To all the kind souls who took the time to write me in support after I came forward. Your words meant more to me than you'll ever know. Two years later, I'm still trying to answer letters.

Throughout my years, I was blessed to have some of the most talented and supportive coaches on this planet:

Bob Beaty, thank you for taking a chance all those years ago. Who could have guessed how far I'd end up going?

Don Jones and Dave Bolger, thank you for helping me grow as a kicker and as a person.

Keith Mead, the world could use more men like you. Even though it's no longer your "official" title, you'll always be "coach" in my heart.

Rocky Long, it was truly an honor to play for you. I will carry the lessons Lobo football taught me through the rest of my life.

My UNM coaches—Everett Todd, Dan Dodd, Jeff Conway, Bob Bostad, Lenny Rodriguez, Jason Strauss, Grady Stretz, Danny Gonzales, Curtis Luper, Osia Lewis, Troy Reffett, and Gavin Bevis—I could not have asked for a better group of leaders.

Last but not least . . .

The group of men who made up the UNM football team from 2002 to 2004—you were the best teammates a girl could ever ask for. I love you guys.

And my family—3 up, 3 down, you were there through it all. I couldn't have done any of it without you. The five of you are the greatest blessings in my life.